W9-ASL-767

JOURNEY
TO
CHAOS

JOURNEY

TO

CHAOS

Samuel Beckett's Early Fiction

RAYMOND FEDERMAN

UNIVERSITY OF
CALIFORNIA PRESS
Berkeley and Los Angeles 1965

823.91
B396 F

University of California Press
Berkeley and Los Angeles
Cambridge University Press
London, England

© 1965 by The Regents of the University of California
Library of Congress Catalog Card Number: 65–25284
Printed in the United States of America

For **ERICA**

65217

PREFACE

As indicated in the title, this book deals primarily with Samuel Beckett's early fiction—that is, the works he wrote, in English or French, prior to *Molloy*. These consist of the collection of short stories *More Pricks Than Kicks*, the English novels *Murphy* and *Watt*, the unpublished French novel *Mercier et Camier* and short story *Premier amour*, and the three *Nouvelles*, "L'Expulsé," "Le Calmant," "La Fin." These are discussed here in the order in which they were written and show Beckett's creative evolution until 1947, when he began to write his famous trilogy.

Recently I learned that in 1932 Beckett had written an earlier version of *More Pricks Than Kicks* in the form of a novel, which remains unfinished and unpublished, entitled *Dream of Fair to Middling Women*. Whenever possible, summaries of works analyzed in this book have been incorporated in the text, but because of the particular relationship between *Dream of Fair to Middling Women* and *More Pricks Than Kicks*, and the rarity of the latter, detailed summaries of these two works are given in the appendix. Moreover, a complete chronology of Beckett's works is included in the bibliography.

The purpose of this study is to show both the gradual disintegration of form and content in Beckett's work, and how it is perfected into an aesthetic system in his better-known novels, *Molloy, Malone meurt, L'Innommable,* and the recent *Comment c'est.* I believe that to gain a deeper understanding of these complex and abstract works it is essential to investigate the earlier fiction, which has not received the critical attention it deserves. Therefore, this study of Beckett's early creations is intended as an introduction to the whole of his fiction, with references to the later works used to show the interplay between novels, the process of self-generation of the characters, and thematic development.

It is not my intent to pass judgment on these works, for though there is a definite progression from one work to the next, this does not imply that the earlier works are inferior to the more recent ones. It does emphasize that as early as 1932 Beckett committed himself to a paradoxical creative system to which he remained stubbornly faithful in his effort to achieve originality. It is this paradoxical creative system, which progressively draws toward the formulation of a new reality as it negates common realities, which captured my attention. My discussions are limited to the works themselves, and do not attempt to relate the life of the author to, or to identify the author with, his creations.

Reading the novels in chronological order, it becomes apparent that Beckett's fictional "journey to chaos" followed specific stages: that of his English fiction, that of his early French experiments, and that of his later French works. Only the first two stages are examined here as they prepare for the later period. Part one of the book follows the gradual alienation of the characters from social reality. This represents a forsaking of life not only as it is known in our modern society, but as it is depicted in traditional fiction. In other words, social reality is meant here in the sense of conventional realism. Part two analyzes how Beckett's early French heroes undergo dehumanization as they are exiled (expelled) into what I have called fictional absurdity. This expression describes the unorthodox situations Beckett creates in his French fiction, situations that sustain themselves beyond the norms of rationality, with little reliance on conventional elements of characterization, plot, action, and so on. Eventually the fictitious world of Samuel Beckett becomes so incongruous, so unrealistic, so chaotic, that one wonders how intelligibility and aesthetic unity are achieved.

Some parts of chapters i and ii were revised from articles published in *French Review* (Feb., 1965), *Arizona Quarterly* (Summer, 1964), and the Avon Book anthology of literary essays *On Contemporary Literature* (copyright 1964 by Richard Kostelanetz). My thanks go to the editors of these for permission to reprint.

I wish to thank Mr. Samuel Beckett and his publishers for kind permission to quote from the following copyright material: *More Pricks Than Kicks,* copyright 1934 by Samuel Beckett and Chatto and Windus, Ltd.; *En Attendant Godot,* copyright 1952 by Editions de Minuit; *L'Innommable,* copyright 1953 by Editions de Minuit; *Nouvelles et Textes pour rien,* copyright 1955, 1958 by Editions de Minuit; *Comment c'est,* copyright 1961 by Editions de Minuit; *Proust,* copyright 1957 by Grove Press; *Murphy,* copyright 1957 by Grove Press; *Watt,* copyright 1959 by Grove Press; *Molloy,* copyright 1955 by Grove Press, translated by Beckett and Patrick Bowles; *Malone Dies,* copyright 1956 by Grove Press; *The Unnamable,* copyright 1958 by Grove Press; *Waiting for Godot,* copyright 1954 by Grove Press; *Endgame,* copyright 1958 by Grove Press; *Poems in English,* copyright 1961 by Samuel Beckett and Grove Press; "The Expelled," ("L'Expulsé") copyright 1962 (*Evergreen Review,* Vol. 6, no. 22), translated by Beckett and Richard Seaver, Grove Press.

I would like to express my deep appreciation to Professor Neal Oxenhandler of the University of California, Los Angeles, for his encouragement and many suggestions while I was working on this book. I am also indebted to my former colleagues of the University of California, Santa Barbara—Professors Hugh Kenner, Helmut Bonheim, and

Michel Rybalka—with whom many valuable hours were spent discussing the works of Samuel Beckett. This book would never have reached its present form if my wife, in the process of editing the manuscript, had not challenged every word and every thought. Finally, I am extremely grateful to Mr. Samuel Beckett, who, during an interview in Paris in the summer of 1963, granted me permission to quote from the manuscripts of his unpublished works.

R. F.

State University of New York
at Buffalo, 1965

CONTENTS

Nous naissons
tous fous.
Quelques-uns
le demeurent.

EN ATTENDANT GODOT

What but
an imperfect sense of humour
could have made
such a mess
of chaos.

MURPHY

INTRODUCTION

comment c'était je cite
avant Pim avec Pim après Pim
comment c'est trois parties
je le dis comme
je l'entends

BECKETT. *Comment c'est*

We must never forget
that though the author can
to some extent choose his disguises,
he can never choose
to disappear.

w. c. booth, *The Rhetoric of Fiction*

I

THE FICTION OF MUD

The novels of Samuel Beckett seem to defy all classification, evade all possible definition. By their unorthodox form, their lack of elements essential to the nature of fiction, their deceptive use of language, their apparent incoherence, and above all their ambiguous suggestiveness, they lead to contradictory interpretations. However, a patient reading of these works reveals new concepts of fiction, and an original vision of man's existential dilemma. This vision was shaped progressively over a period of three decades during which Beckett exploited, in a large number of works (poetry, drama, fiction),[1] a complex and paradoxical method of creation. The ultimate result of these experiments was the unusual work entitled *Comment c'est* (1961).

To comprehend this novel, the unprepared reader must rid himself of all preconceived notions he may have of the novel form. On first reading, *Comment c'est* appears as a confusing and incoherent mass of words which gains order and meaning only in the light of Beckett's previous self-generating fiction. A close look at the bulk of Beckett's novels shows that from one work to the next a deliberate

[1] A chronology of Beckett's works appears at the end of this volume.

process of disintegration reduces form and content, setting and characters, to a system whereby "composition takes place during decomposition." [2]

Most works of fiction achieve coherence through a logical accumulation of facts about specific situations and more or less credible characters. In the process of recording, or gradually revealing mental and physical experiences organized into aesthetic and ethical form, these works progress toward a definite goal: the discovery of knowledge. The novels of Samuel Beckett seem to advance in exactly the opposite direction, and give the impression of being conscious efforts to reduce or retract all given norms. A Beckett novel progresses by unexpected leaps and bounds, from impasse to impasse, toward apparent chaos and meaninglessness. Whereas a traditional hero performs a series of related actions which inevitably produces a psychological change in his attitude and personality, a change that eventually results in tragic or comic denouement, Beckett's people begin and end their fictional journey at the same place, in the same condition, and without having learned, discovered, or acquired the least knowledge about themselves and the world in which they exist. Theirs is a journey without beginning or end, without purpose or meaning. Though these creatures succeed in creating an illusion of progress, both for themselves and for the reader, they merely occupy time and space—the time it takes for the book to be read, and the space it requires for the story to be told. Ultimately their actions, motions, and verbal contortions are negated by the fact of having been performed or spoken.

In his last novel, *Comment c'est*, Beckett reaches the outer boundary of fictional absurdity and disorder, without, however, falling into complete nonsense. This novel presents itself as a literary incongruity which invalidates all rules of conventional fiction. For what is this book which tells no story, has no plot, has neither beginning nor end, and, though divided into three distinct parts (before Pim, with

---

[2] Ruby Cohn, *Samuel Beckett: The Comic Gamut* (New Brunswick: Rutgers University Press, 1962), p. 285.

Pim, after Pim), could go on with a fourth or a fifth or an infinite number of parts, as the anonymous narrator himself suggests? What is this novel which appears formless, which could be read from any page either forward or backward, which reveals the mechanism of its own creation, of its own difficult progress, while noting its aesthetic imperfections ("quelque chose là qui ne va pas")?[3] Who is this naked being crawling a few meters at a time face down in the mud of some no-man's-land toward his victim Pim, in part one, establishing a strange and cruel relationship with Pim in part two, and then in turn becoming himself that victim in part three as he awaits his own tormentor, Bem or Bom, to reach him? Who are these creatures whose names change unexpectedly from Pim to Pem to Pam, from Krim to Krem to Kram, from Bim to Bem to Bom? Who is this weird creator-hero (tormentor-victim) who mumbles, out of a twisted mouth, a distorted language which hardly resembles human speech: ". . . brefs mouvements du bas du visage pertes partout" [brief movements of the lower part of the face losses everywhere]? Who dictates these words, who forces them into the narrator's mouth? What is this story that unravels and repeats the same set of expressions for 177 pages of punctuationless prose[4] presented in a series of almost unrelated paragraphs (poetic stanzas?) of a most illogical syntax? Where is this unrealistic universe? Where, in man's experience, is this world of endless dimensions, of darkness and mud, where only a few incongruous objects are still recognizable: a can opener, a cord, a sack full of sardine and tuna fish cans?

To approach Beckett's universe through this novel is disconcerting and frustrating. Readers of fiction are accus-

---

[3] Beckett, *Comment c'est,* passim. Beckett's French works are published by Les Editions de Minuit in Paris, the English works by Grove Press in New York. Unless otherwise indicated, quotations in French and in English and page references are from these editions. As *Comment c'est* was not yet available in English, translations of Fench quotations from this work are my own.

[4] Three periods appear in the original edition of this work (pp. 29, 31, 35). No doubt a careless inadvertence on the part of the printer.

tomed to finding, even in the most fantastic novels, if not a familiar landscape, at least identifiable characters and landmarks which offer physical verisimilitude to man and to the real world. Surrealist literature may present distorted images in twisted verbal expressions, yet these visions of the subconscious reflect external reality. The most daring works of science fiction may posit unbelievable situations, yet despite their grotesque inventions and exaggerations the fantastic relates to the natural world. In other words, whether it pretends to imitate, reshape, evaluate, or interpret reality, or whether it intends to explain the world rationally and formulate ethical values, to remain coherent a work of fiction must rely on realistic norms and logical forms. In this respect the novel must necessarily conform to a certain aesthetic order to avoid dwindling into unintelligibility. The reader apprehends and accepts such fiction only within the frame of his own knowledge of reality and language. Are we then to assume in reading Beckett's "antinovels" that he consciously avoids all ethical statements, all affirmations of a meaningful and rational world, and strives toward a deliberate expression of artistic chaos? Beckett himself stated in a recent interview: "I am working with *impotence, ignorance.* I don't think impotence has been exploited in the past. . . . My little exploration is that whole zone of being that has always been set aside by artists as something unuseable—as something by definition incompatible with art." [5]

The fundamental idea behind Beckett's fiction may be termed an affirmation of the negative. This paradoxical artistic undertaking becomes an investigation, an exploitation of *opposites.* Beckett substitutes ignorance for knowledge, impotence for creativity, lethargy for efficiency, confusion for understanding, lunacy for rationality, doubt for certainty, illusion for reality. These opposites are his fields of exploration. To build novels on such premises is to commit oneself to absurdity and failure. By their very form

[5] As quoted by Israel Shenker in "Moody Man of Letters," *New York Times,* May 6, 1956, sec. 2, p. 3.

and content the novels of Samuel Beckett question the validity of those criteria by which fiction is rendered useful and believable—useful as a social, psychological, and even a political or religious document; believable as the story of rational human beings existing in a sensible world.

While inventing stories and characters that annihilate their own shape and existence, Beckett offers a means of destroying, but also of purifying, the traditional novel. His creative method unmasks the counterfeit aspects of fictional realism and confronts the reader with a bare illusion: the artistic device, the artistic lie through which writers transform reality into fiction. Moreover, since reality (according to Beckett) is incomprehensible and doubtful, the validity of fiction becomes doubly suspect. Thus, instead of creating a world that simulates reality and contains social and psychological implications, Beckett presents situations that reject all concepts of truth, all epistemological claims. The reader is faced with a fraudulent condition: the image of a stubbornly garrulous creature (narrator-hero) sitting in a room, planted in a pot, crawling in the mud, or simply locked in his own delirious mind—a voice muttering and inventing with whatever words are still available, an absurd and totally false subreality.

If the muddy landscape presented in *Comment c'est* bears little resemblance to whatever knowledge one may have of real or fictional worlds, it is because this novel is not a projection of reality, but an experiment in willful artistic failure: the rejection of reality. It reveals in the course of its narration the chaos and agony of its creative movement. One can read this book as a satire on fiction—a masochistic expression of the futility of the creative act, or for that matter of all human actions. *Comment c'est* is a world of abstractions and illusions which poses as fiction, just as conventional fiction pretends to pass for reality. If this book is successful, it is because it achieves what it set out to do: expose its own failure. Beckett consciously avoids creating a finite and realistic world. He performs this feat by parodying that which he is intent on destroying, and only through comic devices does he avoid falling into cynicism. Fiction appears as a game both for the author, who repeatedly comments ironically on the progress of his novel, and for the protagonist, who deliberately distorts his own existence in progress. As creator-hero each new Beckett creation is able to attack his fellow characters. Each successive novel playfully mocks Beckett's preceding achievements, and in turn ridicules the whole of literature.

This technique implies an intricate aesthetic structure, and *Comment c'est* may appear at first complex and unintelligible; but it is extremely simple in both form and content. It has been stripped of all the elements considered necessary to fiction. It is virtually made of *nothing:* an absurd and grotesque situation, an irrational and less than human figure who barely preserves the attributes of man, a few basic sentences repeated to the point of meaninglessness, and all this in a language hardly coherent. Yet the novel progresses almost logically, and is constructed word by word "into a beautifully and tightly wrought structure, a few dozen expressions permuted with deliberate redundancy accumulate meaning as they are emptied of it, and offer themselves as points of radiation in a strange web of utter illusion." [6] This deceptive structure is based on nothing tangible. While the narrator-hero progresses painfully—

pousse tire la jambe se détend le bras se plie toutes ces articulations jouent la tête arrive au niveau de la main sur le ventre repos	[push pull the leg slackens the arm folds all articulations play the head arrives at the level of the hand on the belly rest
l'autre flanc jambe gauche bras gauche pousse tire la tête et le haut du tronc décollent autant de friction en moins retombent je rampe l'amble dix mètres quinze mètres halte [p. 23]	the other side left leg left arm push pull the head and the top of the trunk rise as much friction in less falls I crawl the amble ten meters fifteen meters stop]

[6] Hugh Kenner, *Samuel Beckett: A Critical Study* (New York: Grove Press, 1961) , p. 189.

—one realizes that the physical contortions of this twisted creature have suddenly become verbal contortions. These no longer reflect the difficult progression of a naked body crawling in the mud, but of a mind laboring with words in an effort to communicate an uncommunicable experience. The reader is confronted with the agonizing growth of the novel, and the creator's mind now appears naked as it struggles with an inadequate form and language to perform a futile creative act. Failure and nothingness, the goals of this novel, become aesthetic experiences; the action of writing becomes a metaphor for the novel itself. As he proceeds toward his inevitable failure, the narrator-hero suffers the creation before the reader's eyes. He calculates what remains to be done, recognizes the uselessness of what has been written, acknowledges the errors and lies of his fiction, and finally concludes with satisfaction: "bon bon fin de la troisième partie et dernière voilà comment c'était fin de la citation après Pim comment c'est" [good good end of the third part and last this is how it was end of the quotation after Pim how it is] (p. 177). What is presented then is a controlled image of a world in chaos, a world in the process of disintegrating, in the process of *not* becoming.

The narrative consists of utterances: confused recapitulations of the narrator's journey (his vain creative effort) toward Pim, of his suppositions and hopes as to how it will be with Pim, of his recollections as to how it was with Pim. Pim's obsessive presence governs the narration, gathers the past, present, and future into a single statement: HOW IT IS. This recurring statement negates all possible change, all possible hope of progress and order. Recently Beckett stated: "The confusion is not my invention. . . . It is all around us and our only chance now is to let it in. The only chance of renovation is to open our eyes and see the mess. It is not a mess you can make sense of." [7] Progress and order are mere illusions in this novel, as implied ironically in the title, *Comment c'est* (*commencer,* to begin) , and, since the narra-

<hr/>

[7] As quoted by Tom F. Driver in "Beckett by the Madeleine," *Columbia University Forum,* IV (Summer, 1961) , 22–23.

tor begins and ends his fictional journey in the same situation, the only "chance" of order in this calculated "mess"
lies with Pim. Pim is the point around which every word,
every gesture, every speculation rotates. Yet to know who
Pim is, whom he represents, or if he exists at all, is totally
irrelevant since, as the narrator points out, it is possible that
there are a million Pims, Bems, or Krems, all of them
interchangeable with ". . . les 999 997 autres que de par sa
place dans la ronde il n'a jamais l'occasion de rencontrer"
[. . . the 999 997 others whom from his position in the
round he never has the occasion of encountering] (p. 145).
Obviously, Pim and the others serve merely as excuses for
the novel's existence, for this doubtful story to be written,
uttered, or silenced.

The whole novel lies in the realm of uncertainty. This
fantastic world of mud, of absurd physical and mental per-
mutations, exists simply as a metaphorical impression which
can crumble into chaos whenever the narrator chooses:
". . . ces histoires de voix oui quaqua . . . ces histoires de
sacs déposés oui au bout d'une corde . . . ces histoires de
là-haut oui . . . de la foutaise" [these stories about voices
yes quaqua . . . these stories about deposed bags yes at the
end of a cord . . . these stories of above yes . . . bullshit]
(p. 175). This tale is no longer governed by the conditions
of reality or the logic of language. Yet, while composing his
story, the narrator-hero occasionally remembers a vague anterior existence which he situates somewhere "là-haut dans
la vie dans la lumière," before the mud came. These remnants of realistic memories, presented as concrete images
dispersed throughout the narration, are so incompatible
with the narrator's main stream of incoherent thoughts that
they emphasize the fraudulence of his present condition.
Images such as these—

nous sommes sur une véranda à   [we are on an open-work ve-
claire-voie aveuglée de verveine   randa blinded by vervain the
le soleil embaumé paillette le   embalmed sun spangles the red
dallage rouge parfaitement   tile perfectly]
                    [p. 19]

or elsewhere—

je me donne dans les seize ans et il fait pour surcroît de bonheur un temps délicieux ciel bleu oeuf et chevauchée de petits nuages je me tourne le dos et la fille aussi que je tiens qui me tient par la main ce cul que j'ai [p. 35]	[I give myself about sixteen years of age and to add to the happiness of the moment the weather is delicious egg blue sky ridden with little clouds I turn my back on myself and the girl also whom I hold who holds me by the hand what a lucky ass I am]

—jar the reader as though out of context with the narrator's predicament. His only concern is for the story to continue, regardless of its absurdity. For this reason, he concentrates on Pim, on his quest for Pim, on his relationship with Pim (even if Pim is an illusion), and finally, in part three, on his own futile existence as he now replaces Pim and awaits the coming of Bem or Bom, or an alter ego, who supposedly progresses slowly toward him in the mud. All the rest (reality, rationality, memory) is superfluous to the narration, even though the reader may feel a certain sense of security every time he encounters one of these images.

By the end of part three, the novel has taken on a circular shape. It has acquired such momentum in absurdity and irrationality that it could easily go on for an infinite number of parts, simply repeating the same process, the same words and gestures, much as the two bums of *Waiting for Godot* could repeat their absurd comedy, return to the same place every night, for an infinite number of acts, fully aware that Godot will never come. Faced with this endless condition, in complete despair, the narrator-hero suddenly affirms that the story he told and experienced was an illusion, a lie, that it was completely false, that none of it really occurred, that none of it was ever performed, spoken, or written:

si tout ça tout ça oui si tout ça n'est pas comment dire pas de réponse si tout ça n'est pas faux oui	[if all this all this yes if all this is not how shall I say no answer if all this is not false yes
tous ces calculs oui explications oui toute l'histoire d'un bout à l'autre oui complètement faux oui	all these calculations yes explanations yes the whole story from beginning to end yes completely false yes

ça s'est passé autrement oui
tout à fait oui mais comment
pas de réponse comment ça s'est
passé pas de réponse qu'est-ce
qui s'est passé pas de réponse
QU'EST-CE QUI S'EST PASSÉ
hurlements bon

it happened otherwise yes en-
tirely yes but how no answer
how did it happen no answer
what happened no answer
WHAT HAPPENED howlings
good

il s'est passé quelque chose oui
mais rien de tout ça non de la
foutaise d'un bout à l'autre oui
cette voix quaqua oui de la
foutaise oui qu'une voix ici oui
la mienne oui quand ça cesse de
haleter oui   [p. 174]

something happened yes but
none of all this no bullshit from
beginning to end yes this voice
quaqua yes bullshit yes that a
voice here yes mine yes when it
stops panting yes]

What happened is that a novel has been written, no matter
what its form, content, or purpose may have been. Beckett
has fulfilled his role as author, and the narrator-hero has
performed his role as fictional being. A book now exists, a
book on whose cover one can print ROMAN.

A novel such as *Comment c'est*, which discloses the secret
of its creation as it progresses, which exposes its own shortcomings, imperfections, and failure, cannot be created without some antecedent, at least from within the frame of the
author's previous works. To arrive at such complete disintegration of form and content, to achieve such transparency of
language, to succeed in eliminating the most essential elements of the novel, and yet apparently preserve a form of
narrative, a pattern must precede the creation. It must
emerge from some concrete origin. Any writing, whether it
leads to a reduction or an augmentation of given norms,
must have a point of departure either in reality or in
fiction.

To grasp Beckett's vision in *Comment c'est*, to accept this
novel without brushing it aside as a mere literary hoax, to
experience fully the mental and physical deterioration of
man as it occurs in Beckett's universe, it is necessary to
return to the beginning of his creations. As one proceeds
backward into the strange and desolate landscape of

Beckett's fiction, moving chronologically against the grain from *Comment c'est* to the prose fragment entitled "From an Abandoned Work," to the thirteen *Textes pour rien,* to the trilogy of *L'Innommable, Malone meurt, Molloy,* to the three *Nouvelles* ("L'Expulsé, Le Calmant, La Fin"), to the unpublished short story *Premier amour* and unpublished novel *Mercier et Camier,* to the English novels, *Watt, Murphy,* and finally to the 1934 collection of short stories *More Pricks Than Kicks,* itself preceded by a rough, unfinished, unpublished first draft entitled *Dream of Fair to Middling Women,*[8] one notices how the fictional setting becomes more and more familiar, more recognizable and rational as it regains the many realistic features Beckett has systematically removed, destroyed, or juggled away in the course of his creative journey. Proceeding backward along this literary path, one observes how the characters recover those physical and human attributes that had been gradually eliminated from their existence, and how these figures regain a functional position in social reality. It is as though they were returning from a descent into the infernal limbos of their own extravagant minds—the region of irresponsibility and unreality. At the same time, their environment, the external world, and society acquire a semblance of order and stability. Thus, in retrospect, from the sterile country of *Comment c'est* to the bourgeois Dublin of *More Pricks Than Kicks,* the reader has the impression of recapturing a lost sense of logic and rationality, and his doubt, his interest, are stabilized as he discovers that Beckett's universe may have had a sensible origin. In other words, however paradoxical and preposterous the ultimate result may be, physical and moral alienation began in a stable and realistic social region only to progress step by step into fictional absurdity.

Most relevant to this literary progression is Beckett's shift from the English to the French language around 1945.

[8] These works are listed in the order in which they were written. For exact date and place of publication, see the chronology of Beckett's works in the bibliography.

Puzzled critics have offered several explanations for this language change, none too satisfactory. Some say that Beckett decided to write in French to escape the overpowering influence of his friend James Joyce; others, that he chose a second language to gain greater objectivity; and a German critic quotes Beckett as saying, "Parce qu'en français c'est plus facile d'écrire sans style." [9] Yet a close examination of Beckett's French prose reveals an original and personal style which results from a subjective point of view. Perhaps the best answer to this puzzling question was furnished by Beckett in the jesting reply he made to another interviewer: "Pour faire remarquer moi" [to make notice *me*],[10] deliberately distorting the syntax of his adopted tongue.

Reading Beckett's English fiction, one cannot fail to notice the author's preoccupation and fascination with languages (he knows French, German, Italian, Spanish, Latin, Greek). His abuse of intricate syntactical structures, his Joycean playfulness with words, puns, archaisms, foreign expressions, technical vocabulary, and even punctuation eventually produced a deterioration of meaning. In his last English novel, *Watt*, Beckett carried the complexity of language to extremes, accumulated words to the point of redundancy, and succeeded thereby in exposing the flagrant ambiguity and evasiveness of the English language. If this experimentation led Beckett into a creative impasse, it was, nevertheless, successful because its primary purpose was to reveal the inadequacy of language as a means of artistic communication.

Having, however, committed himself to a creative system that negates not only the validity of the novel form, but that of language as an expressive medium, Beckett could no longer fall prey to a language that forced him to say that which he deliberately avoided. By turning to French, he found a way of renewing his purpose, of liberating his

---

[9] Niklaus Gessner, *Die Unzulänglichkeit der Sprache* (Zurich: Juris-Verlag, 1957), p. 32 n.
[10] *Transition 48*, II (1948), Contributors' Notes, p. 147.

writing from linguistic suggestiveness, thus perpetuating his creativity in the critical vein he had chosen.

It is recognized that the French language, with its demand for clarity and precision, its strict grammatical structure, its words that always relate exactly to the concepts they describe, does not allow a writer to say what he does not want to say. Since Beckett, by choice, was attempting to formulate nothingness into words, to state what cannot be stated, meaninglessness, it was essential for him to rely on a language that could be trusted. Moreover, French was better suited to his intent because it is basically compatible with the expression of abstract ideas, tends explicitly toward the formulation of a substratum of meaning (that of essences rather than substances), whereas English is more appropriate to the expression of concrete facts, of common realities. Therefore, the shift from English to French corresponds not only to Beckett's exile from his Irish land and tongue, but marks also a willful rejection of realism as an inherent aspect of his novels in favor of a more abstract and elusive type of fiction.

However, if the simple and colloquial diction Beckett adopts for the seemingly incoherent interior monologue of his French heroes appears better suited to their irrational and dubious line of thought than does the pedantic and academic language of his English prose, nonetheless any speculation about Beckett's shift from English to French encounters an insoluble paradox. Since Beckett eventually reverts to English for the rendition of his French texts, one can only conclude that, whatever his reasons for turning to French, they are automatically canceled by the act of rewriting the works in English. Thus, whether one deals with Beckett as an Irish writer who translates his work into French, or as a French writer who translates his work into English, to grasp the progressive disintegration of form, setting, and characters, to apprehend the continuity of thought in Beckett's universe, one must examine his works beyond the boundaries of a single language or region. For, when dealing with Beckett's literary production, it is no longer only a national literature that concerns the critic, but rather a more universal problem: one of expression, of communication, of the dilemma of existence above and beyond all physical and linguistic limitations. Furthermore, with a learned polyglot such as Beckett, to appreciate his linguistic dexterity both French and English texts must be consulted. Only then can one note to what extent Beckett's bilingual ability serves the expression of his complex thoughts.

To apprehend the overall structure and the intricate thematic scheme of the Beckettian universe, one cannot limit oneself to the study of a single novel or play, in either French or English; the whole of his fiction must be examined as a continuous flow of words, as a homogeneous creation. When viewed chronologically it is a world in constant motion, in a constant state of being reshaped while gradually being destroyed.

Beckett's novels may give the impression of being the same story told over and over again. Nonetheless, from one work to the next a conscious effort is made to reduce fictional elements to a still barer minimum. This reduction is exemplified by the interplay between each new work and its predecessors. A new Beckett novel or play represents a critical reflection on previous achievements. Each novel, each play, overlaps the others, each character serves as a prototype for his heirs. All the members of Beckett's family share the same idiosyncrasies, the same grotesque physical traits, present the same lethargic and eccentric attitudes, suffer the same existential anguish. As a result they often speak the same words, perform the same actions, reappear from one novel to the next, criticize, mock, parody, insult, and imitate one another, until their names and personalities become interchangeable.

The major difference between Beckett's first work of fiction, *More Pricks Than Kicks*, and the 1961 *Comment c'est* is one of gradual disintegration. The characters are progressively removed and alienated from a social environment. In the process they lose identity and individuality and attain complete physical and moral irresponsibility as they are transformed into anonymous, universal beings. But basically, and despite the language difference, their eccentricity and antisocial attitude remain constant. It is undoubtedly for this reason that the curious creature of *The Unnamable* is able to claim all Beckett's previous creations as his own. In fact, he considers them as steps toward the establishment of his unnamable condition: "All these Murphys, Molloys and Malones do not fool me. They have made me waste my time, suffer for nothing, speak of them when, in order to stop speaking, I should have spoken of me and of me alone" (p. 21).

Looking at the bulk of Beckett's work over the past thirty years or so, one discovers an underlying thematic structure that gives aesthetic unity to the whole of his literary production. However, Beckett's fiction has evolved in three distinct stages, each not only finding a parallel in the deterioration of form and language, but corresponding also to a specific step in the characters' alienation from social reality. The works of fiction written in English before 1945—primarily *More Pricks Than Kicks, Murphy,* and *Watt*—form the first period. They show Beckett's concern for abstract intellectual concepts, and are overburdened with literary and philosophical allusions. These novels and stories are set in a realistic setting (Ireland, Dublin, London) governed by social and historic limitations. Each evolves within the boundaries of conventional fiction and only gradually departs from realism. These English experiments rely for their structure on characterization, description, dialogue, and even sketchy plots which unfold within the restrictions of a specified time and place. Thus, in spite of linguistic extravagance and ludicrous situations, they remain in the domain of traditional fiction. Only in *Watt* can one observe a departure from the conventional narrative in the curious juxtaposition of two worlds: the stable world of man, fictional realism; and the deceptive world of the imagination, fictional absurdity (see the preface for a definition).

Though Beckett presents his English fiction from an objective third-person point of view, repeatedly he feels the need to intrude in the narration to express his dissatisfaction with conventional techniques. His attitude is sardonic, bitter, and antagonistic. Consequently, the narratives are punctuated with numerous ironic and self-conscious parenthetical remarks on the part of the author who attacks both the characters he creates—as replicas of men—and the fiction in which they appear—as an inadequate reflection of reality. These works become social satires in which Beckett ridicules and destroys established order, whether social, religious, ethical, or aesthetic. Subjected to the whims of their creator, the characters meekly express their need for private ideologies, and seek to escape the physical world. But because they doubt their own ability, and are too lethargic to act, they remain caught in the mediocrity of everyday life. They struggle in vain to free themselves from an overly organized system whose reality they question and whose absurdity they recognize, and where they find it impossible to acquire absolute knowledge through either empirical means or reason. Unable to cope with the material world and the natural functions of their bodies, tormented by objects, habits, memory, and time, they retreat into private asylums (minds or madhouses) from which they gaze out in stupefied perplexity. Eventually, under the unflinching hand of their creator, they suffer a paralysis of body and mind which brings a failure of verbal communication, and which indicates their deterioration as well as that of fiction.

It is through this process of the slow mental and physical breakdown of his creations that Beckett builds his fiction. This disintegration is only sketched in his English novels, and such figures as Belacqua Shuah (the protagonist of *More Pricks Than Kicks*), Murphy, and Watt, despite their eccentricities, are reasonably motivated by and humanly concerned with daily life. Their dilemma comes from existing in a world where they can no longer distinguish reality from illusion. Particularly obsessed by the dualism of body and mind, unable to reconcile matter with intellect, they vainly attempt to detach physical from mental forms, reality from fiction, thereby aspiring to a state of complete intellectual irresponsibility: a state of lunacy. In this, they prepare for the subsequent stages of Beckett's universe. But because these English protagonists are subdued by social reality they never succeed in becoming true outsiders like the derelicts of Beckett's later French fiction, who exist in total mental alienation. Instead, they remain lethargic citizens (Oblomovs) [11] who refuse to observe social commitments or to perform useful activities. They prefer to watch, with a certain self-satisfaction, the physical decomposition of their bodies. Their actions consist mostly of a few eccentric gestures which lead to grotesque situations, but which do not permit them to forsake the external world and its impositions. Such predicaments may appear comical to the reader, but for the heroes themselves these abortive gestures produce mental confusion and an acute awareness of failure. Incapable of coping with the world, strangers to their own bodies, unstable in their own minds, these indolent characters repeatedly express death wishes or the desire to return to an uncommitted prenatal condition.

[11] The parallel between Beckett's heroes and Goncharov's lethargic hero has been noted on several occasions. See Melvin Friedman, "The Achievement of Samuel Beckett," *Books Abroad*, XXXIII, no. 3 (Summer, 1959), 278–280. Colin Wilson, *Religion and the Rebel* (London: Victor Gollancz, 1957), also compares "Goncharov's Oblomov (the Russian Hamlet who just cannot bring himself to do anything)" with Beckett's heroes. Peggy Guggenheim in her intimate memoirs, *Out of This Century* (New York: Dial Press, 1946), refers to Beckett, "the tall, lanky Irishman of about thirty with enormous green eyes that never looked at you," as Oblomov, a nickname she claims to have given him when she first met him in Paris in 1937: "I called him Oblomov from the book by Goncharov that Djuna Barnes had given me to read long before. When I met him I was surprised to find a living Oblomov. I made him read the book and of course he immediately saw the resemblance between himself and the strange inactive hero who finally did not even have the will-power to get out of bed" (p. 197). Most of Peggy Guggenheim's remarks about Beckett in her memoirs and also in a more recent book entitled *Confessions of an Art Addict* (New York: Macmillan, 1960) have little relevance to the understanding of Beckett's work, aside from the allusion to Oblomov.

At this point in his literary career Beckett turned to the French language and launched his creations: into fictional exile. The works that represent the second stage of his creative evolution consist of three unpublished manuscripts: the novel *Mercier et Camier,* the story *Premier amour,* the three-act play *Eleutheria,* and three published short stories, "L'Expulsé," "Le Calmant," "La Fin," which were incorporated in the 1955 publication of *Nouvelles et Textes pour rien.* This material marks Beckett's first important attempt to write in French. It is a decisive departure from both intellectualism and realism. Written between 1945 and 1947, these works share a similarity of mood, humor, setting, vulgarity, and obscenity. Their notable aspects are a colloquial tone, a striking simplicity of language, form, and content, a strange juxtaposition of a pseudorealistic environment and grotesque, irrational characters. After the novel *Mercier et Camier,* which retains a narrator, Beckett turns to the first-person narrative, which he then maintains in all subsequent French fiction, gradually shaping the creator-hero of his more recent novels.

These early French works have been overlooked by critics, no doubt because they are not readily available,[12] and yet they represent an important transitional stage in Beckett's creative evolution. The study of these works, however, is essential to the understanding of Beckett's later achievements, for not only do they show a further step in the process of human and fictional disintegration, but they serve as a logical bridge between Beckett's earlier use of social realism and his later reliance on fictional absurdity.

The most appropriate comment on this group of works is found in the title of one of its stories: "L'Expulsé." While all the protagonists of Beckett's English fiction strive to reach some refuge away from the fiasco of society, and temporarily attain such asylum, the hero of the early French works, after having enjoyed a brief stay in what appears to

[12] I am fortunate to have typescripts available of the original manuscripts of *Mercier et Camier, Premier amour,* and *Eleutheria,* as Beckett refuses to publish these.

have been a bourgeois home or a mental institution, are suddenly *expelled*. Yet they do not return to life in society among their fellowmen, but rather face a much more distressing existence outside reality, within the solitude of their incoherent minds, within the unpredictable world of fiction. These outcasts seem to be preparing themselves for a journey, an obscure quest the purpose of which they do not understand, but which they feel compelled to undertake. At the onset of this journey they suffer the embarrassing experience of being kicked into the gutter from the safety and comfort of their refuge. As they set out aimlessly in search of a place, a room, a bed, a container, a coffin, or simply a story in which to exist as fictitious beings, they curse the anonymous creator (father or author) who is responsible for their expulsion into life, into being, and into fiction. While relating the sad and often obscene story of their existence, they wander through the streets, the parks, the outskirts of an unidentified city in which they feel completely out of place, and where they encounter people (members of an organized society) with whom they can no longer identify as human beings. These wandering derelicts have indeed been expelled from the world of man and are now condemned to exist in the illusory world of fiction, whose rules are not necessarily rational. While trying to adapt to this unfamiliar and deceptive condition, they seek to recapture memories of their past, sometimes to invent a past for themselves, to rationalize their irrational predicament, and even to plan a possible return to the world of men—that is, the world of conventional fiction. They soon realize, however, that they no longer function as human beings or as traditional heroes; they have become puppets superimposed on a realistic setting with which their absurd fictional existence is incompatible.

The story in which these narrator-heroes appear is the sole justification for their presence and existence. And yet, they are unable to sever all ties with the real world. Though they are Beckett's first real bums, their survival still depends on the charity of others, on social recognition, on the objects they drag along, on the memories they preserve of a former life, and above all on their own inventiveness. Before they can wander outside the city, outside the material world, before they can plunge into the hallucinatory region where Beckett's more recent French creatures dwell, before they can indulge in creative delirium like Molloy, Malone, The Unnamable, or the narrator-hero of *Comment c'est,* they must learn to become self-sufficient, they must break away from their incomprehensible past and the vague memories that still cling to them. They must learn to become inventors of fiction so that they can create a world in which to exist fictionally. More fortunate than their predecessors in the English fiction, whose stories and existences are controlled by the omniscient author, these early French heroes acquire a creative power that permits them to situate themselves in the stories they narrate. However, though they struggle to achieve the perfect status of creator-hero, they do not succeed in attaining total fictional detachment and irresponsibility. Too often their obsession with the material world prevents them from enjoying the mental, physical, and fictional freedom Beckett grants his more recent creations. These early French wanderers have reached only the periphery of the desolate and moribund region in which Beckett's later heroes vegetate.

Having established the thematic and aesthetic structure of his universe, Beckett is able to reduce the novel form to ultimate nothingness. Thus, progressing into Beckett's French fiction, one discovers that the regressive pattern—the deliberate movement away from rationality and realism—is accentuated from one work to the next. In *Molloy, Malone meurt, L'Innommable,* the *Textes pour rien,* and the fragment "From an Abandoned Work," the disintegration of man, of form, and of language follows an irrevocable course which produces in *Comment c'est* the image of a reptilian creature muttering disconnected sounds as it crawls in the mud of a fantastically unreal landscape. This creature's thoughts and actions reach such incoherence that one marvels how any aesthetic order is maintained. Page after page the narration is undermined, insidiously stripped of its essential attributes, and while the narrator-hero struggles toward an inevitable and yet impossible silence, the story, the setting, the language, deteriorate into meaninglessness and chaos.

Beckett's early English fiction is presented as Swiftian social satire, and is often sardonic. There the protagonists express their dissatisfaction with the world through extravagant actions which produce a striking contrast with their conventional personalities. The early French works introduce ambiguous figures who appear to be suspended between the real world and an absurd region they eventually identify as the world of fiction. Beckett's more recent French heroes are also eccentrics, but because they have lost contact with social reality, because they can no longer be held responsible as rational human beings, their eccentricity appears compatible with their grotesque predicament. Aside from finding themselves alienated from reality and submerged in absurdity, these derelicts become conscious of their illusory condition, aware of their roles as fictional beings, however futile such roles may be. They acquire a certain creative freedom, a certain lucidity which places them outside the moral and rational standards to which their predecessors are bound. Thus, while the characters of Beckett's earlier works remain bitterly antagonistic to society, its institutions and people, the French heroes assume complete indifference toward the human condition. As they are gradually dehumanized, they become more and more irresponsible and uncommitted to the affairs of man. Their sole concern is the self, but a self that transcends physical and material life to encounter in the region of pure intellect the anguish of metaphysical existence. Conscious of the gratuity of their condition, Beckett's creator-heroes invent surroundings and lives for themselves, however trite, meaningless, absurd, or fantastic these may be. They improvise their existence on the theme of self, with little respect for human norms. Their fictional progress becomes a dizzying performance which, like jazz improvisations, exploits its own imper-

fections as it discovers new zones of being. These creatures'
shapes, thoughts, words, and actions are as unpredictable as
the notes of a jazz musician's instrument, and they achieve
coherence largely by virtue of that unpredictability.

At the third stage of its evolution, Beckett's fiction follows a culminating process that draws toward a single image, a single expression repeated stubbornly to an irrational
infinity. It strives toward the ambivalent creation of a
unique and universal being caught in absurd immortality,
in total ignorance and impotence, a voice that finally cries
out: ". . . ça va être le silence, là où je suis, je ne sais pas,
je ne le saurai jamais, dans le silence on ne sait pas, il faut
continuer, je vais continuer" (L'Innommable, p. 262). This
closing statement of the novel gains an even more pathetic
note in the English version where Beckett adds: ". . . you
must go on, I can't go on, I'll go on" (The Unnamable, p.
179 [italics mine]).

It is also at this stage that Beckett extended his experimentation to the theater, where he succeeded in presenting
plays devoid of plot, decor, action, psychological development, climax, denouement, and in which he even eliminated
some of man's most essential functions. The theater, however, more than the novel, cannot function without the
presence of human elements. Therefore, the dramatist is
never quite able to present complete physical disintegration
on stage. Yet in spite of this restricting condition, Beckett
succeeded in abstracting the human body from his dramas
by relying on only the use of voices. To achieve this he
turned to the almost obsolete medium of radio and wrote
plays, All That Fall, Embers, Words and Music, Cascando,
in which physical reality is suggested by sounds. In the stage
play Krapp's Last Tape he replaced human relationship,
essential to dramatic impact, with a character confronted by
a voice speaking from a tape recorder. On two other occasions, seeking another method for annihilating the human
condition, Beckett presented short dramatic pieces in which
human speech is totally excluded: the two mimes, Acte
sans paroles.

As of 1947, the mood, the tone, and the structure of Beckett's universe were set, the central themes had been explored, and the characters were on their way to alienation and disintegration. Beckett then proceeded from one work to the next to perfect the distorting and destructive pattern he had devised. In less than four years (1947–1950) he wrote the bulk of those French works that have brought him recognition: *Molloy, Malone meurt, En Attendant Godot,* and *L'Innommable,* in that order. Beginning in 1951 these works were released for publication at yearly intervals, but only after detailed revisions—as can be seen from earlier excerpts published in various magazines.[13] The thirteen *Textes pour rien* written in 1950 show Beckett's anguish as he reached a creative impasse from which he seemed unable to extricate himself. He then began the translation of his French texts into English: *Waiting for Godot* (1954), *Molloy* (1955), *Malone Dies* (1956), and *The Unnamable* (1958). In 1953, approximately ten years after it was written, the novel *Watt* was released for publication, out of sequence, and in 1955 *Nouvelles et Textes pour rien* appeared. All these works had been written prior to 1950. Only in 1957 did Beckett produce a new work in French, the remarkable play *Fin de partie,* which he translated into English as *Endgame.* Then followed three short plays written first in English: two radio plays, *All That Fall* (1957) and *Embers* (1959), and the one-act stage play, *Krapp's Last Tape* (1958).

It seemed that Beckett had turned completely to the theater, and was incapable of returning to the novel form. In 1957 appeared only a fragment of fiction, appropriately entitled "From an Abandoned Work." [14] Was Beckett mark-

[13] Excerpts from *Malone meurt* appeared in *Les Temps Modernes* (Sept., 1951), pp. 385–416; excerpts from *L'Innommable* appeared in *Nouvelle Nouvelle Revue Française* (Feb., 1953), pp. 214–234.

[14] It is difficult to know exactly when Beckett wrote this prose fragment, but by its tone and style it appears contemporaneous with *L'Innommable* and the *Textes pour rien* of 1950. However, unlike these, this fragment was first written in English. It was published in *Evergreen Review,* I, no. 3 (1957), 83–91.

ing time? Were the critics correct in assuming that he had nothing more to say, nothing more to do? In 1958, oddly enough, his name appeared as translator of the *Anthology of Mexican Poetry* compiled by Octavio Paz. It took Beckett eleven years from the *Textes pour rien* of 1950 to produce another major work of fiction, the unusual novel *Comment c'est*.

If this book marks a departure from Beckett's earlier fiction, it nonetheless exploits the same process of physical and mental reduction of the characters, uses the same narrative technique as the trilogy, and represents another logical step in fictional disintegration. The important innovation here lies with linguistic distortions—the complete lack of punctuation, the unusual syntax, and the poetic diction.[15] Since the publication of *Comment c'est*, Beckett has produced four more dramatic pieces: the one-act play *Happy Days*, which had an unsuccessful world première in New York in the fall of 1961, and two short radio plays, *Words and Music* (in English for the BBC) and *Cascando* (in French for the RTF—Radio Télévision Française). *Play*, Beckett's most recent work, opened in Ulm, Germany, in the spring of 1963 in Beckett's own German version. *Happy Days* was recently published in Paris in Beckett's French translation entitled *Oh les beaux jours*. Beckett is now working on the English rendition of *Comment c'est*.[16]

Though he has gained wider recognition as a dramatist, it is as a novelist that Beckett achieves greater literary stature. With the novel *Comment c'est* he has brought fiction to the brink of artistic chaos. This work reduces language to its most primitive form, strips setting and characters to complete physical and mental nakedness, and in so doing

[15] Discussing this novel, Ruby Cohn ("Comment c'est: de quoi rire," *French Review*, XXXV, no. 6 [May, 1962], 563) states: ". . . this work, stripping away plot and characters, is as close to poetry as to fiction; even typographically the text appears in irregular verses."

[16] Excerpts from *Comment c'est*, in English, translated by the author, appeared as "From an Unabandoned Work," *Evergreen Review*, IV. no. 14 (Sept.-Oct., 1960), 58–65, and in *Paris Review*, no. 28 (Summer-Fall, 1962), 113–116.

mocks the creative act. Its originality suggests the impossibility of writing subsequent novels without being repetitious or imitative.

In a recent conversation with Samuel Beckett in Paris, I asked him what his plans were, what project or what new novel he had in mind. He answered: "I have nothing more to say. . . . I am empty." Reporting on a similar conversation with Beckett some years ago, Hugh Kenner wrote: "If one thing was clear to him in April 1958, it was that *The Unnamable* and the *Textes Pour Rien* had placed him in an impasse where he could not possibly write another novel. Accordingly in January 1961 he published a sort of novel, *Comment c'est*. There is neither perversity here, nor inadvertence, but stubborn policy." [17]

This is HOW IT IS with Beckett's fiction, and one may wonder what curious shape his next novel will take.

[17] Kenner, *op. cit.*, p. 25.

SOCIAL REALITY: LETHARGY, DOUBT, AND INSANITY

Hell is the
static lifelessness of
unrelieved viciousness.
Paradise the static lifelessness
of unrelieved immaculation.
Purgatory a flood of movement
and vitality released by
the conjunction of
these two elements.

BECKETT, "Dante . . . Bruno. Vico . . Joyce."

The creature of habit
turns aside from the object
that cannot be made
to correspond with
one or other of
his intellectual prejudices.

BECKETT, *Proust*

II

BELACQUA AND THE INFERNO OF SOCIETY

As represented in Beckett's early English fiction, social reality corresponds to a traditional and realistic setting in which
conventional characters remain helplessly caught in "the
muck" of life's routine. The fictitious heroes Belacqua
Shuah, Murphy, and Watt seek to forsake this environment
not only through mental alienation, but by aspiring to an
existence no longer controlled by rational and logical conditions, an existence situated in a fictional surrounding appropriate to their eccentric temperament. Recognizing that
"the nature of outer reality remains obscure" (*Murphy*, p.
177), deceptive, and incomprehensible, unable to reconcile
themselves to the unavoidable dualism of matter and mind,
they try to negate all notions of reality, thereby rejecting the
mediocrity of social life. To succeed in this ascetic quest, to
reach this apparently blissful condition, these protagonists
must learn to exist beyond their own physical and emotional
needs, indifferent to the human body, exiled from the society of man. None of Beckett's early heroes is capable of

such complete moral and physical detachment. Therefore, they find themselves constantly oscillating between the world of man (social reality) and the make-believe world of the mind (fictional absurdity). In their struggle to free themselves from worldly concerns they endure a succession of embarrassing failures which confines them to social reality and forces them into acts of self-destruction.

The three major figures of Beckett's English fiction, Belacqua, Murphy, and Watt, share one obsession, one desire—to find a refuge away from the sociorealistic "fiasco," somewhere beyond the restrictions of organized society, and ultimately beyond the boundaries of traditional fiction. In other words, subconsciously they aspire to the absurd condition Beckett later grants his French creations. Too lethargic to participate in the social game, doubting the validity of external reality, neglecting the natural demands of the human body, these protagonists attempt to escape the common world to enjoy the fancies of their imagination. They seek as their ideal an institution (or fictional setting) where they can vegetate, uncommitted to the tedious activities of everyday life, an insane asylum where lunatics indulge in their "own pernicious little private dungheap" (*Murphy*, p. 177), and where mental chaos is equated with creative freedom. Thus, while physical needs are cared for, the mind can perform its extravagances, unconcerned with bodily functions, relieved of doubtful notions and memories.

The better-known novels of Samuel Beckett, *Molloy, Malone meurt, L'Innommable*, and the recent *Comment c'est*, are, as Martin Esslin states, "*sui generis*, unclassifiable, disturbing, funny, cruel, and inspiring"; they defy all attempts at interpretation, and are not even easily accessible.[1] To gain insight into the structure and meaning of these complex, unrealistic works, one must investigate Beckett's early English fiction, which contains, in a more traditional form, the essential elements of his later achievements. For

[1] "Samuel Beckett," in *The Novelist as Philosopher*, ed. John Cruickshank (London: Oxford University Press, 1962), p. 144.

though they rely on linguistic dexterity and intellectual exhibitionism, Beckett's early works can be apprehended on the level of conventional realism. Such is the case with Beckett's first extensive work of fiction, the now rare collector's item, *More Pricks Than Kicks*,[2] a work ignored by Beckett's critics.

Published in 1934, the book consists of a collection of ten short stories loosely related through a common protagonist, Belacqua Shuah, whose eccentric actions and amorous adventures are described comically in a picaresque manner, from his days as a student until his death and burial as a thrice-married man. Although these stories lack consistent overall structure, unifying plot, and recurrent motifs, they acquire thematic unity through the hero's personality; in spite of the ambiguous changes he undergoes from one story to the next, he remains faithful to his indolence, his extravagance, his antisocial attitude, and above all his sensual desires. Thus *More Pricks Than Kicks* can easily pass for a novel rather than a series of disconnected episodes. In fact, an unfinished, unpublished first version of this book exists in novel form. Entitled *Dream of Fair to Middling Women*,[3] a good portion of its material was used in *More Pricks Than Kicks,* though a careful examination of the two texts reveals the extent to which Beckett reworks his manuscripts. The hero of the first draft was also named Belacqua.

As the firstborn of Beckett's family of outcasts, Belacqua stands as the prototype for all his successors. His actions, obsessions, and idiosyncrasies prepare the personalities of the later eccentrics. Compared, however, with Beckett's French derelicts, most of whom spend their absurd existence vegetating in some nameless, moribund landscape, Belacqua is a normal and traditional hero. Primarily concerned with the physical self, he functions as a social man who has to

[2] Beckett, *More Pricks Than Kicks* (London: Chatto and Windus, 1934), 278 pp. For a synopsis of this work, see the appendix. Page references given in the text are from the original edition.

[3] Unpublished novel written about 1932. For a discussion and synopsis of this work, see the appendix.

cope with all the trivialities of life in society. If Beckett's more recent creatures dwell in a timeless and spaceless region no longer limited by realistic norms, Belacqua's fortunes evolve in a pattern controlled by chronological events. His environment remains identifiable and realistic. Moreover, he has a past, an ancestry, an education, and rational beliefs that determine his behavior. He has basic emotional and sexual relationships with numerous ladies and enjoys "many a delightful recollection of their commerce" (p. 54). He succeeds in marrying three of them. These are worldly pleasures of which Beckett's senile French heroes are deprived; for them marriage, love, sex, and the remembrance of such activities are reduced to grotesque gestures or obscene thoughts. However, being thus cornered by social, physical, and marital impositions, Belacqua assumes a lethargic, sardonic, and particularly a cowardly posture in all his actions. He is, as Beckett describes him, "an indolent bourgeois poltroon, very talented up to a point, but not fitted for private life in the best and brightest sense . . ." (p. 234).

Belacqua, like his creator, is a Dubliner, descendant of "the grand old Huguenot guts" (p. 230), a Trinity man, a poet, student of Dante, and somewhat of a dilettante. He, too, has traveled abroad, and likes to brag about it to the point that one of his early conquests complains, "You make great play with your short stay abroad" (p. 25). Indeed, Belacqua is very much inclined toward self-exhibitionism, and, as Beckett himself tends to do in his early works, he abuses the knowledge, the erudition, the foreign languages with which he is familiar. His speech is punctuated by Latin, German, Italian, and French expressions, so much so that the author feels obliged to apologize for his hero: "Pardon these French expressions, but the creature dreams in French" (p. 112). However, the comparison between author and protagonist ends here.

Throughout the book, Belacqua appears as a neurotic pedant who cannot reconcile himself to having been born, and to having to adjust to social conventions. He prefers to enjoy prenatal memories in a state of idleness, to entertain romantic notions as a rejected artist, and to indulge in self-pity. Consequently, he shows very little respect for the Dublin institutions, his fellow citizens, and his family. In the opening story, "Dante and the Lobster," he refers to one of his relatives as that "lousy old bitch of an aunt" (p. 11), and throughout the stories shows a particular distaste for the people with whom he comes in contact, even his lady friends.

Belacqua refuses to play the social game, but out of cowardice submits to its rules. His only defense and self-justification is indolence; when forced to act, his behavior is marked by irresponsibility and eccentricity. He rents flashy cars which he can hardly drive; he cannot bear to sit on a person's right side; he is very particular about his food, and meticulous about the preparation of his meals; he loves burnt toast and "a good green stenching rotten lump of Gorgonzola cheese" (p. 8), and, were it not for his cowardice, he would go so far as to assault the grocer who tries to cheat him of his pleasure:

He looked sceptically at the cut of cheese. He turned it over on its back to see was the other side any better. The other side was worse. They had laid it better side up, they had practised that little deception. . . . Belacqua was furious. The impudent dogsbody, for two pins he would assault him.
'It won't do' he cried, 'do you hear me, it won't do at all. I won't have it.' He ground his teeth. [pp. 8–9]

Such obsessions hardly ingratiate Belacqua to the reader; in this he is unlike most later Beckett heroes who, despite their deformity, depravity, vulgarity, and cruelty, beg for compassion. Belacqua is detestable, and as a result his own creator constantly ridicules him. Worst of all, he drinks heavily and evades all commitments "by pleading that he had been drunk at the time, or that he was an incoherent person and content to remain so, and so on" (p. 46). His overindulgence in gin and tonic often places him in bizarre situations. Under the influence of alcohol, he does not hesitate to undress in the street to enjoy the trickling of rain on his bare chest. In another instance, while walking, drunk, down the street "his feet pained him so much that he took off his perfectly good boots and threw them away" (p. 113). When intoxicated Belacqua is quite unpredictable; once he buys four seats in heaven from a woman peddler in a pub who tells him, "For yer frien', yer da, yer ma an' yer motte" (p. 57), but does not offer one to Belacqua who hardly deserves paradise. Whereas Beckett's later heroes may consider themselves in purgatory, Belacqua finds himself hopelessly caught in the inferno of society.

Belacqua Shuah may not be a typical Beckett hero, but one can detect in his physical defects and mental deficiency many attributes of Beckett's later creations. He is afflicted with all sorts of minor torments: his face is broken out with impetigo; he has spavined gait and ruined feet, from which he suffers continuously, and eventually he undergoes a toe and neck operation; his temperament is marked by anxiety and morbidity, he suffers fits of depression, has suicidal inclinations, and shows a flagrant aspiration to lunacy. His eccentricity and moral irresponsibility become prominent traits of his successors.

If Belacqua seeks to escape the "real" world of men, but repeatedly finds himself thrown back into the grips of reality, by contrast Beckett's later derelicts no longer need to forsake a social or human environment. They exist outside society, outside reality, and struggle merely to reconcile themselves to the condition imposed upon them by their creator. There may be little glory in being reduced to such an inhuman status, but in the middle of their illusory condition Beckett's French characters suffer *heroically*.

Belacqua never achieves a heroic state because he insists on acting too humanly. To become a true Beckettian hero, he would have to renounce all ties with society, all affinities with the human condition, and be willing to accept the consequences of social alienation. This requires a courage of which Belacqua is not capable. Therefore, his erratic actions, his social antagonism, his cynicism, his faculty for acting with insufficient motivation, and "his gratuity of conduct" (p. 122) may show a potential aspiration toward genuine fictional existence, but too often it is marked by cowardliness. When caught, he meekly surrenders to the laws and regulations of society, and presents a hypocritical and submissive front. His eccentricity may be a gesture of revolt, or simply a means to escape his environment, yet it is never carried far enough, or conducted with enough conviction, to be effective.

Throughout the book, whenever he is faced with the embarrassing outcomes of his irresponsible actions, Belacqua quickly retreats into a humble and apologetic attitude. In the story "A Wet Night," while on his way to a Christmas Eve party, already quite drunk and disorderly, Belacqua comes face to face with a policeman. The comic encounter exemplifies his submissive behavior:

Subduing a great desire to visit the pavement he catted, with undemonstrative abundance, all over the boots and trouser-ends of the Guard, in return for which incontinence he received such a dunch on the breast that he fell hip and thigh into the outskirts of his own offal. . . .

Sprawled on the sidewalk, Belacqua clumsily collects his thoughts:

He bore no animosity towards the Guard, although now he began to hear what he was saying. He knelt before him in the filth, he heard all the odious words he was saying in the recreation of his duty, and bore him not the slightest ill-will. . . . It distressed him to learn that for two pins the Guard would frog-march him to the Station, but he appreciated the officer's dilemma.

Undoubtedly, Belacqua would gladly redeem himself:

'Wipe them boots' said the Guard.
Belacqua was only too happy, it was the least he could do. Contriving two loose swabs of the Twilight Herald he stooped and cleaned the boots and trouser-ends in the best of his ability. . . .
'I trust, Sergeant,' said Belacqua, in a murmur pitched to melt the hardest heart, 'that you can see your way to overlooking my misdemeanour.'   [pp. 95, 96, 97]

The policeman orders him to move on, and, as he walks away clutching the crumpled newspaper with which he cleaned the boots, Belacqua curses the officer under his breath, but waits until he is safely around the corner and out of sight before dropping the litter to the pavement.

Unlike the hero of *More Pricks Than Kicks,* most Beckett characters show little respect for the numerous policemen who abound in Beckett's fiction. Instead they mock and play tricks on them, insult them openly, and in one instance two of Beckett's bums (Mercier and Camier) go so far as to attack and eventually kill a policeman. Belacqua would never dare indulge in such acts of rebellion. Like many protagonists of contemporary novels, he is one of these "crackpots thumbing their noses at society from the safety of some sordid room," [4] or the safety of their own solipsism. Yet, though he brags of having furnished his mind that he may live there in peace, Belacqua finds that his bodily functions, his physical needs, and his relationships with the outside world prevent him from enjoying mental privacy. Therefore, he expresses his desire for escape by three un-fulfilled wishes: to return to a prenatal condition (which is impossible), to commit suicide (which he attempts but fails to conclude successfully), and to be confined to an insane asylum (which is denied him because he remains too rational). Unable to realize his hopes, constantly frustrated, and "being by nature however sinfully indolent, bogged in indolence" (p. 44), Belacqua is caught in the trap of his own weaknesses, in the limbo of his incapacity. He never achieves fictional freedom (the freedom of controlling his mind and actions) and finds himself totally subjected to the rules of social reality.

It is in the fourth canto of Dante's *Purgatorio* that Beckett encountered the prototype for the hero of *More Pricks Than Kicks.* Dante's Florentine friend, the slothful Belacqua, not

[4] K. W. Gransden, "The Dustman Cometh," *Encounter,* IX (July, 1958), 84.

only shares his name with Beckett's protagonist, but "colui che mostra sè più negligente / che se tigrizia fosse sua serocchia" (IV, 110),[5] also offers his indolence and symbolic fetal position as a recurrent attitude and posture for Belacqua Shuah, who in turn becomes a model for later figures in Beckett's universe.

Belacqua, hiding in the shadow of a rock on the steep slope of the mountain that Dante and his guide painfully ascend, is described in the following way: "E un di lor, che mi sembiava lasso / sedeva e abbracciava le ginocchia, / tenendo il viso giù tra esse basso" (IV, 106–108).[6] Dante's Belacqua, who has failed to repent, assumes a lethargic fetal position in order to review his former terrestrial life before he is allowed to enter paradise. In moments of drunkenness or depression, the hero of *More Pricks Than Kicks* also adopts "the knee-and-elbow" position of the indolent souls in purgatory—not, however, to recapture fleeting memories or to evaluate his life, but to obliterate reality. All Beckett's creatures are described or describe themselves in that position at one time or another. The protagonists of Beckett's two English novels, Murphy and Watt, in their inability to cope with reality, long to return to the womb, and often unconsciously assume the appropriate pose. The anonymous narrator of "L'Expulsé," one of Beckett's early French stories, after having been kicked into the gutter from the comfort of his paternal home, explains: "Under these circumstances, nothing compelled me to get up immediately. I rested my elbow on the sidewalk, funny the things you remember, settled my ear in the cup of my hand and began to reflect on my situation, notwithstanding its familiarity." [7]

[5] Dante, *The Divine Comedy*, "Purgatorio," Bilingual Edition, ed. John D. Sinclair (London, 1948), p. 62. "He who shows himself more indolent / than if sloth were his sister."

[6] *Ibid.*, p. 60. "And one of them, who seemed to me weary sat clasping his knees / and holding his face low down between them."

[7] Beckett, *Nouvelles et Textes pour rien*. Quotation from the translation by Richard Seaver in *Evergreen Review*, VI, no. 22 (Jan-Feb., 1962), 9.

Condemed to wander aimlessly, he repeatedly regrets having been expelled not only from his home but from the womb.

The wandering Molloy also compares himself with Dante's Belacqua: "I was perched higher than the road's highest point and flattened what is more against a rock the same colour as myself, that is grey . . . crouched like Belacqua, or Sordello, I forget" (*Molloy*, p. 12). Sordello, one recalls, is also in the circle of the indolent souls in purgatory. But, although Dante ascribes to Belacqua the characteristic Florentine shrewdness, of Sordello he says, "Come ti stavi altera e disdegnosa / e nel mover delli occhi onesta e tarda!" (VI, 62–63).[8] Thus, if Molloy confuses Belacqua and Sordello, it is because Beckett's heroes share attributes of both these Dantesque figures; they retain a mixture of wit, indolence, pride, scorn, and dignity. However, while the protagonists of Beckett's early English fiction aspire to the "Belacqua bliss," as Murphy calls it, and hope for salvation or for an end to their misery, the undying heroes of Beckett's French works seem to have evolved beyond that hope. Caught in a zone where memories of happier days are failing them, and where the hope of possible salvation is negated, they resign themselves to their futile and static plight: "Their path begins and ends at Belacqua's rock; their movement is, like Zeno's arrow, a state of rest." [9] In Beckett's last novel, *Comment c'est*, once more the pitiful narrator-hero compares himself with Dante's Belacqua, but this time his grotesque posture mocks the literary reference:

endormi je me vois endormi sur le flanc ou sur le ventre c'est l'un ou l'autre sur le flanc lequel le droit c'est mieux le sac sous la tête ou serré contre le ventre serré contre le ventre les genoux remontés le dos en cer-	asleep I see myself asleep on the side or on the belly the one or the other on the side which one the right side it's better the bag under my head or tight against the belly tight against the belly knees folded the back

[8] Dante, *op. cit.*, p. 82. "How lofty and disdainful was thy bearing / and what dignity in the slow moving of thine eyes."

[9] Walter A. Strauss, "Dante's Belacqua and Beckett's Tramps," *Comparative Literature*, XI, no. 3 (Summer, 1959), 259.

ceau la tête minuscule près des genoux enroulé autour du sac Belacqua basculé sur le côté las d'attendre oublié des coeurs où vit la grâce endormi [10]

arched the head minuscule near the knees coiled around the bag *Belacqua toppled over on his side tired of waiting forgotten by hearts where Grace still exists asleep* (Italics mine.)]

In *More Pricks Than Kicks,* Belacqua's wish to return to the womb implies a conscious but feeble revolt against the physical world. His animosity is directed against the conditions of the social and material environment in which he exists, and which dictate a pattern of behavior. Because man has a body he must act to satisfy the needs of that body. Belacqua craves to exist in total mental alienation, or to be back "in the caul," in the dark forever; but since life (or matter, in the form of a body) is inflicted upon man at birth, Belacqua cannot escape physical existence, nor can he avoid his social fate. Consequently, he resigns himself to his condition, curses the day he was born, and, like Dante's slothful friend in purgatory, chooses to spend the duration of his lifetime in the least demanding manner. All Beckett's creatures share this penchant for conscious inaction and idleness. They refuse to allow the body its most natural functions, either for its sake or for the sake of belonging to an organized system. But when Molloy, Malone, The Unnamable, or the narrator-hero of *Comment c'est* take on the fetal posture, it is no longer, as with Belacqua Shuah, a gesture of revolt against the material world, but a resigned expression of metaphysical anguish. They are lonely beings curling like worms in a desolate plot of earth.

In the *Divine Comedy,* Belacqua's fate is to remain in purgatory, or, more precisely, antepurgatory, since he has committed the sin of having delayed repentance, for a period equal to the duration of his prior earthly lifetime. Accordingly, his purgation is also delayed, and the Florentine is not permitted to ascend the mountain to paradise until the heavenly bodies have circulated around him as often as they

[10] Beckett, *Comment c'est,* p. 29.

did during his physical existence. It is, no doubt, to emphasize the indolence of Belacqua that Dante insists on the steepness and length of the ascent. Dante's former friend conceals his resignation and lack of motivation in a state of complete lethargy. Yet when asked why he sits there in idleness, his answer contains no anguish, for he knows that his present condition is limited.

Such a predicament appears ideal for those Beckett heroes who, like Dante's Belacqua, seek to spend the duration of their lifetimes (from womb to tomb) oblivious to reality, unconcerned with the world, satisfied merely to indulge in the whims of their imaginative and somewhat irrational minds. For Belacqua Shuah, the prospect is even more desirable since he firmly believes in the possibility of escaping his present condition, either to be locked in a mental institution or to enjoy the eternal bliss of an afterlife. Thus, if he can compare his existence to that of Dante's friend, it is because it progresses toward a definite end: lunacy or death. In fact, he and Murphy, who shares the same naïve belief, are the only two Beckett protagonists to encounter death; the later heroes vegetate endlessly and hopelessly in absurd immortality.

In Beckett's French novels and plays the line of demarcation between present and future, between life and death, has been abolished. The heroes exist in a region that extends beyond the limits of birth and death. It is an existence that can never end, since it really never began, an existence that allows no progress, no change. Caught in this static condition, these undying creatures convince themselves that their clumsy motions will lead them out of their present state, yet they are aware that these movements are mere illusions—illusions of progress created from despair and fictional necessity. These derelicts are deprived of any choice. They exist outside physical, social, and psychological restrictions, but they are also exempt from death. For them fictional life is death in progress. Therefore, if their actions seem more absurd than those of Belacqua, it is because they have neither motive nor purpose, or, as Maurice Blanchot puts it:

Il n'y a rien d'admirable dans une épreuve à laquelle on ne peut se soustraire, rien qui appelle l'admiration dans le fait d'être enfermé et de tourner en rond dans un espace d'où l'on ne peut sortir même par la mort, car, pour y tomber, il a fallu précisément déjà tomber hors de la vie.[11]

Belacqua Shuah, on the contrary, is convinced that his feeble actions and motions will undoubtedly bring an end to his physical misery. Because his life is finite he is able to toy with the notion of physical reality, and he boasts of having achieved mental freedom. In this respect he is *de mauvaise foi* in his claims, and his anguish remains strictly intellectual, for he can always end his discontent—either by resuming a normal life among his fellowmen, or by committing suicide. His distress is self-imposed even though unjustifiable; his attitude is hypocritical because he can choose an alternative to his condition. He exists within a system that provides him with safety margins: the reality of physical life on the one hand, and that of death on the other. The essential difference then between his predicament and that of Beckett's ageless bums rests on a temporal basis. Belacqua's condition, like that of Dante's souls in purgatory, is limited, and contains the hope of redemption, whereas the waiting and the suffering of Beckett's more recent and tragic heroes are infinite in their absurdity. The heroes no longer hope for a quick death and a blissful afterlife, nor do they return to social reality.

Whether or not the hero of *More Pricks Than Kicks* succeeds in escaping the social inferno to enjoy what he imagines to be a delightful mental purgatory is totally inconsequential since his existence is abruptly curtailed by a death that cures him of the naïve hope he had for an afterlife. Belacqua's immediate successor, Murphy, suffers from a similar delusion. He, too, aspires to the "lee of Belacqua's rock and his embryonal repose" (*Murphy,* pp. 77–78), and, moreover, claims that he is able to penetrate the ideal zones of his mind. Like Belacqua Shuah, he

[11] Maurice Blanchot, *Le Livre à venir* (Paris: Gallimard, 1959), p. 260.

equates mental existence with a purgatorial state, and neither of them is willing to recognize the infinite anguish that
inner life or afterlife can produce. In fact, Murphy thinks
"so highly of his post-mortem situation, its advantages were
present in such detail in his mind, that he actually hoped he
might live to be old" (*ibid.*, p. 78) in order to enjoy as
restful a state as that of Dante's friend. Beckett refers to
Murphy's systematized hope as "his Belacqua fantasy," and
adds that "it belonged to those that lay just beyond the
frontier of suffering, it was the first landscape of freedom"
(*idem*). For the heroes of Beckett's early English fiction this
desired condition lies either within the mind, beyond the
restrictions of the human body, or in some endless afterlife,
beyond the limits of earthly existence.

Neither Murphy nor Belacqua achieves mental freedom
or immortality in some paradisiac region. Murphy's body
and mind are disintegrated in a gas explosion, and his ashes
swept away on the floor of a London pub. As for Belacqua
Shuah, he, who had often looked forward naïvely to meeting
all his girl friends in some peaceful heaven ("What a
hope!"), must endure a final sarcastic derision even as he
lies marble cold on his deathbed: while his widow flirts with
his best friend, the author comments, "Death had already
cured him of that naïveté" (p. 264).

Though he declines to participate in the social and physical effort of existence, Belacqua is conditioned by the demands of external reality. While seeking mental isolation,
he curses the moment of his birth, and longs for physical
annihilation. He expresses this longing not only by his
desire to return to the womb, but also through repeated
suicidal wishes. For Belacqua death remains an alternative
that can end both physical and mental distress. His anxiety
and his obsession with self-destruction constitute "a breakdown in the self-sufficiency which he never wearied of arro-
gating to himself, a sorry collapse of my little internus
homo, and alone sufficient to give him away as inept ape of
his own shadow" (pp. 45–46). His suicide attempts stem

from his inability to cope with life either socially or intellectually. Even before Albert Camus' 1942 essay, *Le Mythe de Sisyphe*,[12] Beckett expressed intuitively the relationship between absurdity and suicide. All Beckett's exiled heroes consider suicide at one time or another as a means of ending their absurd existence, but, aside from Belacqua and Murphy, no Beckett hero succeeds in dying. Instead, Beckett's French derelicts remain suspended in a state of endless expectancy, and often devise means of parodying self-destruction.

In the story "Love and Lethe" the sexual act is presented as an ironic substitute for suicide. Belacqua has managed to convince his girl friend, Ruby Tough, that she should commit the act of *felo de se* with him. Together they proceed to a deserted spot at the top of a mountain. Belacqua carries, in a bag, a revolver and bullets, some veronal, a bottle of whisky with glasses, and the suicide note which he describes "as the notice . . . that we are fled" (p. 128). In spite of its implied seriousness the situation quickly turns to grotesque comedy.[13] When they reach the chosen place, Ruby, who has removed her skirt in order to "storm the summit" with more ease, succeeds in pouring half the bottle of whisky down

[12] In 1942, Camus (*Le Mythe de Sisyphe* [Paris: Gallimard, 1942], p. 18) wrote: "Un monde qu'on peut expliquer même avec de mauvaises raisons est un monde familier. Mais au contraire, dans un univers soudain privé d'illusions et de lumières, l'homme se sent un étranger. Cet exil est sans recours puisqu'il est privé des souvenirs d'une patrie perdue ou de l'espoir d'une terre promise. Ce divorce entre l'homme et la vie, l'acteur et son décor, c'est proprement le sentiment de l'absurdité. Tous les hommes sains ayant songé à leur propre suicide, on pourra reconnaitre, sans plus d'explications, qu'il y a un lien direct entre ce sentiment et l'aspiration vers le néant." He was formulating philosophically what Beckett, a decade earlier, suggested artistically and intuitively in his first work of fiction, and which became an essential theme of his later works.

[13] Horace Gregory (*The Dying Gladiators* [New York: Grove Press, 1961], p. 168) points out the interesting similarity of Beckett's story "Love and Lethe" to Graham Greene's short story "A Drive in the Country," where the protagonist takes a girl for a drive with the intention of "forcing her into a suicide pact." Mr. Gregory adds, however, that the comic turn Beckett gives his story makes it more successful than "converting it into a slick magazine story melodrama," as Graham Greene does.

Belacqua's throat, and she herself swallows the other half. The hero is then incapable of carrying out his suicide scheme, fires the gun "in terram," and together they find a justification for their failure by indulging in the act of love. Beckett, with his usual irony, cannot prevent himself from peeping at the lovers and from interjecting a lyrical but sarcastic comment:

So that they came together in inevitable nuptial. With the utmost reverence at our command, moving away on tiptoe from where they lie in the ling, we mention this in a low voice.
It will quite possibly be his boast in years to come, when Ruby is dead and he an old optimist, that at least on this occasion, if never before nor since, he achieved what he set out to do; *Car*, in the words of one competent to sing of the matter, *L'Amour et la Mort*—caesura—*n'est qu'une mesme chose.*
May their night be full of music at all events.   [pp. 137–138]

Belacqua's suicide having failed, only one other alternative remains: "A mental home was the place for him" (p. 123). It is the author who makes this suggestion, but Belacqua himself is quite aware of his mental deficiency. Suitably enough the two-word suicide note which he proudly displays for Ruby's inspection reflects his awareness. Painted in large letters on an old license plate, it reads: "TEMPORARILY SANE."

Insanity, or a similar condition that does not require rational commitments, is the state most desired by Beckett's people. "We are all born mad. Some remain so," proclaims Estragon in *Waiting for Godot*,[14] as though madness were the preferred condition for man's passage through life. Beckett's creatures mistrust the vague notions they have of the past; they strive for a mental posture that can free them from rationality and whatever doubtful memories they preserve. These rootless beings alienate themselves from society through a conscious denial of their memory's validity. They repeatedly question the time and place that should determine their present condition: "You're sure it was here!"—"What?"—"That we were to wait."—"He said by

---

[14] Beckett, *Waiting for Godot* (New York: Grove Press, 1954), p. 51.

the tree." Yes, but is it the right tree, and what kind of tree is it? And is it the right day? "You're sure it was this evening?"—"What?"—"That we were to wait."—"He said Saturday . . . I think."—"But what Saturday? And is it Saturday? Is it not rather Sunday? Or Monday? Or Friday?" [15] In their state of anguished expectancy, Beckett's heroes stand as witnesses for the failure of logic, reason, or whatever mental process man utilizes for the discovery and understanding of the external world. Thus, by pretending insanity, or merely aspiring to such a state, they reject all notions of reality and the sum of human knowledge. This self-imposed alienation produces ignorance, meaninglessness, and mental chaos.

Most Beckett protagonists would willingly relinquish future and past, or even the hope of eventual redemption, to enjoy the privileges of lunacy. These are perhaps best defined in *Malone Dies* when Macmann, a creation of Malone's delirious mind, arrives in an asylum and the anonymous keepers explain:

You are now in the House of Saint John of God, with the number one hundred and sixty-six. Fear nothing, you are among friends. Friends! Well well. Take no thought for anything, it is we shall think and act for you, from now forward. We like it. Do not thank us therefore. In addition to the nourishment carefully calculated to keep you alive, and even well, you will receive, every Saturday, in honour of our patron, an imperial half-pint of porter and a plug of tobacco.   [p. 84]

If Macmann is allowed to enter a mental institution, it is because he has reached such a state of physical and mental deterioration that there is no question as to his admittance into the world of lunacy.

Life in an insane asylum provides a certain physical irresponsibility, a certain mental freedom that few humans ever enjoy. For not only are lunatics given the daily care necessary for the human body, but they are left free to indulge in their private fancies. In Beckett's universe, the madman's existence is not only comparable to ascetic isolation, but also

[15] *Ibid.*, pp. 10, 11.

to that of the secluded artist locked in his ivory tower. It is not accidental then if several of Beckett's heroes think of themselves as writers (Molloy, Moran, Malone) and present their mental delirium as artistic creation.

In *More Pricks Than Kicks,* all Belacqua's actions and reflections are intended to negate what others consider rational or logical. His refusal to submit to the concepts that govern knowledge, his claim to a lack of memory and understanding, his extravagance, his fear of the conventional, and his distaste for material life are all aspirations toward mental alienation, toward lunacy. But Belacqua is far from being totally deranged, and though he contemplates life in an insane asylum as the most ideal type of existence, his physical and social obsessions prevent him from entering "the spacious annexe of mental alienation." [16]

Belacqua cannot forsake the "big world," therefore he is not permitted to enter the Portrane Lunatic Asylum and must continue to play the fool in a world that appears to him even more foolish than he is. Though "a mental home" is recommended for him, he fails to be admitted to such an institution. He remains outside the tall wall surrounding the Portrane Lunatic Asylum and resigns himself to contemplating the "big red building" from a nearby hill. He says to one of his conquests, Winnie, as they observe the lunatics playing gently below in the courtyard: "My heart's right there" (p. 27). Winnie remarks that the lunatics seem very "sane and well-behaved," and her companion agrees wholeheartedly.

Since neither suicide nor insanity can save Belacqua from his social fate, and since he depends too much on his past, his memories, and his acquired knowledge of which he is very proud, when confronted with the absurdity of life he suffers moments of anxiety and fits of depression. In spite of his eccentricity he functions too rationally to be granted mental or even fictional freedom. To reach such a state, he would have to learn to practice the kind of asceticism mas-

---

[16] Beckett, *Proust* (New York: Grove Press, 1957) , p. 19.

tered by Beckett's later heroes, which consists of freeing oneself from the physical by withdrawing into the mental world. Surrounded by "aesthetes" and "impotents," as he calls his fellowmen, involved in the petty activities of daily life, submitting to the regulations of society, cornered by his own habits, and, cowardly, obeying the orders of lawmakers and law enforcers, Belacqua leads a schizophrenic existence that denies both physical and mental escape. Neither lethargy, drunkenness, suicide, nor madness can save him from habitual and conventional impositions. Therefore, faced with this dilemma which appears to be a conspiracy of what he calls "the Furies," he suffers moments of utter panic.

The major cause of Belacqua's anxiety, perhaps his most stubborn enemy, is time. In Beckett's universe, time, clocks, and those elements of nature that mark the passing of time with obsessive recurrence, are closely associated with the characters' notions of reality. If the heroes of Beckett's more recent works are able to toy with temporality, to distort or negate time's dimensions and eventually escape its empire, it is because they exist outside the material world. Belacqua, however, must submit to its tyranny. He may feel a particular revulsion toward clocks, yet he cannot avoid their stubborn presence.

Belacqua endures one of his most dreadful moments when, in the story "What a Misfortune," his second-wife-to-be, Thelma bboggs, announces that his wedding gift has arrived:

'The first thing I did was to set it.' [She said.]
    The hideous truth dawned on his mind. 'Not a clock' he implored, 'don't say a grandfather clock.'
    'The grandfather and mother' she did say 'of a period clock.'
    He turned his face to the wall. He who of late years . . . would not tolerate a chronometer of any kind in the house, for whom the local publication of the hours was six of the best on the brain every hour, and even the sun's shadow a torment, now to have this time-fuse deafen the rest of his days. It was enough to make him break off the engagement.   [p. 183]

Belacqua's only solution to avoid "the hideous truth" is to think that "he could always spike the monster's escapement and turn its death's-head to the wall" (p. 183). But this would be too simple and would bring only temporary relief. Throughout the stories, Beckett hardly gives a moment's respite to his hero. Numerous parenthetical remarks remind both the reader and Belacqua of time's impositions: "Now the sun, that creature of habits, shone in through the window" (p. 241), or elsewhere, "let us call it winter, that dusk may fall now and a moon rise" (p. 18). An even more poignant allusion to clocks is interjected when, in the early hours of morning, upon leaving Alba Perdue's apartment, Belacqua strikes a match to look at his watch: "It had stopped. *Patience, a public clock would oblige*" (p. 113 [italics mine]).

Beckett inserts these parenthetical statements within the narration not only to reinforce the irony of his social satire, but to emphasize particularly the inevitable passing of time and its importance on Belacqua's actions:

> Anxious that those who read this incredible adventure shall not pooh-pooh it as unintelligible we avail ourselves now of this lull, what time Belacqua is on his way, Mrs. Tough broods in the kitchen and Ruby dreams over her gloria, to enlarge a little on the latter lady.   [pp. 119–120]

This ironic aside not only ridicules human activities, but makes jest of the narrative technique itself. By subjecting his characters and their actions to linear temporality, Beckett emphasizes the absurd need man has for "passing the time."

Man's slavery to time is a primary affliction which Belacqua must endure as a member of society, and accordingly he must also submit to habit. Time and habit are two of his darkest bêtes noires. In his 1931 essay on Proust, Beckett explained that "habit is a compromise effected between the individual and his environment, or between the individual and his own organic eccentricities, the lightning-conductor of his existence. Habit is the ballast that chains the dog to his vomit" (*Proust*, pp. 7–8). Belacqua is often subjected to all sort of cruelty, although his inability to accept the habitual results primarily from his failure to effect the "compromise" between himself and his "environment," between himself and "his own organic eccentricities."

In the story "Dante and the Lobster," after having reduced all human relationships to their most trivial aspects, Belacqua is deeply troubled when he learns that lobsters are boiled alive—a fact quite unbearable to the human mind until grasped and accepted as a mere convention beyond all rational reflection. Belacqua's life may be governed by habits, but because his mind refuses to accept human actions at face value and proceeds to intellectualize these actions pedantically, he suffers strokes of mental confusion. This contributes to what Beckett calls the "sorry collapse" of his "little internus homo." Yet Belacqua must submit to the shocking discovery that lobsters are always boiled alive:

'Have sense' she said sharply, 'lobsters are always boiled alive. They must be.' She caught up the lobster and laid it on its back. It trembled. 'They feel nothing' she said.

In the depths of the sea it had crept into the cruel pot. For hours, in the midst of its enemies, it had breathed secretly. . . . Now it was going alive into scalding water. It had to. Take into the air my quiet breath.

Belacqua looked at the old parchment of her face, grey in the dim kitchen.

'You make a fuss' she said angrily 'an upset me and then lash into it for your dinner.'

She lifted the lobster clear of the table. It had about thirty seconds to live.

Well, thought Belacqua, it's a quick death, God help us all.

It is not.   [p. 20]

"It is not" a quick death! This objection, no doubt formulated by the author as an answer to the hero's resigned statement, echoes throughout Beckett's work as the perpetual lament of all the crippled, blind, mute, infirm, deformed beings who stubbornly resist total disintegration, and are never permitted to die completely. Belacqua seems to recognize the doomed lobster as a paradigm for man. His horrified reaction when his aunt tells him that lobsters are boiled alive and "feel nothing" is more a gesture of fear than one of revolt or compassion.

The ordeal of the lobster that "crept into the cruel pot," and whose strange death startles Belacqua, forecasts the ordeal of the many Beckett creatures who, in subsequent works, are also helplessly placed in pots, garbage cans, or urns. Though Belacqua does not end in a pot, but in a coffin, his death is just as disconcerting as that of the lobster. While in a hospital room waiting for a neck and toe operation he suffers anguish and disgust at the thought of knowing that "at twelve sharp he would be sliced open—zeep!—with a bistoury" (p. 230). As he observes the busy nurses, doctors, cleaning women, and elevator boys performing their duties with solemnity, going in and out of his room to feed him, remove his tray, bandage his sores, take away his chamber pot, prepare for his operation, all done as a ritual, a series of habitual gestures, Belacqua reflects on the uselessness of their motions, their routine, the absurd game they are playing in the process of preserving life. He sees himself caught in this too-well-organized system, and yet is incapable of reacting violently. He surrenders to the situation by "closing his eyes"—a most feeble (lobsterlike) effort. His only consolation, he muses, is that his "sufferings under the anesthetic will be exquisite" but unfortunately he will "not remember them" (p. 231). Faced with the absurdity of the moment, he ponders a little question: should he assume the attitude of Heraclitus weeping, or that of Democritus laughing?

> It is true that he did not care for these black and white alternatives as a rule. Indeed he even went so far as to hazard a little paradox of his own account, to the effect that between contraries no alternation was possible. But was it the moment for a man to be nice? Belacqua snatched eagerly at the issue. Was it to be laughter or tears? It came to the same thing in the end, but which was it to be now? [pp. 235–236]

He chooses laughter, for it comes to the same thing, since laughter and tears negate each other in the end.[17] His course

[17] Belacqua's paradoxical situation symbolizes Beckett's own dilemma as an artist faced with the absurdity of what he sees around him in the world. All Beckett's works offer the same ambiguous mixture of tragic and comic elements. One never knows whether to laugh or

is clear. He arms his mind with laughter; but, as the title of the story ("Yellow") implies, it can be only a cowardly laughter, *un rire jaune,* that overcomes the frightened Belacqua.

Though everything is meticulously prepared for Belacqua's operation, yet, "By Christ! he did die" of the anesthesia—"They had clean forgotten to auscultate him" (p. 252). The irony of the situation is stretched beyond Belacqua's accidental death and is carried to the scene of his funeral and burial. Thus, even as a corpse Belacqua remains a target for Beckett's sarcasm.

Throughout the book Belacqua receives a most unsympathetic treatment from his creator. Yet his complete disregard for personal property, neglect of the human body and its natural functions, passion for bicycles, aversion to clocks, fear of policemen, his physical ailments, extreme indolence, recurrent wishes for death or a return to the womb, and leanings toward mental instability identify him as a true member of Beckett's family. However, Belacqua's pedantry, arrogance, egocentrism, and morbidity reject the compassion aroused by Beckett's later heroes. No doubt few readers will grant human status to these irresponsible, irrational, obscene, smelly-mouthed, smelly-footed, half-paralyzed creatures, and yet in the middle of their misery these derelicts preserve enough wit and humanity to evoke pity, whereas Belacqua Shuah appears totally repulsive.

Though Beckett introduces himself as a personal friend of his hero ("We were Pylade and Orestes, for a period, flattened down to something very genteel"), eventually he rejects Belacqua: "He was an impossible person in the end. I gave him up in the end because he was not serious" (p. 46). One may wonder if Belacqua Shuah was "not serious" enough as a person or as an artistic creation to deserve such a

---

weep at the characters' misery and their grotesque predicaments, and they themselves are constantly oscillating between laughter and tears. It is appropriate that Beckett subtitled his most famous work, *Waiting for Godot,* "a tragicomedy."

judgment. In any event, Belacqua is the only protagonist who fails to reappear in subsequent Beckett fiction. The two burlesque heroes of the jettisoned novel *Mercier et Camier* receive a derogatory mention in *The Unnamable,* but not Belacqua: "To tell the truth I believe they are all here, at least from Murphy on, I believe we are all here," even the "pseudocouple Mercier-Camier" (p. 6).

If Beckett gave up Belacqua in the end "because he was not serious," nevertheless it would be a mistake to ignore this hero completely. He deserves to be remembered because through him are focused the essential themes of the works to come. *More Pricks Than Kicks* is not technically as accomplished as other Beckett achievements. It is overburdened with clever and obscure allusions, abuses foreign expressions and wordplays, relies heavily on linguistic pedantry, and may be categorized in part as intellectual exhibitionism— the work of a young but talented writer who had yet to find himself. The book fails to express clearly the later Beckett concerns, hardly exploits the various literary and philosophic references it borrows, lapses too much into subtle craftsmanship—but should one agree with Hugh Kenner, who states that "none of this needs to be revived, though it is enlightening to know it exists," [18] and simply reject this revealing and unusual beginning of Beckett's literary career? One finds in *More Pricks Than Kicks* more than "the detritus of the mind of an academic bohemian preoccupied with its own cleverness and inclined toward macaronic effects. . . ." [19] This harsh judgment, again formulated by Hugh Kenner, extends to all Beckett's early efforts in prose and poetry prior to the publication of *Murphy* in 1938, yet of all these early experiments, *More Pricks Than Kicks* most truly deserves rediscovery. This work contains in essence much of the eccentric humor and strangely striking absurdity that was to be subsumed

[18] Hugh Kenner, *Samuel Beckett: A Critical Study* (New York: Grove Press, 1961), p. 41.
[19] *Ibid.,* p. 40.

under a more effective and original class of comedy in those later works that established Beckett's reputation. Belacqua is a remarkable creation in his own right; his problems of adjusting to his environment are no less interesting because he does not arrive at the same solution as do his progeny and heirs in Beckett's French fiction.

'You, my body,
my mind . . .
one must go.'
BECKETT, *Murphy*

III

MURPHY'S SEARCH
FOR AN ASYLUM

In 1938 Beckett published his first novel, *Murphy*, which at
that time went completely unnoticed.[1] Yet James Joyce, one
of the first to recognize Beckett's originality as a novelist,
and who had been presented with a copy of *Murphy*, de-
lighted Beckett by quoting from memory a whole section of
the book.[2]

[1] Beckett, *Murphy*, first published by Routledge (London, 1938),
282 pp. Reprinted by Grove Press (New York, 1957), and Calder
(London, 1963). At the time of its first publication *Murphy* received
no attention except for two paragraphs in the *Times Literary Supplement* (March 12, 1938, p. 172, col. 1, and March 26, 1938, p. 220,
col. 2) under the headline of "Political and Social Novels." According
to Beckett a good part of the original edition was destroyed by bombs
early in World War II. All quotations and page references from this
work are from the Grove Press edition.

[2] As mentioned by Richard Ellmann, *James Joyce* (New York: Oxford University Press, 1959), p. 714. Mr. Ellmann notes that his
information comes from a 1954 interview with Samuel Beckett. The
section referred to is the disposal of Murphy's body. It is un-
questionable that Joyce had great admiration for the young Beckett,
and it is no small tribute to Beckett to have his name—even though
playfully distorted—appear in the pages of *Finnegans Wake* ([New
York: Viking Press, 1939], p. 112): "You is feeling like you was lost
in the bush, boy? You says: It is a puling sample jungle of woods.
You most shouts out: *Bethicket* me for a stump of a beech if I have
the poultriest notions what the farest he all means" (italics mine).

Compared with *More Pricks Than Kicks,* which remains an unsuccessful experiment in spite of its subtle craftsmanship, *Murphy* is a remarkable achievement, not only for its linguistic dexterity and sophisticated humor, but particularly for its philosophical implications reinforced by the technical fluidity of the narration. The aesthetic and intellectual qualities of *Murphy* are even more apparent when viewed in the light of Beckett's subsequent creations. For in *Murphy* one discovers the unifying links between Beckett's earlier fiction and those recent novels and plays in which he achieves full mastery of his craft.

From *Murphy* one is able to extricate most of the thematic lines and technical devices that eventually shape Beckett's later fiction, and were barely exploited in *More Pricks Than Kicks.* Undoubtedly these two works share a similarity of tone, humor, and point of view, develop identical motifs and situations, present settings equally realistic and identifiable, introduce congenial characters concerned with the same problem: the dilemma of existence within social reality. As such these two works not only show literary affinity, but represent logical steps in the establishment of Beckett's fictitious universe.

Belacqua Shuah and Murphy stand as prototypes for their successors, and their obsessions and eccentricities become artistic inspirations for Beckett's French creator-heroes, even though the narratives in which these two early protagonists appear differ markedly in structure, setting, and tone from the more recent works. It is essentially in *Murphy* that the important Beckettian themes find their initial expression and unity. Human loneliness, physical distintegration, mental alienation, intellectual fiasco, creative failure, and above all the unavoidable dualism of mind and body, reality and fiction, are brought together and explored for the first time as the essential elements of a new type of fiction.

This novel can be read as the first step of an epistemologi-

The pun on Beckett's name and the whole passage shows the old master poking fun at his young disciple's confusion as he faithfully copies under Joyce's dictation.

cal quest whose purpose is not the discovery of some philo-sophical or psychological truth, but the negation of all concepts formulated by man to rationalize his existence. Moreover, the ultimate end of this quest is not the creation of a coherent and harmonious fictional "slice of life," but the paradoxical creation of controlled artistic chaos. By his behavior and predicament Murphy holds an important place in Beckett's creative evolution. He sets the foundation, the groundwork, for the human and fictional deterioration of Beckett's later characters. It is as a result of Murphy's search for mental freedom that Beckett's later derelicts are able to participate in the fiction not only as heroes but as creators as well—a dual role that permits them to transcend the social realism that restricts Beckett's earlier heroes.

In *More Pricks Than Kicks,* Belacqua's feeble rebellion against society was insufficient to give the stories overall aesthetic and intellectual unity. Hardly developed beyond a few extravagant situations, the book remained a series of unrelated sketches—instead of becoming a coherent novel as originally planned [3]—because the author was unable to resolve the problem he set for his protagonist: how to recon-cile the self to the inevitable split between the physical and the mental worlds, between external reality and the sub-reality of fiction. Belacqua fails in all his undertakings be-cause he insists on being too committed socially and emo-tionally to his physical surroundings, even though he boasts of having achieved mental freedom. For this reason, Beckett turns against his hero and makes of him a laughable and contemptible being whose obsessions and actions appear as futile as they are bizarre. Yet Belacqua's failure reflects Beckett's unsuccessful attempt to shape the form and con-tent of these stories into a unified structure.

Basically, Murphy faces the same dilemma as his predeces-sor. He too struggles to establish some sort of compromise between the physical and mental worlds. But what was in *More Pricks Than Kicks* a superficial conflict between an egocentric individual and his social environment becomes in

[3] See the appendix.

Murphy the basis for a tightly wrought intellectual and artistic composition. The hero, Murphy, is a more typical Beckettian figure, and much more sympathetic than Belacqua Shuah because he succeeds in temporarily finding a means of existing either in his body or in his mind without having to reconcile the two. Not only is Murphy able to retreat within the region of his skull, thereby ignoring the natural function of his body, but eventually he manages to enter an insane asylum, thereby negating the rational demands of the social system.

This solution may indeed appear as an oversimplification of the concept of dualism, but it furnishes Murphy with a convenient means of resolving an intricate metaphysical dilemma while allowing him to escape worldly concerns. In other words, he aspires to mental freedom by way of mental disorder. But the method he devises to forsake his body and external reality gives the narration its inner coherence, for while he succeeds in transferring himself from the physical to the mental world, he offers his creator the means of achieving aesthetic unity in a novel apparently doomed from the start—on the one hand, it deliberately avoids realism, yet, on the other, it evolves in a realistic setting. Thus the dualism of mind and body, projected into the duality of form and content, becomes the core of this novel's structure.

Moreover, the dualism set forth in *Murphy*, and used as the central theme, is the primary source of the intentional ambiguity inherent in most of Beckett's subsequent works. Whether it shapes the various incongruous couples in the French plays, or initiates the recurrent juxtaposition of two worlds, of two incompatible realities in the novels, or takes on more subtle and complex nuances throughout Beckett's fiction, this dualism reverts to the original ambivalence established in *Murphy*. As one progresses further into Beckett's universe, it becomes evident that the absurdity of the characters' existence and the irrationality of their thoughts result from gradually having the abstract and illusory conditions of fictional life supersede the physical and concrete aspects of reality. Beckett's more recent creations exist in a state that defies credibility or any pretense at lifelike situations, merely because they are no longer subjected to human verisimilitude. Though not explicitly stated in *Murphy*, this subservience of the physical to the mental, of the real to the illusory, prefigures Beckett's total rejection of traditional realism in favor of a more abstract and fanciful type of fiction. Whereas most novels attempt to transfer a simple artistic illusion into a transcendent reality, Beckett's fiction evolves in exactly the opposite direction. Finding its initial impulse in realistic situations, which are then progressively undermined and disintegrated in the course of the creation, it draws toward the paradoxical affirmation that the sole validity of fiction lies in its aesthetic fraudulence. Consequently, as depicted in Beckett's universe, the real world and the physical reality of life appear as mere illusions of an inferior order while the mental and fictional world transposes itself into an apparently authentic *surreality*.[4]

Much of the artistic innovation in *Murphy* rests on the ambivalence of its form. Though the novel exploits a realistic setting and identifiable places, the extravagant actions of the characters, the playful language, and particularly the unorthodox narrative technique emphasize the makeshift quality of fiction. By repeatedly breaking through an omniscient point of view to comment on the narration and the characters, by interpolating a number of parenthetical remarks that involve the reader directly, Beckett skirts realism and credibility.

Having demonstrated quite comically how Murphy defrauds "a vested interest every day for his lunch, to the honourable extent of paying for one cup of tea and consum-

---

[4] The term *surreality* is used intentionally to suggest Beckett's possible affinity with surrealism. For an interesting discussion of the subject see the introduction of Judith Radke's unpublished doctoral dissertation, "Doubt and the Disintegration of Form in the French Novels and Drama of Samuel Beckett" (University of Colorado, 1961).

ing 1.83 cups approximately," Beckett turns to the reader
and suggests mockingly, "Try it sometime, gentle skimmer"
(p. 84), thus drawing the reader into the fictional game.
Elsewhere, he describes in odd terms the manner in which
Wylie kisses Miss Counihan—"A kiss from Wylie was like a
breve tied, in a long slow amorous phrase, over bars' times
its equivalent in demisemiquavers. Miss Counihan had
never enjoyed anything quite so much as this slow-motion
osmosis of live's spittle . . . —and concludes by saying,
"The above passage is carefully calculated to deprave the
cultivated reader" (pp. 117–118). These self-conscious remarks indicate to what extent Beckett controls his fiction in
a deliberate effort to frustrate those who may accept his
words at face value. Here and there the reader is given a
slight concession—for instance, when the author suggests
that he work out for himself "the number of seconds in one
dark night" (p. 224)—but more often Beckett takes away
with one hand what he has given with the other. He spares
no one, and his irony ranges from subtle parody to open
defiance. Having made a suggestive statement about Murphy's sexual needs, he quickly adds, "This phrase is chosen
with care, lest the filthy censors should lack an occasion to
commit their filthy synecdoche" (p. 76). Not only must the
reader endure the author's sarcasm but, being made aware
of the fiction's fraudulence, he is denied any self-
identification with its characters lest he become as ridiculous
and unauthentic as they are.

The characters themselves do not escape their creator's
biting irony as he repeatedly interferes with their pseudoexistence. Beckett makes it clear that his creations are mere
"puppets" who "whinge [sic] sooner or later" (p. 122), and
therefore he does not hesitate to call them liars, mock their
actions, contradict their statements, and even interrupt
whatever confidences they entrust to their fellow characters.
On several occasions Beckett presents these confidences "ob-
liquely" in what he calls an "expurgated, accelerated, improved and reduced" form. Throughout the narrative the
characters are not only described but judged in derogatory

terms. Introducing a new character Beckett states, "This creature does not merit any particular description" (pp. 84–85), and, further on, speaking of the same figure, "Ticklepenny was immeasurably inferior to Neary in every way, but they had certain points in contrast with Murphy in common. One was this pretentious fear of going mad" (p. 89).

All the characters in the novel are given peculiar qualities: Miss Counihan is "quite exceptionally anthropoid," and Beckett finds it also "superfluous to describe her, she was just like any other beautiful Irish girl, except as noted, more markedly anthropoid. How far this constitutes an advantage is what every man must decide for himself" (p. 118); Neary is not only humorously alluded to as a "Pythagorean" and a "Newtonian," but one of his fellow characters describes him as "a bull Io, born to be stung, Nature's gift to necessitous pimps" (p. 216); Miss Dwyer is "a morsel of chaos," Wylie an "analphabete," Miss Dew a "Duck"; Miss Carridge is described as having body odor, "thin lips and a Doric pelvis," and Dr. Angus Killiecrankie as an "Outer Hebridean . . . devout Mottist." Cooper's "only visible humane characteristic was a morbid craving for alcoholic depressant. . . . He was a low-sized, clean-shaven, grey-faced, one-eyed man, triorchous and a non-smoker. He had a curious hunted walk, like that of a destitute diabetic in a strange city. He never sat down and never took off his hat" (p. 54). Of all these caricatures, Cooper is perhaps the one who most nearly resembles Beckett's French derelicts. However, it is Murphy, the protagonist, who receives the most fastidious attributes. Described as "a chronic emeritus . . . a strict non-reader . . . a seedy solipsist . . . an out-and-out preterist . . . a vermin at all cost to be avoided," one learns that Murphy has "a huge pink naevus on the pinnacle of the right buttock" (p. 29), and that women are attracted to him because of "his surgical quality" even though "Murphy's front did not bear out the promise of his rear" (p. 98). As one of the chandlers comments in the novel: " 'E don't look rightly human." Perhaps the most appropriate description of Murphy is furnished by his friend Neary who refers to him as "that long hank of Apollonian asthenia . . . that schizoidal spasmophile" (p. 49).

Such qualifications not only heighten the comic tone of this novel, as Ruby Cohn so aptly demonstrates in her study,[5] but also show some dehumanization of the characters. Even Murphy's charming mistress, Celia, the most sympathetic figure in the novel, is introduced in a manner that reduces her to a mere list of caricatural notations. The method is reminiscent of that used by another skillful Irish satirist—Lawrence Sterne. In fact, numerous pages of *Murphy* read like those of *Tristram Shandy*. Here is Celia's description:

Age.	Unimportant.
Head.	Small and round.
Eyes.	Green.
Complexion.	White.
Hair.	Yellow.
Features.	Mobile.
Neck.	13¾″.
Upper arm.	11″.
Forearm.	9½″.
Wrist.	6″.
Bust.	34″.
Waist.	27″.
Hips, etc.	35″.
Thigh.	21¾″.
Knee.	13¾″.
Calf.	13″.
Ankle.	8¼″.
Instep.	Unimportant.
Height.	5′ 4″.
Weight.	123 lbs.

[p. 10.]

It is evident from this charted presentation of Celia that Beckett is not attempting to create a realistic portrait of his characters. The device he employs suggests an opposite aim: a deliberate rejection of realism. Celia (or for that matter

[5] *Samuel Beckett: The Comic Gamut* (New Brunswick: Rutgers University Press, 1962).

all the other "puppets" in the novel) is above all a *body* which can be gauged according to specific measurements, such as those furnished to a tailor for a suit of clothes. Yet basically the human body is a cumbersome aspect of man's existence which Beckett's characters seek to forsake.

As expressed candidly by one of the characters in *Murphy*, "There is a mind and there is a body" (p. 218), and Beckett emphasizes the incompatibility of the two. Whereas man in reality attempts to reconcile matter and spirit and tries to work out a system of interaction between them, the essential idea in Murphy, as demonstrated by the protagonist's actions, is to escape the limitations of the body in order to enjoy freedom in the mind. Accordingly, Beckett skillfully segregates the physical and mental aspects of fictional existence and daringly categorizes the conditions of what he calls "the big world" and "the little world." Yet this does not imply that mental being is preferable to physical being, and though Murphy strongly favors the "sanctuary" of his mind over the "chaos" of his body, he soon realizes how impossible it is to escape the physical world. For this reason, even when Beckett undertakes to examine his hero's mind as though it were an autonomous mechanism, he does so in satirical terms: "It is most unfortunate, but the point of this story has been reached where a justfication of the expression 'Murphy's mind' has to be attempted" (p. 107). A section follows which is devoted to this investigation—a section to which the author makes several later references ("as described in section six") whenever he mentions Murphy's mental world. Having interrupted his novel to describe in semicomic and semiphilosophic terms the zones of Murphy's mind, Beckett concludes by saying, "This painful duty having now been discharged, no further bulletins will be issued" (p. 113). Though this section of the novel suggests symbolic implications, one cannot ignore the subtle irony with which it is presented nor the possibility that it may be an artistic hoax, an irrelevant statement of playful intent.

In any event, it is certain that the antirealism of this novel finds its expression in the irreconcilable dualism of body

and mind, of form and content, as exemplified by such
extravagant digressions as the analysis of Murphy's mind,
the grotesque descriptions of the characters, and the numerous parenthetical comments Beckett inserts in the narration,
even though the novel's setting remains intentionally realistic.

Murphy appears as a farce, an intellectual comedy set in
the same identifiable world that Belacqua Shuah was trying
to forsake, the only difference being that now most of the
action takes place in London, except for brief moments in
Cork and the Dublin of *More Pricks Than Kicks*. As in the
preceding work, little effort is made to give the characters a
semblance of credibility and the story a sense of authenticity. Though they preserve their Irish personality and wit,
all the characters are superficially portrayed, while the story
edges on absurdity. Formal unity is maintained through
consistent tone, recurrent motifs, and the common obsession
of the characters who are all involved in some search. The
minimal plot unfolds along this series of quests, all closely
related. Every character seeks a counterpart in Murphy,
while Murphy seeks his own physical counterpart in the
region of his mind. If the final outcome of the search is
fruitless, it is because it evolves on two different levels. Yet
Murphy is the center of action, or, as Wylie puts it, "Our
medians . . . or whatever the hell they are, meet in
Murphy" (p. 213).

Murphy's adventures follow a ridiculously simple and
linear plot. Pressed by his mistress, the prostitute Celia, to
take a job so that she may come off the streets, he evades her
persistent requests by pleading that he cannot go against the
prognostications of his horoscope. Eventually, however, he
obtains a position as male nurse in the Magdalen Mental
Mercyseat Asylum and disappears from the outside world.
In the asylum he enjoys friendly relationships with the
inmates and identifies with them. With the help of a fellow
employee, the homosexual Ticklepenny, he appropriates a
little garret in one of the buildings where he indulges in his

favorite pastime: propelling himself into the zones of his mind by rocking naked, tied with seven scarves to a rocking chair. While Murphy seeks mental freedom, Celia and four others (Miss Counihan, a former ladylove of Murphy; Neary, a professor friend of Murphy, under whom he studied in Cork; Wylie, a former pupil of Neary, who plans to marry Miss Counihan; and Cooper, a kind of private detective employed by Neary) undertake a search for the missing Murphy, each for his own egotistical reasons:

Murphy then is actually being needed by five people outside himself. By Celia, because she loves him. By Neary, because he thinks of him as the Friend at last. By Miss Counihan, because she wants a surgeon. By Cooper, because he is being employed to that end. By Wylie, because he is reconciled to doing Miss Counihan the honour, in the not too distant future, of becoming her husband.
[p. 202]

When finally the searching party discovers Murphy's refuge, it learns that the hero has not only succeeded in finding his "loved self," but also in totally escaping, his body and mind having been premeditatively or accidentally pulverized by a gas explosion in his garret. The five friends faithfully proceed to perform Murphy's rather unusual last wish:

'With regard to the disposal of these my body, mind and soul, I desire that they be burnt and placed in a paper bag and brought to the Abbey Theatre, Lr. Abbey Street, Dublin, and without pause into what the great and good Lord Chesterfield calls the necessary house, where their happiest hours have been spent, on the right as one goes down into the pit, and I desire that the chain be there pulled upon them, if possible during the performance of a piece, the whole to be executed without ceremony or show of grief.'
[p. 269]

Cooper is put in charge of delivering the package to its proper destination. However, on the way he stops in a pub, gets drunk, starts an argument with a customer, and in the heat of the verbal exchange throws the paper bag at the man's face: "By closing time the body, mind and soul of Murphy were freely distributed over the floor of the saloon:

and before another dayspring greyened the earth had been swept away with the sand, the beer, the butts, the glass, the matches, the spits, the vomit" (p. 275). After the grotesque disposal of her lover's remnants, Celia resumes her former profession, and is last seen nursing her paternal grandfather, Mr. Willoughby Kelly, as he flies a kite from his wheelchair in Kensington Gardens.

In spite of its dubious plot, *Murphy* remains a traditional novel. Undoubtedly the characters are intentionally presented as caricatures, to fulfill the author's primary purpose of creating a work that mocks realism and rationalism. Therefore, the novel becomes a calculated intellectual exercise that coldly mirrors the world of man while subtly revealing the fraudulence of fiction. Beckett's experiment is successful because it maintains a deliberate split between form and content.

In his 1929 essay on Joyce, Beckett attacked those who criticized the incomprehensibility of Joyce's *Work in Progress* by saying: "If you don't understand it, Ladies and Gentlemen, it is because you are too decadent to receive it. You are not satisfied unless form is so strictly divorced from content that you can comprehend the one almost without bothering to read the other." [6] In *Murphy,* one could accuse Beckett of divorcing form and content, although he does so to reinforce the theme of his novel: dualism of mind and body. Consequently, instead of achieving aesthetic unity through a logical plot based on the rational actions of the characters, Beckett relies on a substratum of leitmotifs and the fluidity of the language.

The language in *Murphy* shines by its precision and its fluency. From the opening sentence which sets the mood—"The sun shone, having no alternative, on the nothing new" (p. 1)—to the closing paragraph which falls in place like the final curtain on a perfect drama—

[6] Beckett, "Dante . . . Bruno. Vico . . Joyce," *Our Exagmination Round His Factification for Incamination of Work in Progress* (London: Faber and Faber, 1936), p. 13.

Celia caught him on the margin of the pond. The end of the line skimmed the water, jerked upward in a wild whirl, vanished joyfully in the dusk. Mr. Kelly went limp in her arms. Someone fetched the chair and helped to get him aboard. Celia toiled along the narrow path into the teeth of the wind, then faced north up the wide hill. There was no shorter way home. The yellow hair fell across her face. The yachting-cap clung like a clam to the skull. The levers were the tired heart. She closed her eyes.

All out. [p. 282]

—each sentence flows unrestrained toward the appropriate pun or comic turn, shifts from sarcasm to mocking lyricism. From the opening scene where the naked Murphy is introduced tied to his rocking chair in the process of projecting himself into the zones of his mind, to the closing scene where Mr. Kelly is seen flying a kite from his wheelchair, the novel moves effortlessly in an "amplitude of diction" which makes "easy jest of its own virtuosity." [7] Every event finds a counterpart in some distorted situation, images echo each other, motifs are woven in and out of the narrative toward an elliptical goal.

The novel's structure is built on the recurrence of various attributes: Celia's prostitution, Cooper's curious ailments, Neary's need for intoxicant and friendship, Mr. Kelly's passion for flying kites, Wylie's for sex and money, Miss Carridge's repulsive body odor, Ticklepenny's homosexuality, Murphy's rocking chair and obsession with his horoscope. All these peculiarities are linked to the protagonist's refusal to take a job, his rejection of physical reality, and his eventual acceptance of a position in an insane asylum. Thus, while the schizophrenic Murphy succumbs to the delusion of his mind, the other characters follow in a pursuit that relates to what Beckett calls "Murphy's course of inaction," and that gives unity to the hero's split personality.

Murphy may appear elusive to the other characters in the novel, but he is unable to escape his own physical self. The controlling factors of social reality prevent him from evading the needs of his body. Furthermore, his rationality, and

[7] Hugh Kenner, *Samuel Beckett: A Critical Study* (New York: Grove Press, 1961), p. 50.

particularly his awareness of time, give a semblance of continuity and coherence to his extravagant actions. Through
numerous interjections, used partly to create an unconven-
tional narrative but mostly to emphasize the limiting aspects
of reality, Beckett reveals the futility of having to subject the
events of fiction to temporality. If this novel maintains a
linear shape that follows a precise temporal scheme, it is
because the hero himself is subjected to physical reality and
fails to escape his body in order to enjoy timelessness in the
mind. For this reason, Beckett constantly checks Murphy's
actions with direct references to time: "It must have been
while the chandlers were mocking Murphy that the shocking thing happened. That day, Friday, October 11th, after
many days, Miss Carridge found her bread . . ." (p. 132) ;
or elsewhere: "Late that afternoon, after many fruitless
hours in the chair, it would be just about the time Celia was
telling her story, M. M. M. stood suddenly for music, Music,
MUSIC . . ." (p. 236) . By relating each event in time to a
corresponding incident, Beckett regulates the progress of a
rather non sequitur narration while expressing his antagonism for what he calls, in his essay on Proust, "that double-
headed monster of damnation and salvation—Time." [8]
Often in *Murphy* that monster takes on human attributes:
"It was as though Time suddenly lost patience or had an
anxiety stroke" (p. 278) , or, in a bold personification, mocking man's perpetual enemy: "Let us now take Time that old
fornicator, bald though he be behind, by such few sad short
hairs as he has, back to Monday, October the 7th, the first
day of his restitution to the bewitching Miss Greenwich" (p.
114) .

As in *More Pricks Than Kicks,* these imprecations against
time are mainly gratuitous. Time is not, as in the work of
Proust or Joyce, an integral theme of this novel; it is merely
superimposed on the characters' actions, and though it is
true that they cannot escape or alter its conventional divi-
sions into hours, days, or months, it is also true that the

[8] Beckett, *Proust* (New York: Grove Press, 1957) , p. 1.

various dates Beckett presents are totally irrelevant to the progress of the narration. Yet the author takes every opportunity to specify the chronological development of events:

Celia's triumph over Murphy, following her confidence to her grandfather, was gained about the middle of September, Thursday the 12th to be pedantic, a little before the Ember Days, the sun being still in the Virgin. Wylie rescued Neary, consoled and advised him, a week later, as the sun with a sigh of relief passed over into the Balance. The encounter, on which so much unhinges, between Murphy and Ticklepenny, took place on Friday, October the 11th (though Murphy did not know that), the moon being full again, but not nearly so near the earth as when last in opposition.   [p. 114]

Such precision, however, hardly justifies the need to subject the narration to strict temporality. In a novel that mocks rationality, it suggests an ironic purpose. One may wonder what relevance these dates and the movements of heavenly bodies have to the absurd course of action Murphy follows, unless they are meant to emphasize his incapacity to escape the physical world.

In the everyday world, and even in fiction that pretends to pass for reality, time is closely related to man's notion of reality. Though Murphy's actions appear irrational, he cannot function outside time, and therefore cannot escape his physical environment. Unable to free himself from his body, habits, and memories, he fails to enjoy timelessness as do Beckett's later derelicts. On some occasions, particularly when it means coming home to Celia for dinner, Murphy acts with extreme punctuality: "The punctuality with which Murphy returned was astonishing. Literally he did not vary in this by more than a few seconds from day to day. Celia wondered how anyone so vague about time in every other way could achieve such inhuman regularity in this one instance" (pp. 69–70). What Celia does not know is that Murphy's "inhuman regularity" is carefully calculated. While supposedly on the "jobpath" Murphy often returns to Brewery Road where he and Celia have rented a furnished room, and, "with hours to spare," simply waits around the corner for time to pass till he stands "with his key in the door waiting for the clock in the market tower to chime" (p. 74). In other words, Murphy's punctuality, as Beckett's precise use of time, is a fraud.

Only once, just before his mysterious death in the M. M. M. Asylum, does Murphy come close to enjoying complete escape from time. After a most exciting and truly absurd chess game with one of the lunatics (appropriately named Mr. Endon—Greek for *within*), and having been defeated, Murphy drops his head among the pieces and succumbs to a moment of unexpected pleasure:

Murphy began to see nothing, that colourlessness which is such a rare postnatal treat, being the absence (to abuse a nice distinction) not of *percipere* but of *percipi*. His other senses also found themselves at peace, an unexpected pleasure. Not the numb peace of their own suspension, but the positive peace that comes when the somethings give way, or perhaps simply add up, to the Nothing. . . . Time did not cease, that would be asking too much, but the wheel of rounds and pauses did, as Murphy with his head among the armies continued to suck in, through all the posterns of his withered soul, the accidentless One-and-Only conveniently called Nothing.   [p. 246]

The nothingness Murphy is here enjoying is that classical, mystical experience that all Beckett's French heroes seek in the depth of their own delirious consciousness. However, in this novel Beckett cannot grant his protagonist total reprieve from time ("that would be asking too much"); but for "an-out-and-out preterist" like Murphy this sense of nothingness he momentarily experiences marks the success of his quest. It is the epiphany toward which his whole mental being has been striving. For a brief moment Murphy finds himself cut off from reality and time, isolated beyond the boundaries of his physical self. His refusal to accept the activities of the external world, to particpate in the "colossal fiasco" of society (a refusal sealed by his course of constant inaction), could lead only to a state of mental vacuum. Nothingness is Murphy's goal, the last refuge where a "seedy solipsist" like him can achieve mental alienation. But to reach such an ideal state, he must undergo severe crises of doubt—Cartesian doubt, in fact. He must reject all physical appearances and construct out of chaos his own mental and fictional environment. It is around this philosophical concept that Beckett builds his novel, but it is also around this concept that he leads Murphy to intellectual and creative failure.

To retrace Cartesian doubt in *Murphy,* one must return to Beckett's first published work, a 98-line poem with 17 footnotes, whose protagonist is René Descartes, "soliloquizing in a Dublin accent." [9] This poem, which bears the ambivalent title *Whoroscope,*[10] represents Beckett's first attack on that "Janal, trinal, agile, monster of Divinity," [11] that most implacable of man's enemies, the "whore" of time. But this witty and rather obscure intellectual feat also shows Beckett's early fascination with Cartesian doubt and the concept of dualism.

Descartes, it seems (as Beckett points out in a footnote), refused to reveal his birthday for fear some astrologer might disclose the secret of his nativity. But, Ruby Cohn suggests in her brilliant analysis of this poem: "Time took its cheap revenge, killing the great mind and body just as he was praying for a 'second starless inscrutable hour.' The time of the punning title is that trollop, a human lifetime, *ab ovo* to death." [12] *Whoroscope,* like most of Beckett's subsequent works, expresses a deep feeling of repulsion and doubt for everything that lies outside the mental universe—that region Beckett often calls "the last ditch." Through Descartes' reflections in the poem about his breakfast eggs, which he liked (another footnote points out) "hatched

[9] Kenner, *op. cit.,* p. 41.

[10] Beckett, *Whoroscope* (Paris: Hours Press, 1930), 6 pp. Reprinted in *Poems in English* (London: Calder, 1961, and New York: Grove Press, 1961). The poem was awarded first prize for the best poem on Time in a contest sponsored by Nancy Cunnard's Hours Press in Paris.

[11] Beckett, *Proust,* p. 22.

[12] Ruby Cohn, "Preliminary Observations," *Perspective,* XI, no. 3 (Autumn, 1959), 120. For a detailed analysis of this poem see also Ruby Cohn's discussion in *Samuel Beckett,* pp. 11–16.

from eight to ten days," [13] Beckett formulates what become
the most consistent peculiarities of his later heroes: an aversion to external reality, an indifference to the activities of
the human body, a derisive attitude toward time and habit,
and a lack of self-knowledge.

As Beckett's people retreat further and further into private consciousness (from which, according to Descartes, all
human knowledge originates), these peculiarities turn more
and more into obsessions, *idées fixes.* Thus the Descartes
figure of *Whoroscope,* for whom " . . . the shuttle of a
ripening egg combs the warp of his days," [14] appears as a
prototype for Beckett's later creatures, or, to abuse Descartes' own definition of man, Beckett's "things that think."
The protagonist of *Whoroscope* shares many characteristics
with his successors, but in this poem Beckett limits himself
to an ironic portrayal of the philosopher, which he conveys
by alluding to events of Descartes' life. In later works,
particularly in *Murphy,* Beckett exploits Cartesian doubt,
which is only vaguely implied in *Whoroscope.* For example, Descartes' questioning of the egg:

> What's that?
>   An egg?
>
> . . . . .
> What's that?
>
> A little green fry or a mushroomy one?
> Two lashed ovaries with prostisciutto?
> . . . .
>
> What's that?
> How long?
> Sit on it.

and finally concluding:

> Are you ripe at last,
> my slim pale double-breasted turd? [15]

[13] Beckett, "Whoroscope," *Poems in English* (New York: Grove Press,
1961), p. 15.
    [14] *Ibid.,* p. 16.
    [15] *Ibid.,* pp. 11, 13, 15.

As suggested by Beckett, the egg symbolizes the dualism of matter and spirit, but, to quote Ruby Cohn once more, "For all his caution . . . Descartes broke the egg, severing mind and body so effectively that all the king's horses and all the king's men couldn't put them back together again. The final irony, then, is that the egg hatches into modern time, for which only a *W* horoscope can be cast." [16] In fact, it is in *Murphy* that the "whoroscope" enters into play, the horoscope that governs Murphy's course of action is delivered to him by the prostitute Celia.

One aspect of Cartesian philosophy which could not fail to attract Samuel Beckett was the premise of doubt. The idea that truth can be reached by first doubting and rejecting all preconceived opinions, the willingness of the seventeenth-century philosopher to question all sources of human knowledge—these are aspects of Cartesianism which Beckett found most compatible with his own questioning of reality. To reevaluate his position in the universe and regain the lost meaning of reality, man must begin anew, disregarding tradition and given notions. Only then can he raise his own edifice solidly on a single foundation. Of this essential Cartesian concept, only the subconcept of doubt can serve Beckett's creative purpose, for as soon as a system draws toward rational reconstruction Beckett's destructive aesthetic principle blocks its advance. He strives for a creative process that, as it proceeds, negates its own form and content—a process whereby, to quote Beckett's own paradoxical terms, "A step forward is, by definition, a step back." [17] Therefore, Beckett cannot possibly accept the whole of Descartes' *method*. His pessimistic and somewhat romantic mind refuses to engage in the methodical reconstruction proposed by the rationalist philosopher. Moreover, Descartes' theory led him to affirm God's existence and His perfection. Beckett's people do not withdraw into consciousness to receive spiritual salvation or gain im-

[16] Cohn, *Samuel Beckett,* p. 16.
[17] Beckett, "Dante . . . Bruno. Vico . . Joyce," *Our Exagmination . . .* , p. 22.

mortality. Their escape is merely a gesture of refusal, and God does not interfere with their system. If occasionally they debate God's existence, "knowing themselves as defective creatures . . . deeply suspicious of their creator," [18] they usually arrive at such conclusions as: "The bastard! He doesn't exist!" [19]

Nonetheless, there is no question that Descartes' initial rejection of external reality and his views on the dualism of mind and body serve as underlying inspirations for much of Beckett's works. When Descartes states

> From the very fact that I know with certainty that I exist, and that I find that (absolutely) nothing else belongs (necessarily) to my nature or essence except that I am a thinking being, I readily conclude that my essence consists solely in being a body which thinks (or a substance whose sole essence or nature is only to think) . And although perhaps, or rather certainly, as I will soon show, I have a body with which I am very closely united, nevertheless, since on the one hand I have a clear and distinct idea of myself insofar as I am only a thinking and not an extended being, and since on the other hand I have a distinct idea of the body insofar as it is only an extended being which does not think, it is certain that this 'I' (that is to say, my soul, by virtue of which I am what I am) is entirely (and truly) distinct from my body and that it can (be or) exist without it . . . [20]

he is formulating what Beckett incorporates quite freely as a central theme of his fiction, and what he expresses in *Murphy* in less philosophical but certainly much more humorous terms than Descartes:

> Thus Murphy felt himself split in two, a body and a mind. They had intercourse apparently, otherwise he could not have known that they had anything in common. But he felt his mind to be bodytight and did not understand through what channel the intercourse was effected nor how the two experiences came to overlap. He was satisfied that neither followed from the other. He neither thought a kick because he felt one nor felt a kick because he thought one. Perhaps the knowledge was related to the fact of the

[18] Frederick J. Hoffman, *Samuel Beckett: The Language of Self* (Carbondale: Southern Illinois University Press, 1962) , p. 63.

[19] Beckett, *Endgame* (New York: Grove Press, 1958) , p. 55.

[20] Descartes, *Meditations*, trans. Laurence J. Lafleur (New York: Liberal Arts Press, 1951) , "Sixth Meditation," pp. 69–70.

kick as two magnitudes to a third. Perhaps there was, outside space and time, a non-mental non-physical Kick from all eternity, dimly revealed to Murphy in its correlated modes of consciousness and extension, the kick *in intellectu* and the kick *in re*. But where then was the supreme Caress? [p. 109]

Murphy does not attempt to comprehend how the two parts of his being establish "intercourse," nor does he try to reconcile the body-mind cleavage through some philosophical concept as Descartes does. For this reason Murphy remains ambiguously caught between the physical and the mental. Eventually in subsequent works Beckett resolves Murphy's puzzlement over the "bodytightness" of the mind by gradually negating the functions of the body in favor of an affirmation of the mind—the only place where man can conceive himself free. In other words, rather than creating in his characters harmonious interactions between the two parts of what Hugh Kenner calls "The Cartesian Centaur," Beckett chooses to obliterate the body and all its demands, which range from gastronomic needs to sexual desires, thereby forcing the mind to vegetate in its own void. The ultimate goal of Beckett's entire literary production is to create a fictional being that can exist completely detached from the physical reality of the body, a creature that can function outside human knowledge as a consciousness inventing its own fictitious surroundings. Only after a slow process of physical distintegration, and an intense probing into man's inner self, does Beckett produce such a creature: the bodiless voice of *L'Innommable* muttering incoherent thoughts in fictional absurdity. For Murphy, however, the dualism of mind and body remains a dilemma. In his efforts to cope with this metaphysical problem, Murphy is often led into inescapable situations that cannot be fully apprehended through Descartes' system.

Having formulated distinctly the concept of mind (or soul) without presupposing the concept of body, and vice versa, Descartes concluded that two separate beings or substances exist outside each other's influence. The body is always divisible, whereas the mind remains totally indivisible. Thus Descartes was confronted with the fact that man consists of two mutually exclusive natures, and that reciprocal action between these two is unjustifiable. Yet the body and the mind act and react upon one another and form a unified being. Descartes explained this interaction by granting the body a useful "vital will" (which oddly enough he located in the pineal gland), whose function it is to intervene and guide the motions of the body and set a connection between the physical and the mental.

However ingenious this reconciliation may be, it requires a physical effort and a moral responsibility which Beckett's lethargic heroes are not at all willing to furnish. For Murphy, whose primary concern is to escape the external world in order to enjoy the "closed system" of his mind, a more suitable proposition than Descartes' needed to be found. For this, Beckett turned to another Cartesian philosopher, the Belgian Calvinist Arnold Geulincx, whose naïve method of reconciling the body and mind dualism is more compatible with Murphy's indolent personality, for it demands less physical exertion on the part of its adherent.

The Occasionalist Arnold Geulincx (1624–1669), like his contemporary Malebranche (both mentioned in other Beckett works, as well),[21] felt that self-examination (*in-*

---

[21] Geulincx is not only mentioned by name in *Murphy*, but Beckett quotes from his "beautiful Belgo-Latin" what becomes Murphy's motto: "*Ubi nihil vales, ibi nihil velis*" (p. 178). In the story "La Fin," the anonymous narrator remembers that his "précepteur . . . m'avait donné l'*Ethique* de Geulincz" (p. 105 of *Nouvelles et Textes pour rien*), and Molloy also mentions the Occasionalist philosopher while paraphrasing one of Geulincx's more striking images: "I who had loved the image of old Geulincx, dead young, who left me free, on the black boat of Ulysses, to crawl towards the East, along the deck. That is a great measure of freedom, for him who has not the pioneering spirit" (p. 68). In *Comment c'est*, Beckett turns to another Occasionalist, and makes this statement: ". . . nous voilà partis nez au vent bras se balançant le chien suit tête basse queue sur les couilles rien à voir avec nous il a eu la même idée au même instant du Malebranche en moins rose les lettres que j'avais . . ." (p. 37).

In a recent article, "Philosophical Fragments in the Works of Samuel Beckett," *Criticism*, VI, no. 1 (Winter, 1964), Ruby Cohn examines in detail these various allusions to Geulincx and shows how the Occasionalist theory underlines much of Beckett's philosophical attitude.

specto sui) is the base of all ethics. However, in contrast to Descartes, he insisted that only private thoughts belong to the individual, whereas the body functions as part of the material world, and therefore actions are purely accidental. Whatever connection exists between mind and body, he says, is achieved through the miraculous power of God. Man no longer needs to make a conscious effort to understand the actions of his body, nor does he need to establish logical rapport between the mental and the physical world. He simply relies on divine intervention, and gazes out in bewilderment from the safety of the mental chamber, or, to paraphrase one of Geulincx's statements, while the ship moves westward carrying its passenger to his destination, nothing prevents this passenger from walking eastward on the deck. [22] In view of this paradoxical doctrine, it becomes evident why Beckett's creatures are so often indifferent to their bodily actions, and why they observe with perplexed detachment whatever their hands or feet are doing.

Geulincx's solution to the problem of dualism is undoubtedly more suitable to Beckett's point of view than is Descartes' willful reconciliation, and it is sustained throughout the Beckettian universe. If "Murphy's occasionalism is implicit everywhere in the novel," [23] Beckett deliberately performs a subtle alteration to Geulincx's proposition: Murphy

---

About Nicholas Malebranche, she states that he "was the most rigid of the Occasionalist philosophers, denying causality, and insisting that all events were occasions for manifestation of divine power. In this context the dog follows the human beings by a series of independent miracles, and the ironic comment is patent in the disproportion between God's will and dog's act" (p. 38). One may add that the irrational actions of Beckett's creatures can be justified only in function of some divine miracle (no doubt that of their creator), since they themselves hardly make an effort to understand or control these actions.

[22] I am paraphrasing this passage from Geulincx's *Ethics:* "Navis occissime vectorem abripiens versus occidentem, nihil impedit quominus ille in navi ipsa deambulet versus orientem" (Land edition [1891–1893], Vol. III, p. 167).

[23] Samuel I. Mintz, "Beckett's *Murphy:* A 'Cartesian' Novel," *Perspective,* XI, no. 3 (Autumn, 1959), 156. This was the first article to point out Beckett's Cartesianism

does not rely on God's miracle to set up the connection between his mind and body, but on the much more debatable power invested in the horoscope furnished by the astrologer—"Famous throughout Civilised World and Irish Free State"—Ramaswami Krishnaswani Narayanaswami Suk. Thus, if it is true that *Murphy's* intellectual structure is based extensively on Geulincxian Cartesianism (a curious mixture of rationalism and mysticism), it is also true that Beckett's distortion of that philosophical system, whereby divine power is reduced to astrologic delineations, renders Murphy's solution blatantly ironic. All Cartesians were deeply suspicious of astrologers, as Beckett had already pointed out in *Whoroscope*. In allowing Murphy to resolve the dualism of mind and body through the power of astrology, Beckett mocks the Cartesian doctrine on which his novel is based.

Beckett quotes appropriately "in the beautiful Belgo-Latin of Arnold Geulincx" these revealing words: *"Ubi nihil vales, ibi nihil velis"* (p. 178). The complete moral and intellectual resignation suggested by Geulincx—where I can do nothing, I ought not to will anything—leads to a kind of self-negligence, to a state of lethargy reflected in the physical indifference Beckett ascribes to his hero. Since human actions in the external world are free of mental control, it is futile to attempt a reconciliation of the two. This Geulincxian attitude is typical not only of Murphy, but of most Beckett heroes who neglect or reject their social and physical commitments.

It is with Murphy that this attitude finds it initial expression:

However that might be, Murphy was content to accept this partial congruence of the world of his mind with the world of his body as due to some such process of supernatural determination. The problem was of little interest. Any solution would do that did not clash with the feeling, growing stronger as Murphy grew older, that his mind was a closed system, subject to no principle of change but its own, self-sufficient and impermeable to the vicissitudes of the body.   [p. 109]

Whether or not "Murphy's speculations are in the tradition of the seventeenth-century philosophers confronting the difficulties of Cartesian dualism," [24] his willingness to accept "any solution," provided that his mind remains a "closed system," shows to what extent Beckett departs from the Occasionalist theory. It is evident from Murphy's thoughts that his attitude toward Cartesian dualism is purely ironic. For Murphy, the union of mind and body is achieved by neither the function of the pineal gland nor the intervention of God, but by that "corpus of incentives based on the only system outside his own in which he felt the least confidence, that of the heavenly bodies" (pp. 22–23).

Like most Beckettian heroes, Murphy shows deep aversion to any organized system; but for him, since he remains prisoner of his body, astrology furnishes a justification for physical indolence. Murphy does not wish to reconcile body and mind; he wants to find a means of neglecting the former in order to enjoy the privacy of the latter. By refusing to undertake any action that opposes the "celestial prescriptions," he deliberately avoids social involvements. Murphy's reliance on the suggestions of his horoscope becomes the means of protecting "his course of inaction," in particular his refusal to take a job.

Early in the novel, upon Celia's repeated requests, Murphy is almost resigned to setting out on the "jobpath," if the content of his "THEMA COELI" offers the proper conditions. Celia delivers a large black envelope (suggesting blackmail on her part) which contains Suk's prognostications. Listed below a pompous title, Murphy finds all the governing elements of his life, plus a compilation of his lucky attributes: days, gems, colors, numbers, and years. After careful examination of the document, Murphy comments: "Pandit Suk has never done anything better," and immediately his mistress inquires:

'Can you work now after that?' said Celia.
'Certainly I can,' said Murphy. 'The very first fourth to fall on a Sunday in 1936 I begin. I put on my gems and off I go,

24 *Ibid.*, p. 157.

to custode, detect, explore, pioneer, promote or pimp, as occasion
may arise.'

'And in the meantime?' said Celia.

'In the meantime,' said Murphy, 'I must just watch out for fits,
publishers, quadrupeds, the stone, Bright's—'

She gave a cry of despair intense while it lasted, then finished
and done with, like an infant's.

'How you can be such a fool and a brute,' she said, and did not
bother to finish.

'But you wouldn't have me go against the diagram' said Murphy,
'surely to God.'   [p. 34]

Indeed it would be quite incompatible with Murphy's principles to "go against the diagram." Therefore, when eventually he accepts employment in the Magdalen Mental Mercyseat Asylum, it is not because he submits to Celia's requests or to the demands of the material world, but because
subconsciously he follows his horoscope. Though Murphy
becomes aware of this much later when Ticklepenny offers
to introduce him into the M. M. M. institution, his conviction is reinforced when he remembers the mention "of lunatic in paragraph two and custodian in paragraph seven" (p.
93) of his horoscope. It is clear to him, then, that the final
outcome of his quest was predetermined, and that taking a
job as male nurse (custodian) in an insane asylum (the
world of lunatics) does not oppose Suk's prognostications.
On the contrary, his function in the asylum corresponds to
mental alienation, for not only has Murphy escaped bodily
restrictions and social commitments, but he has also fulfilled
his Geulincxian inclination: *"Ubi nihil vales, ibi nihil
velis."*

It seems appropriate at this point to pause a moment, as
Beckett himself does in section six of the novel, to examine
Murphy's mind, since it is there, after all, that the protagonist seeks the answer to his existential dilemma. Ironically,
the description of Murphy's mind is presented under the
motto *"Amor intellectualis quo Murphy se ipsum amat"*
(p. 107).

The most curious aspect of Murphy's mind is that it

creates itself. It is pure Cartesian *cogito*—thought inventing its own vehicle—or, in Beckett's own words, "Murphy's mind pictured itself as a large hollow sphere, hermetically closed to the universe without." Within this sphere Murphy moves freely from light to dark in three distinct zones. Depending on his needs he can temporarily adjust his mental existence to the conditions of any of these three zones: "now to be in the light, now in the half light, now in the dark" (p. 108). Each of these mental regions provides Murphy with a particular vision of external reality.

In the light zone, Murphy takes his revenge on the physical world and all its petty impositions, vexations, and limitations: "Here the kick that the physical Murphy received, the mental Murphy gave. It was the same kick, but corrected as to direction" (p. 111). In this zone, all forms and appearances of the outside world have their equivalents, but these are now "available for a new arrangement." All Murphy's disappointments, frustrations, and shortcomings are hurled back at their originators: "Here the whole physical fiasco became a howling success." In this zone of "reprisal," from the safety of which Murphy takes pleasure in reversing the physical order, he is able to bring together in humiliating situations those fellow characters he despises. He can, for instance, force the repulsive Miss Carridge into being raped by the even more repulsive homosexual Ticklepenny. It is a game whereby Murphy makes available for metamorphosis anyone he chooses, it is the first step to creative freedom. But existence in the light zone requires an intellectual effort Murphy is not always capable of furnishing.

Life in the half-light zone is much more satisfying. Here forms are without parallel; here Murphy needs not return the physical kick. He merely rests in a contemplative state, while neatly arranged forms and experiences are presented to his delight: "This system had no other mode in which to be out of joint and therefore did not need to be put right in this. Here was the Belacqua bliss and others scarcely less precise" (p. 111). Furthermore, existence in this zone does not require much intellectual effort. It provides those who

are able to move from "one unparalleled beatitude to another" with simple aesthetic pleasure. Nonetheless, this
blissful repose has its limitations. One cannot vegetate
indefinitely in a purgatorial condition. One must either
return to the old order, the inferno of society, or proceed
toward a new order, the paradise of creativity, even if it
leads to mental chaos.

Thus if, in the first two zones, Murphy is free either to
take his revenge on his fellowmen and scorn the exterior
world, or simply to wallow in mental beatitude, it is in the
third—the dark—zone that the most desirable aspects of
mental existence are found, for that zone is "a flux of forms,
a perpetual coming together and falling asunder of forms"
(p. 112). This mental station represents the ultimate
escape, the ideal state of nothingness: "Here there was
nothing but commotion and the pure forms of commo-
tions. Here he was not free, but a mote in the dark of
absolute freedom" (p. 112). Here the order of physical experiences is totally destroyed, reduced to its preexistential
condition, to chaos. Here thought and pure intellect
achieve complete irresponsibility. In this ultimate refuge
there is nothing "but forms becoming and crumbling into
fragments of a new becoming, without love or hate or any
intelligible principle of change" (p. 112). In the dark zone
all potentials of creation, recreation, and destruction find
a new aesthetic order. Beckett even seems to suggest that
here lies the only possible point of departure for all true
fiction.

The three zones of Murphy's mind can be compared to
the three stages of Beckett's own creative evolution, the light
zone representing his satirical English fiction, the half-light
zone his early contemplative French experiments, and the
dark zone the seemingly incoherent works of the later
French period. In fact, the final comments Beckett makes
about each zone of Murphy's mind describe quite appropriately and prophetically the three periods of his creation. If
in the first zone "It was pleasant to kick the Ticklepennies
and Miss Carridges simultaneously together into ghastly acts

of love . . . ," and in the second zone "It was pleasant to lie dreaming on the self beside Belacqua, watching the dawn break crooked . . . ," in the dark zone, the El Dorado of mental existence, the nirvana of Beckettism, the paradisaic state of nothingness, "How much more pleasant was the sensation of being a missile without provenance or target, caught up in a tumult of non-Newtonian motion. So pleasant that pleasant was not the word" (pp. 112–113).

Using the rocking chair as transportation, in which he ties himself naked, stripped of all material impediments, hidden in "a mew of West Brompton" which symbolically has been condemned by city officials, Murphy propels himself into the zones of his mind. There he tries to spend more and more time in the dark zone, where he can possibly negate physical reality and achieve "his most transcendent experience, the apprehension of pure intellect, the mind apprehending itself. *'Amor intellectualis quo Murphy se ipsum amat.'* " [25] But if Murphy succeeds in penetrating the dark zone of his mind, he nonetheless fails to attain complete independence and remains subjected to the material world which constantly interferes with his mental freedom. Too socially and rationally inclined toward the old order, that of the big world, he finds himself repeatedly catapulted back to physical reality. Even in the heated garret of the M. M. M. Asylum, which resembles the padded cells of the lunatics, Murphy cannot apprehend the essential issue of the dark zone: to be "in the dark, in the will-lessness, a mote in its absolute freedom" (p. 113).

When Descartes locked himself "dans un poêle" to concentrate on the function of the mind, he did so with a view toward reconstructing external reality through the process of consciousness. Though Murphy's mental escape resembles Cartesian solipsism, his reason is diametrically opposed to that of Descartes. It lacks both ethical and aesthetic motive. In fact, Murphy's mental escapades are totally unjustified. It

[25] *Ibid.*

is not sufficient to free oneself of the human body and physical reality; once within the sanctuary of the mind one must advance toward new forms, even if the ultimate result brings mental confusion. Beyond the notion of doubt, Descartes reconstructed a new ethical and artistic system. Murphy avoids all systems of reconstruction, whether social, moral, philosophical, or aesthetic. In the realm of pure consciousness he submits to the conditions of mental alienation, but fails to equate these with creative freedom. Even though able to retreat within the zones of his mind, Murphy is not capable of maintaining himself in the permanent state of hallucination, irrationality, and chaos which these zones offer, and which would grant him the creator-hero status.

During his stay in the asylum Murphy identifies with the lunatics: "they felt in him what they had been and he in them what he would be" (p. 184) ; but even then he remains an outsider (a rational being) who cannot endure mental alienation. The philosopher, moralist, artist, and even qualified fictional hero must assume the responsibility of intellectual freedom, even if the final outcome results in nonsense and failure. Only the madman is free from such responsibility, and though his fancies may resemble those of the creative artist they need not have aesthetic or ethical order. They are inevitably considered failures by the rational man.

In Beckett's more recent works, madness and creativity are closely related, and therefore to fail artistically and recognize this failure as an essential element of fictional existence is a basic attitude of Beckett's French creator-heroes. Murphy's failure, however, consists of not being able to accept (or acknowledge) *failure* as the primary term of mental existence. In spite of his intellectual escapades within the zones of his mind, he never realizes the creative potentials that would enable him to organize the chaos of his thoughts. It is true that whether Murphy chooses to abdicate the physical in favor of the mental or vice versa, the end result can only be the same, since both his mind and body are doomed to be reduced to ashes. For Murphy, existence appears as a choice between methods of arriving at the same disastrous conclusion. Thus, through his hero's defeat, Beckett suggests more than artistic failure; he exemplifies the futility of human actions as well as man's imperfections in an imperfect world.

Arnold Geulincx's proposition, *"Ubi nihil vales, ibi nihil velis,"* as understood in the light of Murphy's incapacity for acting, justifies the hero's failure to become a genuine creator within his own mind as well as a genuine fictional being within the novel. Murphy is destroyed in the end because he is unable to choose between mental nothingness (chaos and failure) and his own physical desires. He remains a puppet, a caricature of a fictional hero, a common social man for whom

It was not enough to want nothing where he was worth nothing, nor even to take the further step of renouncing all that lay outside the intellectual love in which alone he could love himself, because there alone he was lovable. It had not been enough and showed no signs of being enough. These dispositions and others ancillary, pressing every available means (e.g. the rocking-chair) into their service, could sway the issue in the desired direction, but not clinch it. It continued to divide him, as witness his deplorable susceptibility to Celia, ginger, and so on. The means of clinching it were lacking.   [p. 179]

What Murphy cannot "clinch," cannot accept in the end, even in the service of the "Clinch Clan" ruling over the M. M. M. Asylum, is to exist in the vacuum of his mind, in the vacuum of fiction. His physical contacts with the outside world, with the "nothing new," prevent him from achieving perfection in failure. His eccentricities, like those of Belacqua Shuah, are poor gestures of dissatisfaction, hardly sufficient to produce mental alienation. Moreover, Murphy is prevented from enjoying freedom in the mind because he submits to all the little needs of his body. For instance, he cannot "go without money," and though he claims "providence will provide" when Celia asks how they are going to manage if he does not get a job, he gladly accepts the "small charitable sums" that a certain uncle, Mr. Quigley, sends from Holland.

Murphy cannot live without the assurance of a roof over his head, and all the commodities of daily life. Furthermore, he needs friendship and affection, not to mention love. His sexual appetite and gastronomic desires must be satisfied. He looks forward to his meals with great anticipation, and becomes quite angered when deprived of these or when served the wrong kind of food: "I asked for China and you give me Indian," (p. 83) he shouts at a waitress in a restaurant who brings the wrong cup of tea. Like Belacqua, he is extremely meticulous about his lunch. But where his predecessor had a passion for burnt toast and Gorgonzola cheese, Murphy prefers biscuits whose degustation becomes a daily ritual:

He took the biscuits carefully out of the packet and laid them face upward on the grass, in order as he felt of edibility. They were the same as always, a Ginger, an Osborne, a Digestive, a Petit Beurre and one anonymous. He always ate the first-named last, because he liked it the best, and the anonymous first, because he thought it very likely the least palatable. The order in which he ate the remaining three was indifferent to him and varied irregularly from day to day.   [p. 96]

Murphy even goes so far as to calculate the number of ways in which he can eat his five biscuits. Such petty concerns hardly help him to justify his claims to intellectual freedom. Even in the garret of the M. M. M. Asylum, where he has transferred his rocking chair, Murphy requires all the comfort he is accustomed to, and before moving in he insists that some sort of heating system be installed.

The wandering bums of Beckett's French novels and plays learn to survive in a ditch, in a pot, in a garbage can, totally detached from their fellowmen, happy to suck on stones or dry bones. For them material objects are of little value in their absurd surroundings. Molloy may show as much concern in systematizing his method of sucking stones as Murphy does for his biscuits, but once he has resolved the problem of the sucking order he quickly abandons the whole matter. The process of arranging sixteen stones in four pockets so that each stone can be sucked in order without ever sucking the same one twice before the cycle is completed seems extremely important to Molloy when he first tackles the problem, but in the course of solving it he soon forgets the essential issue, loses interest in his calculation, and finally negates the matter as insignificant. Yet he has pushed the mathematical permutability so far into absurdity and abstraction that it becomes acceptable, attractive, but also negligible in its irrationality. All of Molloy's actions, in fact, constitute a series of small failures contained in the overall motion of Molloy toward ultimate fictional failure, a pattern followed by all of Beckett's French creatures.

Murphy, on the contrary, succeeds in calculating the various ways in which his biscuits can be eaten, but when faced with the unavoidable fact that "the assortment would spring to life before him, dancing the radiant measure of its total permutability, edible in a hundred and twenty ways," he suffers a moment of panic and succumbs to "the demon of gingerbread" (pp. 96–97). For Murphy the reality of things, the physical truth, is too much to bear. The mathematical problem he faces in relation to his biscuits is part of a concrete and rational system; it belongs to the conspiracy of the physical world which threatens him, and which he attempts to escape.

Though Beckett provides his protagonist with a "nonporous" suit of clothes that admits no air from the outer world, and with a most remarkable vehicle (the rocking chair) for his journeys to the mind, only on rare occasions does he succeed in escaping from "the pensums and prizes, from Celia, chandlers, public highways, etc., from Celia, buses, public gardens, etc., to where there were no pensums and no prizes, but only Murphy himself improved out of all knowledge" (p. 105). For whether he penetrates the zones of his mind or enters the insane asylum, eventually Murphy is forced back to reality, because his ascetic aspiration, like that of Belacqua Shuah, is too often based on acts of bad faith.

In the opening chapter of the novel, Murphy is introduced in the process of rocking himself free of his body: "He worked up the chair to its maximum rock, then relaxed. Slowly the world died down" (p. 6). But just as he reaches the boundary of his mind where he can love himself, the materialistic world brutally snatches him back: ". . . a foot from his ear the telephone burst into its rail. He had neglected to take down the receiver" (p. 7). If Murphy does not answer immediately his landlady will come rushing in and discover his bizarre occupation. Murphy's fear of public opinion gives an insincere tone to his claim to mental freedom. His wish to retreat within the mental world may be not a genuine desire to attain mental alienation, but merely a cowardly way to avoid responsibility. For only from the safety of his mind can he turn against those who threaten his existence: the degenerate Ticklepenny who fears madness, the selfish Newtonian Neary, the venal Miss Carridge, the "ruthless tout" Cooper, the stubborn Celia and her threats of a job, the Clinch Clan which rules over the M. M. M. Asylum, the chandlers who mock Murphy's appearance, and all the philosophers, learned men, bureaucrats, and so on—all those to whom "reason stuck like a bur" (p. 94).

In the asylum, Murphy's most violent execrations are reserved for psychiatrists whose function, he discovers, is to bring back "the sufferer from his own pernicious little private dungheap to the glorious world of discrete particles, where it would be his inestimable prerogative once again to wonder, love, hate, desire, rejoice and howl in a reasonable balanced manner, and comfort himself with the society of others in the same predicament" (p. 177). Nothing seems more repulsive to Murphy than the role of these pseudo-priests, and his greatest pleasure and surest salvation is to identify with the lunatics who somehow have escaped into the hermetic zones of their minds. From the depth of his conscious identification with the patients, Murphy is able to express his disgust for psychiatric treatments: "All this was dully revolting to Murphy, whose experience as a physical and rational being obliged him to call sanctuary what the psychiatrists called exile and to think of the patients not as banished from a system of benefits but as escaped from a colossal fiasco" (pp. 177–178). Thus in the light zone of his mind and in the M. M. M. Asylum Murphy enjoys some success in expressing his aversion to outer reality. On these levels he receives full assistance from the author himself, and the Murphy-Beckett couple becomes a partnership engaged in a devastating attack on society. But as soon as Murphy wanders into the half-light zone, or proceeds further into the dark zone, Beckett deserts him and turns against him. Here Murphy is on his own, and because he insists on being too rational, too realistically inclined, he suffers the sarcastic attacks of his creator, who repeatedly forces him back to the world of reality.

Murphy's whole existence, then, consists of a succession of small, embarrassing deceptions, as though Beckett were preventing him from reaching his proposed goal, which paradoxically tends toward failure. Murphy's greatest disappointment occurs a few moments before his death when, after the absurd chess game with the schizophrenic Mr. Endon, he almost experiences perfect mental disorder, and yet does not grasp its potentialities. This is the closest Murphy ever comes to his desired insanity. As he returns to his garret, still under the impact of this traumatic experience, he begins to cast away his clothes piece by piece as though symbolically freeing himself of the last ties with the material world. Finally, when completely naked, "he lay down in a tuft of soaking tuffets and tried to get a picture of Celia. In vain. Of his mother. In vain. Of his father (for he was not illegitimate). In vain" (p. 251). At this point Murphy resembles the wandering derelicts of Beckett's French fiction who spend most of their existence dragging themselves along in a moribund landscape. It seems that Murphy has divorced himself from the rational world. He must now come to terms with the chaos of his mind and become himself a creator. He must assume the responsibility mental alienation imposes upon him. But Murphy is not a lunatic, his condition is self-imposed, and therefore it is up to him to control his mind and give new order to its disorder. Having reached the outer limit of reality, he must now push further into consciousness, further into the realm of fiction, into creativity. But he fails to do so, and his mind remains cluttered with realistic fragments he cannot transform into fiction, cannot organize aesthetically:

He tried again with his father, his mother, Celia, Wylie, Neary, Cooper, Miss Dew, Miss Carridge, Nelly, the sheep, the chandlers, even Bom and Co., even Bim, even Ticklepenny and Miss Counihan, even Mr. Quigley. He tried with the men, women, children and animals that belong to even worse stories than this. In vain in all cases. He could not get a picture in his mind of any creature he had met, animal or human.   [pp. 251–252]

Murphy is not suffering from a lapse of memory—memory in Beckett's universe is not essential to creativity—but from a lack of creative consciousness. In his effort to visualize all the other characters of the novel, all the people of the fictional world in which he himself exists, and even "the men, women, children and animals that belong to even worse stories than this," Murphy almost reaches the state of creative hallucination Beckett grants his later French heroes. It is here for the first time that the concept of procreation of characters by characters appears in Beckett's universe. Eventually Beckett's French progenies perfect this system to such a subtle degree of inventiveness that they are able to claim the fiction as their own. But for Murphy the effort is "in vain." He does not achieve the *objective correlative* of the French heroes. By refusing to accept the fictional predicament, Murphy fails to bypass the limits of realism, to transcend the human condition. And because he has neither gone mad nor apprehended the essential terms of creativity, he cannot remain among the lunatics.

His only alternatives are to run away from the M. M. M. Asylum "before the days staff" returns, and resume physical relations with Celia, or to commit suicide. It seems that

Murphy chooses the latter. He frantically rushes to his garret where, accidentally but conveniently, his mind and
body are annihilated in a gas explosion. However, since
Murphy leaves a suicide note, or at least a sort of last
testament, it is not clear whether his death is truly accidental or premeditated. In any event, he is reduced to
chaos by "chaos" (the etymology of gas, as Beckett suggests,
being from the Latin word *chaos*) at the precise moment
when he is almost in possession of all the chaotic elements
of fiction:

> Scraps of bodies, of landscapes, hands, eyes, lines and colours evok-
> ing nothing, rose and climbed out of sight before him, as though
> reeled upward off a spool level with his throat. *It was his experi-
> ence that this should be stopped, whenever possible, before the
> deeper coils were reached.*   (p. 252 [italics mine])

Murphy turns his back on the possibility of escaping the
real world and of reaching "the deeper coils" of fiction.
Therefore, he cannot survive in the presence of such secrets,
and must be eliminated. Perhaps Murphy's death is not
suicide after all, but murder, and the murderer is Beckett
himself. It is no accident, but rather an ironic gesture of
disgust on the part of his creator, that Murphy's ashes are
dispersed on the floor of a London pub by the drunk
Cooper, and from there swept away with all the detritus of
mankind. Murphy's remains return to where they belong:
the world of crude reality he could not forsake. But Murphy
would not be too disappointed, for he himself had chosen as
glorious a place for his ashes. In his testament he expressed
the wish to have his ashes flushed down the Abbey Theatre
WC.

The obscene disposal of his body represents a flippant
indictment of all those who, like Murphy, seek freedom in
the mind, but refuse to accept the consequences of such a
condition and allow worldly concerns to interfere with intellectual or artistic aspirations. Stephen Spender sums up this
Beckettian point of view in a statement that can be read as
an accusation of Murphy's self-delusion:

Thus Beckett makes his protest against everything that is society, or literature, or status—everything that enables one to evade the perpetual, clogging, physical and mental sense of one's own being, imprisoned in one's body, with that dull cellmate one's soul. He makes of self-consciousness a matter of conscience, and those who feel guilty of escaping from brute self-awareness, into the disguises of success, will feel the force of the worlds he creates as criticism of their evasion.[26]

Murphy gets only a glimpse of fictional madness. He never reaches the realm of creativity, never sinks completely into absurdity and irrationality. The creatures of the French novels—Molloy, Malone, Macmann, L'Innommable, Worm and Co.—succeed in outwitting madness and death. In the zone of nothingness, beyond the familiar landscape of reality, they perform the miracle of self-creation, of self-preservation, and even of self-destruction. Condemned to perpetual absurdity, they achieve total indifference toward their futile existence and toward the process of creation in which they are involved. Murphy, however, is abandoned along this infernal course; his obtrusive body is reduced to dust and dispersed with "the sand, the beer, the butts, the glass, the matches, the spits, the vomit," in the realistic world he could not escape.

[26] Stephen Spender, "What Is a Man's Life, a Joke or Something Sacred?" *New York Times Book Review,* Feb. 25, 1962, pp. 7, 32.

But what
was this pursuit of meaning,
in this indifference to meaning?
And to what did it tend?
These are delicate questions?

BECKETT, *Watt*

IV

WATT'S MENTAL
BREAKDOWN

As shown in the preceding chapters, the characters in *More Pricks Than Kicks* and in *Murphy* function as members of an organized social system. The setting in which they exist mirrors the reality of the everyday world. Places are identified (Dublin, Cork, London), time is specified, and the actions of the characters follow a rational though eccentric pattern that produces "not wholly unrelated reactions and consequences." [1] Though these characters are superficially described and presented as puppets given fictional roles to perform, they are nonetheless portrayed as replicas of man—whose existence is controlled by physical attributes and whose actions are governed by a semblance of rationality. It is true that Belacqua Shuah and Murphy seek to forsake their physical condition, but basically they remain *human* and *coherent*. Therefore, their fictional free-

[1] David H. Hesla, "The Shape of Chaos: A Reading of Beckett's *Watt, Critique*, VI, no. 1 (Spring, 1963). This article presents an interesting interpretation of *Watt*, one that shows great erudition but also discredits all previous interpretations. This indicates to what extent Beckett's work lends itself to contradictory interpretations.

dom is limited by the realistic setting in which they evolve. Caught in a materialistic environment, these protagonists never succeed in becoming independent heroes or self-reliant creator-heroes, as do their successors in Beckett's French fiction. Belacqua's and Murphy's attempts to escape within the mental world, or within the walls of some mental institution, are futile because these protagonists are physically and rationally tied to social reality. Though they entertain notions of an ideal, ascetic existence in some environment other than the traditional fiction in which they appear, they are too human to transcend the common world and become *heroic* figures—heroic in the sense of achieving fictional independence, which in Beckett's universe can correspond to a state of mental disorder, to a state of chaos, absurdity, and irrationality.

In *Watt*,[2] Beckett's last English novel, the characters no longer fall into a single category, but can be segregated into three distinct groups: the human, the heroic, and the lunatic. Essentially this is because between the physical and the mental, the real and the illusory, the rational and the irrational, a clear line of demarcation is established. In Beckett's preceding works this cleavage was merely suggested and caused the characters much of their existential anguish. In spite of repeated attempts, they could not escape the basic restrictions of the human condition—the physical and the rational. When confronted by the unpredictable aspects of the mental or imaginary world, Belacqua and Murphy sought the security of the material world, either to resume social existence or to commit suicide. In *Watt,* the three types of characters are specifically marked by the condition imposed upon them, but there are interrelationships causing unusual aesthetic and philosophic conflicts. Nevertheless, each character is assigned a particular role, and the ambivalent juxtaposition of these various beings permits Beckett to

[2] Beckett, *Watt* (Paris: Olympia Press, 1953). Reprinted by Grove Press, 1959. All quotations and page references from this work are from the Grove Press edition.

exploit a fictional gamut that extends from trivial realism to the ultimate in absurdity.

The humans are commonplace characters who appear only in the opening and closing scenes of the novel, and who are primarily concerned with physical existence. Presented as stereotypes, they function as conventional figures confined within the boundaries of a traditional setting—the world of public gardens, trams, and trains. Among these figures one finds a policeman, a porter, a newspaper agent, railway employees, and even lovers. Perhaps more significant, though also superficially characterized, are Mr. Hackett, Mr. Nixon, Mrs. Nixon, Mr. Spiro, Lady MacCann, Mr. Case, Mr. Nolan, and Mr. Gorman. The first four appear only in the opening scene.

By far the most typically *human* is Mr. Hackett, for whom the world is harmonious and stable, and who is satisfied with his limited existence, lest his daily routine be disturbed. Mr. Nixon and his wife, a bourgeois couple, relate the grotesque and seemingly irrelevant story of their son's birth, and then disappear from the scene. Mr. Spiro introduces himself as a neo-John-Thomist, editor of "the popular catholic monthly," *Crux*. He too seems irrelevant to the narration. Lady MacCann, the only human character to have the privilege of appearing in both the opening and closing scenes of the novel, is "a lady who daily left the neighbourhood by the first train in the morning, and returned to it by the last at night" (p. 240). As for the remaining three, railway employees, their performance is restricted to the closing pages of the novel. Like all other members of the human category, their existence is marked by the seal of habit and conformity.

The heroic are concerned primarily with intellectual matters. It is through the mind that they seek a meaning for their fictitious existence. However, because of the deceptive and absurd qualities of their situation, rather than being heroes in the true sense of the term they become caricatures—subheroes of the absurd. Watt is the most important figure of this group, and much of the narration is devoted to his adventures. A kind of knight-errant, Don Quixote of the irrational, he journeys from the world of the humans to a curious and elusive establishment—the house of Mr. Knott—whose mystery he attempts to elucidate. Though Watt is singled out as the hero of this novel, he belongs to a series of beings who replace one another in Mr. Knott's service according to a complex principle. His function, it seems, is to apprehend the fictional illusion. From the moment he sets out on his journey, he undergoes a mental, physical, and linguistic dehumanization which renders his quest heroic, in spite of its futility. Eventually, his failure to rationalize the Knott world leads him to an insane asylum.

The lunatics have as their spokesman a single individual, Sam, who is entrusted with the all-important function of narrating Watt's adventures. In other words, this madman assumes the creative responsibility. Sam's narration is an attempt to recapture the initial reality from which Watt began his fictional journey. By ascribing this role to a lunatic, Beckett seems to suggest that fiction emerges from a state of insanity, and whatever illusions or delusions are present in the deranged minds of Watt and Sam can serve to recreate an image of reality, or create a new reality, but one that constantly falls into chaos and uncertainty.

Paralleling these three types of beings are the worlds they inhabit: the material world (traditional fiction), where seemingly rational characters are confronted with external reality, with facts and tangibles; the Knott world, where the hero (Watt) and other fellow servants struggle to disentangle elements that are as irrational, as illogical, and as evasive as fiction can permit; and the world of insanity, where human and heroic alike are driven when they fail to reconcile the outer with the inner world, or when they fail to understand the Knott world. This lunatic region has no other logic than the one imposed upon it by fictional necessity, for it is here that creativity originates.

Beckett presents these three worlds as incompatible entities, each with a particular setting, definite rules, and specific conditions. The material world appears reasonable to its inhabitants, and time, habit, laws and conventions, logic, reason, and coherent language provide them with a notion of security and stability. This world is as it appears. By contrast, the Knott world is irrational, unstable, evasive, disorganized, in constant metamorphosis, and therefore cannot be apprehended with the same intellectual and sensory instruments as those of the real world. Whatever this world stands for, it is no longer the reality known to man. Here the equivocal Mr. Knott is master, while around him a succession of servants, such as Watt, performs duties as absurd as their surroundings. This world represents fictional illusion, the region where reality crumbles into disorder and meaninglessness as it seeks a new order and a new meaning. Whoever comes in contact with this world of illusions must either submit to its deceptive conditions and endure complete dehumanization, or retreat to reality. The world of insanity is situated beyond the Knott world in an unidentified insane asylum which shelters Watt after he suffers a mental breakdown as a result of his stubborn efforts to elucidate logically and rationally the illogical and irrational Knott world. In this institution Watt befriends one of the inmates to whom he relates his experiences, and in turn this lunatic, Sam, narrates Watt's adventures. This region represents the zone of creative consciousness.

Thus the humans remain subjected to the ordinary world of appearances, the heroic characters travel to Mr. Knott's house and try to apprehend its absurd system, and the lunatics exist beyond reality and rationality in the chaos of their own minds. To these categories one may add a fourth, represented by the almost unattainable Mr. Knott himself—a kind of grotesque divinity, an elusive deity who reigns over a Kafkaesque establishment.

The humans have no contact with Mr. Knott, nor are they aware of his existence; their deity is God, whose identity they do not question, for "God is a witness that cannot be sworn" (p. 9), declares one of the humans. The heroic regard Mr. Knott as their master, the omnipotent, omniscient controller of their servitude, but also as their fictional goal, the embodiment of their ambitions and hopes. In witnessing Mr. Knott's existence they witness their own existence. That Mr. Knott should appear totally absurd, and remain totally *unknown* to those who strive to elicit his identity, simply reveals the absurdity and meaninglessness of their quest. The futile and yet necessary relationship between Mr. Knott and his servants is as undefinable as the relationship between creator and creation, for "Mr. Knott, needing nothing if not, one, not to need, and two, a witness to his not needing, of himself knew nothing. And so he needed to be witnessed. Not that he might know, no, but that he might not cease" (pp. 202–203). As for the lunatics, they remember Mr. Knott as the cause of their mental disorder, as the instigator of their failure. For them the Knott house and its master are delusions of their deranged minds—delusions to which they must give order in retrospect.

The most puzzling aspect of this threefold structure lies in the fact that it is shaped from the point of view of the lunatics. In his effort to recapture his experiences of the Knott world after he enters the insane asylum, Watt sinks deeper and deeper into confusion and, therefore, "as there seemed no measure between what Watt could understand, and what he could not, so there seemed none between what he deemed certain, and what he deemed doubtful" (p. 132). How then can aesthetic coherence be achieved in this novel, and how can its three worlds be rendered artistically and intellectually compatible?

As the central figure, Watt establishes both physical and symbolic links between the various types of characters, even between those who appear only briefly or inadvertently, and it is primarily as a result of these intramural activities that narrative coherence is maintained. Watt traverses the three regions of the novel while undergoing physical and mental disintegration. He sets out from the world of reality (the human world) in a heroic but clumsy effort to conquer the illusory Knott world, strives to place himself on the same level as Mr. Knott by identifying with him, thereby attempting to achieve the Knott divinity or *fictionality*. But because the world of illusions cannot be apprehended through rational means, he fails miserably and is reduced to lunacy. In other words, Watt goes from a human to a heroic to a lunatic condition, but in the process, and in spite of his intellectual failure, he gives the narration its formal unity. By traveling through the three worlds of the novel, even though these are incompatible, by physically going from the real to the illusory, and by mentally passing from the rational to the irrational, Watt gathers into himself all the loose, digressive, irrelevant, incoherent, and non sequitur elements of the narration. As protagonist he creates in the midst of disorder a semblance of order in a narrative apparently doomed to nonsense since it is entrusted to a lunatic narrator.

Basically the world of insanity is deprived of rationality and coherence, and since the novel is constructed in retrospect from the distorted recollections of Watt as interpreted by the mentally deranged Sam, it seems indeed that the author has committed his work to inevitable failure. Yet Beckett avoids unintelligibility, and creates artistic order—even if such order opposes the primary condition of madness—by relying on a deceptive and unorthodox narrative structure, which consists in not revealing the presence and identity of the narrator until the reader is well engaged into the narration. Only at the beginning of the third chapter is Sam introduced as the narrator and as character as well. Prior to that the novel is omniscient, except for vague intrusions which appear to be on the part of the author himself. Thus an illusion of continuity is achieved despite the novel's misleading form. But once the reader discovers the true identity of the narrator, he is forced to wonder how certain parts of the narration can be accounted for, especially the opening scene which Sam could not possibly have witnessed nor learned of from Watt, since Watt himself merely passes through the world of the Hacketts and Nixons as an inanimate object.

To make matters even more confusing, Beckett deliberately distorts the textual order of the narration. Watt seems to progress on a straight course from the material world to the Knott world, and then on to the mental institution, at least according to the textual perspective, but actually Watt's fictional journey is a regressive movement from insanity to an apparently rational condition. Logically, Watt's adventures should follow this order:

1) Departure by train from the world of reality and arrival at the Knott world.
2) First stage, on the main floor of Mr. Knott's house.
3) Second stage, on the upper floor of Mr. Knott's house.
4) Departure by train from the Knott world and final residence in the insane asylum where Watt encounters Sam.

Yet the events of the novel's four parts are not presented in this sequence. The narration opens by introducing Mr. Hackett and the Nixons who engage in a trivial conversation about the weather, common friends, and personal reminiscences until Watt emerges from a tram in front of the public bench occupied by these three figures. It seems that Watt is an old acquaintance of Mr. Nixon, although the latter is totally ignorant of the former's identity and whereabouts, except that somehow he knows Watt to be "an experienced traveller" who is now "setting out on a journey" (p. 17).

Watt is first seen among human characters in the world of reality, on his way to Mr. Knott's house. After several misadventures and three unfortunate encounters with members of organized society (first with a porter into whom he stumbles on the platform of the train station, then with Mr. Spiro in the train who assails him with theological jargon, and finally with Lady MacCann who throws a stone at Watt for no reason as he proceeds on foot toward his destination), he arrives at the door of Mr. Knott's house.[3] In the dimly lit

---

[3] David Hesla (*op. cit.*) states that Watt's journey to Mr. Knott's house follows the fourteen Stations of the Cross. It is true that at one point in the novel Sam identifies Watt with the "Christ supposed by Bosch, then hanging in Trafalgar Square" (p. 159).

kitchen he is greeted by Arsene, whom he is to replace in the service of Mr. Knott. Before departing, Arsene delivers "a short statement," a bitter, pompous, and digressive speech of some twenty-six pages, whose incoherence announces the form of Watt's own story to come. Arsene's "statement" can be interpreted as a warning against the deceptive Knott world—a prologue to Watt's own fictional failure. But, as Arsene points out, Watt must find out for himself: ". . . you will decide for yourself, when your time comes. Or rather you will leave undecided to judge by the look of you" (p. 45).

The next chapter describes Watt's activities and preoccupations on the main floor of Mr. Knott's house as he struggles to comprehend rationally a system that constantly evades him and that refuses to be understood rationally. Watt questions the *potness* or *whatness* of Mr. Knott's pots, investigates the preparation and serving of Mr. Knott's food—a curious mixture of incongruous ingredients boiled together for four hours and served to Mr. Knott "cold, in a bowl, at twelve o'clock noon sharp and at seven P.M. exactly, all the year round" (p. 88). This brings Watt to analyze the method of disposing of Mr. Knott's leftovers, which in turn brings him to consider in some detail the various members of a hypothetical Lynch family whose duty it is to raise generations of dogs kept in a state of near starvation so that when they are brought daily to Mr. Knott's kitchen door they will devour what is left over from the meals, if such leftovers are available. Watt's speculations reach such absurdity that he is finally forced to abandon the whole question.

These are the problems that confront the hero during his stay on the main floor. But he is also concerned with people, for the Knott world, despite its strangeness, is not totally cut off from the outside world, and some human characters do come in contact with this establishment. Among those who deal with the Knott house are the Galls, father and son, who come all the way from town to "choon the piano"; Mr. Graves, the gardener, with whom Watt occasionally con-

verses; and Mrs. Gorman, the fishwoman, who calls every
Thursday, except when she is indisposed, and with whom
Watt carries on a rather comical love affair. Each of these
figures undergoes a special investigation, but it is particularly the Galls' visit that disturbs Watt—for though he
witnesses the incident that takes place in the music room,
and hears the exchange of words between the piano tuners,
once these two have departed he begins to wonder if the
incident really took place. The more he reflects upon this
matter the more it escapes him, as does everything else in the
Knott world. Finally Watt tries to draw meaning from an
incident which in retrospect appears totally meaningless and
nonexistent.

Much of Watt's attention during this first stage is directed
to his fellow servant, Erskine, whose duties are on the second
floor, closer to Mr. Knott. But even about Erskine he learns
very little. Watt's relationship with his master is also negligible, for he hardly ever sees or comes in contact with Mr.
Knott. Therefore, at the end of his stay on the main floor,
Watt has gained only a confused knowledge of his surroundings, of his master's appearance, identity, activities,
and whereabouts in the house. Nevertheless, Watt hopes
that soon he will learn more, for he knows that when
Erskine leaves it will be his turn to move upstairs, and
someone else will come to replace him downstairs. This
endless cycle has been explained to Watt by the departing
Arsene, who himself had been preceded by Walter and
Vincent. One morning Watt discovers Erskine gone and a
strange man waiting in the kitchen—as Watt himself once
did—a man who resembles "Arsene and Erskine in build,"
and who gives his name as Arthur.

Turning then to the next chapter, one expects to find
Watt on the upper floor of Mr. Knott's house; but to the
reader's great surprise Watt now appears in the insane asylum in the company of Sam in whom he confides, and who
takes it upon himself to narrate Watt's adventures. Thus
there seems to be a gap in the narration concerning when
and how Watt left Mr. Knott's house to enter the asylum

where, according to Sam, he has been residing "for quite some time." Sam describes first his relationship with Watt in the asylum, then proceeds to show Watt's method of expressing himself at that time, which consists of reversing the logical order of words in sentences, of sentences in paragraphs, and even of letters in words. Sam offers several examples of Watt's manner of speech and explains how Watt "spoke also with scant regard for grammar, for syntax, for pronunciation, for enunciation, and very likely, if the truth were known, for spelling too, as these are generally received. Proper names, however, both of places and of persons, such as Knott, Christ, Gomorrha, Cork, he articulated with great deliberation" (p. 156).

It is from Watt's distorted discourse and recollections that Sam gathers the information for his tale. However, he does point out that much of it was lost: "I missed I suppose much I presume of great interest touching I suspect the second stage of the second or closing period of Watt's stay in Mr. Knott's house" (p. 165). Much of the narration about Watt's later experiences in the Knott world, as presented by Sam, appears fragmentary and incoherent. Non sequitur statements, hiatuses, question marks, footnotes, blank spaces, digressions, extensive lists of absurd propositions followed by lists of refutations accumulate as Watt's frantic quest stumbles from linguistic to philosophic impasses, in a last and desperate attempt to pinpoint Mr. Knott's identity. No doubt the disorganized text reflects Watt's mental disorder, rendered even more incoherent as interpreted by Sam's lunatic mind.

The only piece of coherent prose in this chapter consists of an absurd and totally irrelevant story which Arthur relates one day while sitting in the garden with Mr. Knott, Mr. Graves, and Watt. Arthur explains to Mr. Graves the effects of a fabulous drug called Bando,[4] which he claims has changed his whole outlook on life:

[4] No doubt an allusion to the suggestive French slang word *bander* (to have an erection).

From being a moody, listless, constipated man, covered with squames, shunned by my fellows, my breath fetid and my appetite depraved (for years I had eaten nothing but high fat rashers), I became, after four years of Bando, vivacious, restless, a popular nudist, regular in my daily health, almost a father and a lover of boiled potatoes. Bando. Spelt as pronounced. [p. 170]

To illustrate the efficiency of Bando, Arthur proceeds to tell the story of his old friend, Mr. Ernest Louit. Louit's story, as told by Arthur, extends over twenty-seven pages of extravagant prose which parodies academic language as well as academic life. It is a piece of fiction within fiction, totally inconsequential to the rest of the novel. However, the whole of Arthur's story, as with Arsene's speech, can be read as another absurd reflection of Watt's own story. After numerous digressions and superfluous remarks on the part of Arthur, he ends his story quite abruptly as he seems to tire of it, and "Watt was thankful for this, for he too was tired of Arthur's story" (p. 197). In fact, Watt is tired of the whole Knott world, and therefore Sam quickly ends his narration by saying that "Watt had little to say on the subject of the second or closing period of his stay in Mr. Knott's house" (p. 199). At the end of this chapter Sam and Watt separate in the garden of the asylum, and the reader is presented with the disconcerting image of Watt walking backward toward his private pavilion. One may then assume that this is the end of Watt's story.

But in the fourth chapter the reader is brought back to Mr. Knott's house and observes Watt preparing himself for his departure, follows him as he proceeds to the train station where he spends the night waiting for the morning train. When finally the ticket window opens, he buys a ticket for "the further end of the line" (p. 244). When the train arrives, not a single passenger gets on; only a bicycle is unloaded. Watt seems to have suddenly disappeared, and the railway employees (Mr. Case, Mr. Nolan, and Mr. Gorman) remain, staring at one another for a while before resuming their usual daily activities. After an almost perfect circular course which led him to nothing, Watt, who began his journey in the world of the humans, appears to have returned to it.

According to the textual order of events, Watt's tale seems to end in the material world, where the hero is last seen at the train station. Thus an apparent confusion exists as to whether Watt truly travels to the mental institution or remains among the humans. But the chronological order of the narration suggests that Watt has reached the asylum, and therefore is now beyond rationality. There are then two possible endings for Watt's tale: Watt in the asylum, or Watt back in the material world. These two endings are rendered even more ambiguous by the presence of an addendum which suggests that the novel could not be completed, or at least could have been told differently, and consequently should not be taken at face value. Introduced by a curious footnote ("The following precious and illuminating material should be carefully studied. Only fatigue and disgust prevented its incorporation" [p. 247]), the eight-page addendum, rather than clarifying the novel, adds to its structural confusion, and yet appears essential to a narration that cannot find its own logical exit.

In its seemingly unfinished form, *Watt* offers itself as a literary fraud, since it is never known how the protagonist ends his quest or for what reason he undertook it. Beckett sums up Watt's futile efforts (as though subtly commenting on his own fictional experiment) in an odd statement:

For the only way one can speak of nothing is to speak of it as though it were something, just as the only way one can speak of God is to speak of him as though he were a man, which to be sure he was, in a sense, for a time, and as the only way one can speak of man, even our anthropologists have realised that, is to speak of him as though he were a termite.   [p. 77]

Watt's fallacy is to speak of nothing as though it were something, to speak of Mr. Knott as though he were a god, and of himself as though he were, perhaps not a termite, but a being who has suffered a "loss of species." Yet "to elicit something from nothing requires a certain skill and Watt

was not always successful, in his efforts to do so" (p. 177),
and therefore his quest ends in complete nonsense, just as
the novel was narrated in total confusion. This is explicitly
emphasized at the beginning of the fourth chapter: "As
Watt told the beginning of his story, not first, but second, so
not fourth, but third, now he told its end. Two, one, four,
three, that was the order in which Watt told his story.
Heroic quatrains are not otherwise elaborated" (p. 215).
Yet this statement does not clarify matters, for in fact Watt
did not tell his story "Two, one, four, three," as the narrator
claims, but one, two, four, three. [5] This intentional error
confuses the interplay among the various regions of the
novel, between the real and the illusory, and between the
rational and the irrational. This deliberate mixing of the
four parts introduces an element of fraudulence, not only in
relation to Watt's tale, which is already quite dubious, but,
on a wider scale, in relation to fiction itself, as the central
theme of this novel revolves around the perpetual question:
What is reality, what is illusion?

Watt's journey to Mr. Knott's house represents a paradoxical epistemological and fictional quest which results in
ignorance and confusion. The protagonist attempts to apprehend an irrational and unrealistic universe with intellectual tools (reason, logic, and conventional language) which
serve the inhabitants of a real world, and even those of
traditional fiction, to give a semblance of order to their
activities and surroundings, but which no longer function in
the absurd environment of the Knott world. Moreover,
Watt's quest is a metaphorical journey into creative
consciousness—a search for the hidden creator on the part of

[5] Ruby Cohn, in *Samuel Beckett: The Comic Gamut* (New Brunswick: Rutgers University Press, 1962), pp. 90–91, notes that "aside from
the ironic implication against Watt-hero in the reference to *heroic*
quatrains, there is deliberate confusion as to the textual order (I, II,
III, IV), the chronological one (I, II, IV, III), and what may be called
the epistemological one (II, I, IV, III). To order these last numbers,
one might think of II and III as the core of Watt's story, with I and
IV as Sam's frame."

a fictitious being. If Watt fails in his undertaking, he is still the first Beckett hero to advance beyond rationality, the first to transcend death in order to penetrate fictional absurdity and immortality.

As the inner core of fiction the Knott world represents an intermediary state between two eventualities: a return to the material world or an exile into insanity. Those who enter this region must refrain from thinking rationally if they intend to return to their starting point. Watt is unable to submit to this condition, and therefore in his insistence on remaining rational he drives himself to madness. In the process, however, he establishes a connection between the humans and Mr. Knott, on the one hand, and Mr. Knott and the lunatics, on the other. Having traveled from the world of the Hacketts and Nixons to the world of Sam, he relates the rational to the irrational. This union is exemplified not only by Watt's direct contact with the humans and the lunatics, but also by his twofold identification with them.

Though Mr. Hackett never travels to the Knott world, and Watt never comes in direct contact with Hackett, they are implicitly related to each other: "The curious thing is, my dear fellow, I tell you quite frankly, that when I see him [Watt], or think of him, I think of you [Hackett], and that when I see you, or think of you, I think of him. I have no idea why this is so" (p. 19). This Watt-Hackett parallel is made early in the novel by Mr. Nixon as he and Mr. Hackett observe Watt setting out on his journey. At first this equation seems irrelevant, but it is sufficient to recall Mr. Hackett to the reader whenever Watt's actions imitate those of Mr. Hackett. Thus, although Hackett appears only briefly in the opening scene, his presence is felt in Watt, who becomes Hackett's alter ego. The human and rational qualities of Mr. Hackett are transcended into the subhero Watt, just as reality is subsumed into fiction.

As a Watt-Hackett relationship is possible between two characters who have no physical contact and who exist on two different planes, so a similar relationship is established between Watt and the elusive Mr. Knott—servant and master. Though Watt rarely comes in contact with Mr. Knott and gains no knowledge of his identity, he manages to place himself in an ambiguous relationship that reduces Mr. Knott to mere human status and elevates Watt to a heroic condition. This is exemplified in an incoherent statement which emphasizes not only the mental but the linguistic deterioration suffered by Watt: "Dis yb dis, nem owt. Yad la, tin fo trap. Skin, skin, skin. Od su did ned taw? On. Taw ot klat tonk? On. Tonk ot klat taw? On. Tonk ta kool taw? On. Taw ta kool tonk? Nilb, mun, mud. Tin fo trap, yad la. Nem owt, dis yb dis" (p. 168). This statement is reported by Sam as a textual rendering of Watt's speech at the time of their association in the insane asylum. It is from such language that Sam reconstructs Watt's experiences in the Knott world. If one reorganizes the syntax according to Sam's instructions—that is, inverting not only "the order of the letters in the word together with that of the sentences in the period, but that of the letters in the word together with that of the words in the sentence together with that of the sentences in the period" (p. 168)—one obtains a significant discourse: "Sid by sid, two men. Al day, part of nit. Dum, num, blin. Knot look at wat? No. Wat look at knot? No. Wat talk to knot? No. Knot talk to wat? No. Wat den did us do? Niks, niks, niks, part of nit, al day. Two men, sid by sid." From the apparent nonsense of the original passage one is able to extract a meaning which can be paraphrased thus: All day, part of night, two men (Watt and Knott) failed to look at each other, to talk to each other, and yet side by side they ended, dumb, numb, and blind. In the midst of confusion and ignorance an equation is therefore established between master and servant, between seeker and sought—a remarkable equation, for "in rhythm, in symmetry, even often in euphony, this is as formal as anything in the book. As for coherence, it obeys the rule that the terms on either side of an equation may be arranged in any order." [6] The symmetry of Watt's statement (a symmetry born of chaos)

[6] Hugh Kenner, *Samuel Beckett: A Critical Study* (New York: Grove Press, 1961), p. 100.

reveals to what extent the confusion of Watt's mind is controlled, artistically controlled, as is everything else in the novel. Though neither Watt nor Knott succeeds in gaining the least knowledge of the other, they find themselves "side by side" in a vacuum of fictional absurdity.

However gratuitous these equations may be, they are carried into the world of insanity where, as a result of Sam's association with Watt, a Watt-Sam parallel is also established. Accordingly, in retrospect, the Watt-Hackett and Watt-Knott relationships acquire new dimensions, since it is, after all, Sam who reports Watt's experiences. Thus from Hackett to Sam a straight line is drawn which links the lunatic to the seemingly rational being. Through Watt, Sam becomes directly related to Knott and the Knott world, to Hackett and the Hackett world, as intricately related as the creator of fiction is to his creation. Consequently, a Sam-Hackett equation is also possible, an equation that can be defined as the relationship between the irrational and the rational. And if fiction, as exemplified in this novel, is made to become the product of a deranged mind, then the relationship between narrator and narration, between "the teller and the told," can be as unpredictable, as confused and mystifying, as the author chooses. That the suggestive Sam-Hackett equation should immediately bring to mind the author's own name, Sam Beckett, emphasizes to what extent he, the omniscient author, remains a subtle manipulator of fiction.

As narrator-hero Sam is granted a creative freedom that permits him to toy with his own predicament and that of his fellow characters. Undoubtedly Sam Beckett is responsible for the novel, but through an ambiguous reversal of fictional perspective it seems that the narrator-hero is now omnipotent, and that it is he who controls the fiction, while the author submits to the creative whims of this fictitious being. Thus, even though Sam could not possibly have witnessed the opening scene of the novel, nor could he have known Mr. Hackett, the Nixons, and other humans, he is now in a position to assume knowledge and responsibility for all the elements of the narration, simply as a result of his association with Watt. Everything Sam knows about the novel comes from the protagonist: "For all that I know on the subject of Mr Knott, and of all that touched Mr Knott, and on the subject of Watt, and of all that touched Watt, came from Watt, and from Watt alone" (p. 125). However, since Sam is mentally deranged, he cannot be held responsible for the novel's incoherence, nor for Watt's mental deficiency.

By transferring his creative responsibility to one of his creations, Beckett is able to extend his fictitious universe beyond the limits of traditional fiction, beyond the boundaries of realism. If, in his two preceding works, *More Pricks Than Kicks* and *Murphy,* the author felt a need to intrude personally in the narration to affirm his omniscience, in *Watt,* by pretending to hand over the creative power to an ambivalent narrator-hero, and by hiding behind Sam's mask, Beckett can render his fiction as irrational and absurd as he wishes. The further one progresses into Beckett's universe, the more independent the characters become, and the more irresponsible, since they are given control of their own fictitious existences and are no longer subjected to reality and realism. As they achieve the status of creator-heroes, speaking for themselves in the first person, these outcasts turn against the creator who originally forced them into fiction. Yet even though they appear to control the world in which they exist, they cannot escape the hidden creator who drives them on, shapes them into further illusions, tortures them into further miseries, all the while watching from the corner of the eye "la main qui écrit, toute brouillée par—par le contraire de l'éloignement" (*Textes pour rien,* p. 161).

It is evident then that the apparent disorder of Watt's form is carefully controlled, and that its circular shape, reflected in the protagonist's own circular quest, corresponds to the mental breakdown Watt undergoes as he struggles to elucidate the mystery of the Knott world, the mystery of fiction. In the process of questioning his predicament, of calculating, affirming, deducing facts about the elusive world in which he finds himself, Watt accumulates words that empty themselves of their essential meaning. Yet in *Watt* Beckett is concerned with the problem of expression and meaning. Later, in his French trilogy, where the creator-heroes are no longer required to think logically, Molloy is able to state: "For to know nothing is nothing, not to want to know anything likewise, but to be beyond knowing anything, to know you are beyond knowing anything, that is when peace enters in, to the soul of the incurious seeker" (*Molloy*, p. 86) . If Molloy finds peace in knowing that he is beyond all knowledge, Watt, on the contrary, cannot prevent himself from thinking logically, and from seeking knowledge. But because the object of his quest is irrational, the expression of his thoughts becomes incoherent and absurd.

Watt would certainly have preserved his mental stability had he, like Molloy, remained indifferent to the absurd conditions of the Knott world. Prior to entering Mr. Knott's house Watt escapes the absurdity of the material world by being indifferent to it, and by consigning to silence the nonsense of human activities. Until Watt reaches the door of Mr. Knott's house he does not speak a single word, nor does he formulate a single thought. He simply passes through the world of humans as though he were not part of it. From the moment he alights from the tram in front of the public bench occupied by Mr. Hackett and the Nixons, he appears as an object rather than a human being:

On the far side of the street, opposite to where they sat, a tram stopped. It remained stationary for some little time, and they heard the voice of the conductor, raised in anger. Then it moved on, disclosing, on the pavement, motionless, a solitary figure, lit less and less by the receding lights, until it was scarcely to be distinguished from the dim wall behind it. Tetty was not sure whether it was a man or a woman. Mr Hackett was not sure that it was not a parcel, a carpet for example, or a roll of tarpaulin, wrapped up in dark paper and tied about the middle with a cord.
[p. 16]

The description of Watt, as formulated by those who observe him, is quite rational, since these people judge only appearances. Being in no position to question the *whatness* of Watt, Mr. Hackett and the Nixons are forced into factual statements. Though they engage in a long discussion about Watt's identity and activities, they reach only vague conclusions. Watt seems to have neither a past nor a definable personality. All that is known of him is that he owes Mr. Nixon five shillings, that he has a huge red nose, that he has no fixed address, that he is probably a university man and an experienced traveler, that he is considerably younger than Mr. Nixon, and that he is truthful, gentle, and sometimes a little strange. Indeed, very little is known of Watt's existence and destination. Because Mr. Hackett and his companions are satisfied with the superficial aspects of their world, Watt appears incongruous to them. They compare him to a stone, to a carpet, to a roll of tarpaulin, to a sewer pipe. Mr. Hackett finally justifies his incapacity for finding a deeper meaning from appearances by stating that to be "unable to tell what you do not know . . . is a common failing" (p. 22). Watt should have followed this principle during his stay in the Knott world, and then perhaps he would have preserved his mental stability.

This refusal to acknowledge the deeper meaning or meaninglessness of the material world permits those who believe themselves rational to contemplate their environment and actions as rational. Thus, when Watt bumps into the porter on the platform of the train station and brushes aside this man's unfounded insults by offering a childish and idiotic smile, the porter assumes that Watt's silence is a sign of irrationality. On the train, when Mr. Spiro, the phony neo-John-Thomist, bombards Watt with religious questions, again Watt remains silent and unconcerned. On the road to Mr. Knott's house, when Lady MacCann, without any apparent reason, hurls a stone at Watt, once more he refuses to take notice. The actions of the milkman, who "wheels cans, up and down" from one end of the platform to the other in a Sisyphus-like punishment, and those of Mr. Evans (the news agent who helps Watt to his feet after his harsh encounter with the milkman), who lugs his bicycle up the stairs of the station as he comes to work in the morning and down the stairs as he returns home in the evening; Mr. Spiro's obsessions with theological matters, and Lady MacCann's unmotivated attack—all these acts and attitudes seem logical to those from whom they stem, whereas actually they are examples of the futile behavior of mankind.

The inhabitants of the material world are satisfied with their superficial knowledge of reality, and for them Watt's indifference to their world can be interpreted only as lunacy. Because what cannot be expressed or understood logically is nonsense for the humans, and being in "utter ignorance" of Watt's past activities, they judge him according to his appearance and classify him as someone "off his head." What the humans do not realize is that Watt has undergone a metamorphosis that separates him from humanity. As he appears in the novel, Watt is less a replica of man than he is an imaginary creature that preserves only the mental and linguistic ability of man. Those who come in contact with him during his passage through the material world are puzzled by his disturbing, clownlike appearance. They are unaware that his physique no longer reflects the human condition but represents a fictitious caricature on the way to physical disintegration. At one point in the novel Watt is referred to as "the long wet dream with the hat and bags" (p. 246). The image is appropriate, for as he draws nearer the Knott world Watt appears less and less human, less compatible with external reality, and his awkward body seems to function independently of his mind. By the time Watt reaches the door of Mr. Knott's house he has become a mental machine—a personified Cartesian *cogito*.[7]

Finding the front door of the house locked, Watt goes to the back door, which he finds also locked, returns to the front door, which is still locked, goes once more to the back

[7] It is not accidental that the description of Watt's method of advancing illustrates Geulincx's Occasionalist theory whereby the body acts independently of the mind: "The feet fell, heel and sole together, flat upon the ground, and left it, for the air's uncharted ways, with manifest repugnancy. The arms were content to dangle, in perfect equipendency. . . . Watt's was a funambulistic stagger" (p. 31).

door, which he now finds open. As he reflects upon this strange occurrence, it becomes obvious that he has begun his process of mental gymnastics. His mind offers two explanations for this mystery: either the door was not locked and he was at fault, or else someone opened it. Watt's rationalization about the door which may or may not have been locked, and about the hypothetical person who may or may not have opened the door from within or from without, hardly clarifies the matter, but it sets the mood for Watt's experiences to come. Moreover, it points out that Watt's mental process is now in action, and at the same time illustrates the types of problems one encounters in the Knott establishment.

From that point on, Watt, the thinking machine, no longer belongs to the society of humans who contemplate appearances as though secure in the Murphian "half-light zone" of the mind, but to that category of beings who heroically wander into "the dark zone" of the mind to investigate the chaos of forms "coming together and falling asunder" in a constant flux of "becoming and crumbling into fragments of a new becoming." [8] For the duration of his stay in the Knott world, Watt painfully struggles, placing "one mental foot in front of the other," [9] in an effort to apprehend the core of fictional illusion. He continues where Murphy in his own fiction had deserted the challenge.

Mathematically and scientifically, Watt's mind registers, analyzes, computes, calculates, adds, divides, subtracts, like some sort of logic machine that performs unbelievable feats of thinking—for "logic was on his side, and he remained faithful" to it (p. 219). But the old words, the "old credentials," though they accumulate in what appear to be logical sentences, fail to produce a meaningful explanation for the Knott world. Toward the end of his stay in this elusive establishment Watt no longer attempts to extract a meaning

---

[8] Beckett, *Murphy* (New York: Grove Press, 1957), p. 112. The three zones of Murphy's mind have been discussed in chapter iii.

[9] Jacqueline Hoefer, "Watt," *Perspective*, XI, no. 3 (Autumn, 1959), 167.

from his environment, but simply gathers as many words as he can to justify his experiences. His quest reaches such a state of superficiality and absurdity that he contents himself in listing frantically eighty-one possible combinations of Mr. Knott's physical appearance, seventy-two ways in which Mr. Knott can move in his room, and twenty ways in which the furniture can be arranged. Similar lists are made for the numerous ways in which Mr. Knott can wear his clothes, the various combinations in which he can wear his black boots, brown shoes, black slippers, and the unusual ways in which Mr. Knott gesticulates and articulates. It seems that Watt is running out of time, and in a final and desperate effort he tries to record his fleeting impressions with whatever words are still available to him. He rushes incoherently through each incident, through every part of the house, and "so vividly do the short, disjunctive paragraphs convey the final disintegration of Watt's mind that one might suspect the absurdity of the cosmos to be no more than a reflection of the disjunction of Watt's mind—a condition that is known as solipsism." [10]

Watt's failure results from his stubborn attempt to explain logically a world that rejects all explanations:

For there we have to do with events that resisted all Watt's efforts to saddle them with meaning, and a formula, so that he could neither think of them, nor speak of them, but only suffer them, when they recurred, though it seems probable that they recurred no more, at the period of Watt's revelation, to me, but were as though they had never been.   [p. 79]

The problems that confront Watt are insoluble, not only because they are constantly changing, but probably "they had never been." Thus the hero's quest proves a total failure, because he tries to formulate in words what cannot be known—the nonexistent. In spite of his methodical approach and desire for knowledge, Watt comes to realize how impossible it is to explain logically the unexplainable, par-

[10] Ruby Cohn, "*Watt* in the Light of *The Castle*," *Comparative Literature*, XIII, no. 2 (Spring, 1961), 160.

ticularly when the explanation is furnished in retrospect from a state of mental disorder:

> But what was this pursuit of meaning, in this indifference to meaning? And to what did it tend? These are delicate questions. For when Watt at last spoke of this time, it was a time long past, and of which his recollections were, in a sense, perhaps less clear than he would have wished, though too clear for his liking, in another. Add to this the notorious difficulty of recapturing, at will, modes of feeling peculiar to a certain time, and to a certain place, and perhaps also to a certain state of the health, when the time is past, and the place left, and the body struggling with quite a new situation. Add to this the obscurity of Watt's communications, the rapidity of his utterance and the eccentricities of his syntax, as elsewhere recorded. Add to this the material conditions in which these communications were made. Add to this the scant aptitude to receive of him to whom they were proposed. Add to this the scant aptitude to give of him to whom they were committed. And some idea will perhaps be obtained of the difficulties experienced in formulating, not only such matters as those here in question, but the entire body of Watt's experience, from the moment of his entering Mr Knott's establishment to the moment of his leaving it.
>
> [p. 75]

Not only is it difficult for Watt to relate experiences he cannot comprehend, but, as Sam points out, one must also consider the conditions under which Watt tells his story, and moreover allow for "the scant aptitude" of the narrator who himself can hardly maintain order in his own language and thoughts. The themes of ignorance, intellectual deficiency, and creative impotence suggested in *More Pricks Than Kicks* and *Murphy* are now elaborated, and it becomes evident that for Beckett the understanding of reality remains an impossibility. The Beckettian hero is incapable of knowledge. Eventually Watt resigns himself to his epistemological failure and to the fact of never being able to know anything about Mr. Knott and about his stay in the Knott world. Thus Arsene's prediction comes true: "You will decide for yourself, when your time comes. Or rather you will leave undecided, to judge by the look of you."

Reduced to insanity, Watt is unable to give order to his

recollections and to reconstruct the course of his adventures in the Knott world. As with Belacqua and Murphy, insanity and creativity are equated in failure, and failure becomes the ultimate end of all artistic and intellectual endeavors. But Watt's failure is carried one step further than that of his two predecessors: it becomes a failure of communication. Language as it is used in the material world begins to fail Watt in the Knott world. "The old credentials" no longer fit the evasive objects of Mr. Knott's house:

> Not that Watt desired information, for he did not. But he desired words to be applied to his situation, to Mr Knott, to the house, to the grounds, to his duties, to the stairs, to his bedroom, to the kitchen, and in a general way to the conditions of being in which he found himself. For Watt now found himself in the midst of things which, if they consented to be named, did so as it were with reluctance.   [p. 81]

Watt finds himself in a situation whereby matching words with objects becomes an absurd and meaningless activity.[11] The more words Watt accumulates the less meaning he obtains. While turning "little by little, a disturbance into words" and making "a pillow of old words, for a head" (p. 117), Watt empties the language he uses of its logical meaning. It is as though, in the process of seeking a meaning for an illusory condition, Watt were destroying the very environment he attempts to elucidate. He goes so far in his "pursuit of meaning," in his "indifference to meaning," that even when speaking of himself he negates his own identity, his own existence. And yet:

> Watt's need of semantic succour was at times so great that he would set to trying names on things, and on himself, almost as a woman hats. Thus of the pseudo-pot he would say, after reflexion, It is a shield, or, growing bolder, It is a raven, and so on. . . . As for himself, though he could no longer call it a man, as he had used to do, with the intuition that he was perhaps not talking

[11] Though Watt is never explicitly presented as a writer, as with Molloy and Malone, his obsession with words, his insistence on matching words with objects and people, suggest on his part the potentiality of becoming a creator of fiction, one who deals with words, one who creates a meaning and a semblance of reality with language.

nonsense, yet he could not imagine what else to call it, if not a man. But Watt's imagination had never been a lively one. So he continued to think of himself as a man, as his mother had taught him, when she said, There's a good little man, or, There's a bonny little man, or, There's a clever little man. But for all the relief that this afforded him, he might just as well have thought of himself as a box, or an urn.   [p. 83]

Watt does not realize that he no longer functions as a man, in the sense of belonging to humanity, but as a fictional invention, itself composed of words. Nevertheless, he persists in describing logically the indescribable Knott establishment and its master. Obsessed by the *whatness* of things and by his own *Wattness,* he refuses to acknowledge the *Knottness* or *nothingness* of his environment. That Watt's very name suggests the interrogative pronoun *what* as the essential term of his quest, while Mr. Knott's name may be read as a double pun on *knot* and *not,* points to the futility of Watt's quest. The whole novel, in fact, or for that matter the whole creative process, becomes an absurd question which can be paraphrased in this manner: WHAT is this KNOT which in the process of being disentangled leads to NOTH-ING?

Basically *Watt* is a narrative experiment which exploits the inadequacy of language, reason, and logic to reveal the failure of fiction as a means of apprehending the reality of the world. In this novel Beckett implies that the rational is no longer compatible with fiction. *Watt's* content, therefore, is an ironic reflection on its own form as well as a parody of all philosophical concepts that govern man's undertakings. It is an attempt to expose the failure of intellectual and aesthetic method in the modern world, in modern literature, and it thereby directly criticizes Cartesian rationalism. Speaking of Watt, Hugh Kenner states with his usual perspicacity: "He bears the Cartesian cross, the discursive intellect, with its irremediable itch to think explicable worlds into existence, stumbling through corridors of exquisite absurdity toward some talismanic formula with which he can be temporarily at rest." [12] But Watt never finds this mental rest—unless insanity is a restful state. Rationalism is at the base of Watt's mental breakdown. However, if Beckett continues to question the validity of Cartesianism, as he previously did in *Murphy*, he also directs his attack toward another branch of philosophy: logical positivism.

For a man like Beckett, keenly aware of the inadequacy of language, and rejecting whatever system man invents to comprehend the universe, logical positivism offers itself as a most tempting object of satire. What better irony is there than to use logic to destroy logic? Beckett's irony, as expressed by the narrator's comments and as exemplified by the hero's obsessive indulgence with words, is primarily directed at Ludwig Wittgenstein's theory of language. It was Jacqueline Hoefer, in her discussion of *Watt*, who first pointed out that "Watt's method as well as his assumptions about the nature of experience are those of logical positivism, which holds that the only kind of empirical knowledge is scientific, and which has been one of the dominant influences in the philosophy of this century," [13] and who first mentioned Wittgenstein in relation to Beckett.

The Viennese philosopher formulated his most pregnant ideas about the function of logic and language in an early work entitled *Logischphilosophische Abhandlung* (the English translation received the ponderous title, *Tractatus Logico-Philosophicus*).[14] A first rendition of this work in English appeared in 1922 with an introduction by Bertrand Russell, who was responsible for its publication. Whether or not Beckett, a fervent student of philosophy in the twenties and thirties, was familiar with this particular work, or knew of its existence, does not alter the fact that Watt's method of investigating the Knott world parallels that of the logical positivist. However, whereas Wittgenstein claims that reality can be understood only in function of language ("The

[12] Kenner, *op. cit.*, pp. 59–60.

[13] Hoefer, *op. cit.*, p. 167.

[14] Ludwig Wittgenstein, *Tractatus Logic-Philosophicus*, trans. D. F. Pears and B. F. MacGuinness (New York: Humanities Press, 1961).

sentence is a picture of reality") , [15] Watt soon discovers that the reality of the Knott world refuses to be apprehended with the "old words."

There is no direct mention of Wittgenstein or of his work in *Watt,* but one finds in Arsene's speech a rather curious statement, made in a mocking German accent, which cannot fail to relate to a passage of the closing paragraph of the *Tractatus.* While describing the various changes, "the slip," which occurred in his life as a result of having entered Mr. Knott's house, Arsene states: "What was changed was existence off the ladder. *Do not come down the ladder, Ifor, I haf taken it away"* (p. 44 [italics mine]) . Miss Hoefer interprets the name Ifor (if/or) as a play on words which relates directly to logical propositions, and which therefore serves to describe the kind of ladder Arsene has in mind. She goes on to explain how, in order to construct the principles of an "ideal language" with which to comprehend reality, Wittgenstein has to make metaphysical statements; but once the system is mastered, once the ladder of logic has been climbed, metaphysical propositions can be abandoned.[16] This is how Wittgenstein presents his argument:

My propositions serve as elucidations in the following way: anyone who understands me eventually recognizes them as nonsensical, when he has used them—as steps—to climb up beyond them. *(He must, so to speak, throw away the ladder after he has climbed up it.)*

He must transcend these propositions, and then he will see the world aright.

What we cannot speak about we must consign to silence. [17]

[15] *Ibid.,* p. 37 (Proposition 4.01) .

[16] Hoefer, *op. cit.,* p. 181. Miss Hoefer's argument is quite convincing, but could have been reinforced by noting that in *Murphy* Beckett had already used a similar statement: "Do not come down the ladder, they have taken it away" (p. 188) . In this instance the reference is to the ladder that leads to Murphy's garret in the asylum, though it may also imply Wittgenstein's ladder of logic, for in the French translation of *Murphy* the author adds the name *Louis* to the text, possibly as a direct allusion to *Ludwig* Wittgenstein: "Ne descendez pas par l'échelle, Louis, ils l'ont enlevée" (p. 137) .

[17] Wittgenstein, *op. cit.,* p. 151 (Proposition 6.54) . (Italics mine.)

To some extent Watt's quest follows this method; his fallacy is to try to formulate in words, in logical propositions, that which is unspeakable, "to speak of nothing as though it were something," whereas nothingness should be left unspoken, untold, and unwritten. Therefore, if there is an analogy between Watt and *Witt*-genstein, it is undoubtedly meant as a philosophic satire. The relationship between Watt's method of investigating the absurd unreality of the Knott world and Wittgenstein's approach to the concept of knowledge is further ridiculed by Arsene's discussion of "existence off the ladder." In the Knott world such existence can take place only beyond reality, in a region no longer subjected to the rules of logic, but in Wittgenstein's theory nothing can take place outside the realm of empirical experiences, outside the logic of language, for, as he clearly states, "The limits of my language mean the limits of the world." [18]

As defined by Arsene and as experienced later by Watt, the climb "up beyond" the steps of logical propositions fails to bring an understanding of reality. If Wittgenstein suggests that eventually one can discard the ladder of logic to "see the world aright," this suggestion, when taken at face value by those who enter the illusory Knott world, produces an absurd result. To his great consternation, Watt discovers that it is impossible to exist and think rationally "off the ladder," because, as Wittgenstein explains, "thought can never be of anything illogical, since, if it were, we should have to think illogically." [19] Thus, if all meaningful (logical) statements belong in the world of reality, in the material world, then the unrealistic and irrational Knott world must remain meaningless, indescribable, unattainable. Accordingly, all fictional quests can lead only to nonsense and confusion. The Knott establishment, and particularly the elusive divinity of its master, cannot be apprehended, because Mr. Knott, like all imaginary deities, exists in a

[18] *Ibid.*, p. 115 (Proposition 5.6) .
[19] *Ibid.*, p. 19 (Proposition 3.3) .

pseudometaphysical realm. For this reason, the language Watt uses to describe his experiences undergoes the same deterioration as his mind. In the material world of the Hacketts and Nixons—which serves as a frame for the Knott world—Wittgenstein's theory is applicable and justifiable as long as the humans avoid formulating a metaphysical meaning for their environment. The knowledge of reality must be limited to linguistic dimensions.

Thus Beckett disproves Wittgenstein's theory by inventing an imaginary world whose reality lies outside the norms of rationality. Those who seek to elucidate this reality through rational means stumble through "corridors of exquisite absurdity" and ultimately find themselves suspended in an ambiguous state of illusion created by the power of aesthetic fraudulence. For the sake of understanding, the critic can always pigeonhole this subreality into a neat formula, but when the fictional characters themselves attempt to rationalize their predicament, as Arsene and Watt do, they are either forced to stagger back to reality (the world of the humans) or to stumble forward into insanity (the world of the lunatics). By having his protagonist tackle the fictional dilemma as though it were a human problem, philosophically and realistically accessible, Beckett mocks all concepts of philosophy and of traditional realism.

Watt can be read as a satire of philosophy as well as an ironic reflection on the futility of the creative act. For Beckett the outer world of reality is absurd and meaningless because man's activities are absurd and meaningless, and the inner world of fiction is incomprehensible because man's intellectual tools (reason and logic) are no longer compatible with it. Thus Beckett's fiction contains not only its own aesthetic formula, but also its own system of criticism.

Arsene's monologue is a valuable document which, as fiction within fiction, comments on the absurdity of Watt's undertaking. Not only does it parody the philosophic method used by Watt to solve the Knott mystery, but it also predicts Watt's creative failure. Arsene begins his speech by telling the newly arrived Watt of the conditions of life in Mr. Knott's house. He explains how one feels upon entering this deceptive world:

The man arrives! The dark ways all behind, all within, the long dark ways, in his head. . . . All the old ways led to this, all the old windings, the stairs with never a landing that you screw yourself up. . . . All led to this, to this gloaming where a middleaged man sits masturbating his snout, waiting for the first dawn to break. For of course he is not as yet familiar with the premises. Indeed it is a wonder to him, and will remain so. . . . But he being what he has become, and the place being what it was made, the fit is perfect. And he knows this. No. Let us remain calm. He feels this. The sensations, the premonitions of harmony are irrefragable, of imminent harmony, when all outside him will be he. . . . When in a word he will be in his midst at last, after so many tedious years spent clinging to the perimeter. These first impressions, so hardly won, are undoubtedly delicious. What a feeling of security! . . . For he has arrived. He even ventures to remove his hat, and set down his bags, without misgiving, he unbuttons his coat and sits down, proffered all pure and open to the long joys of being himself, like a basin to a vomit.   [pp. 39, 40, 41]

Arsene is describing not only Watt's sensations and actions as he enters Mr. Knott's house, but his own as he remembers them, or thinks he remembers them, now that he has experienced the nothingness of Mr. Knott's establishment and must depart in complete ignorance and disenchantment.

Watt, too, experiences this "imminent harmony" when he first settles in Arsene's place. For now he has escaped the torments of the material world, the torments of the "old ways." The Hacketts, the Nixons, the Spiros, the Lady MacCanns, can no longer ridicule his physical appearance and his strange habits. "What a feeling of security!" However, in Mr. Knott's house Watt will suffer a different type of humiliation—mental failure. But for the time being Watt continues to enjoy this security as he listens to Arsene pursue his reminiscences:

Having oscillated all his life between the torments of a superficial loitering and the horrors of disinterested endeavour, he finds himself at last in a situation where to do nothing exclusively would be an act of the highest value, and significance. . . . It is because

of the nature of the work to be performed, because of its excep-
tional fruitfulness. . . .   [p. 41]

At first Watt convinces himself of the "fruitfulness" of his
work and of his mental activity in the Knott world. As he
performs his absurd duties ("calm and glad he peels the
potato and empties the night-stool, calm and glad he witnesses and is witnessed") (p. 42) he ascribes a usefulness
and importance to his condition until the day comes when
he, too, realizes how futile his activities are. Unexpectedly
the Knott world begins to slip away from underneath the
cover of logic Watt imposes on it. "The fool! He has learnt
nothing. Nothing" (p. 42). Arsene also recalls how he felt
that one day ("It was a Tuesday afternoon, in the month of
October" [p. 42]) when "suddenly somewhere some little
thing slipped." It is a hard moment of realization, bitterly
described, as Arsene expresses his disillusionment and looks
back on that terrible day when he felt "the change—the
change of appearance," as he calls it. Arsene tries to explain
what happened:

It was a slip like that I felt, that Tuesday afternoon, millions of
little things moving all together out of their old place, into a new
one nearby, and furtively, as though it were forbidden. . . . But
in what did the change *consist?* What was changed, and how?
What was changed, if my information is correct, was the sentiment
that a change, other than a change of degree, had taken place.
What was changed was existence off the ladder. Do not come down
the ladder, Ifor, I haf taken it away.   [pp. 43, 44]

Neither Arsene nor Watt recognizes that his false notions of
reality have been removed, and that he has slipped from a
human condition to a fictional status. Existence off the
ladder is but another illusion, as is everything else in the
Knott world. Arsene learns nothing from his stay in Mr.
Knott's house, except perhaps that the means of acquiring
knowledge are lacking. Therefore, as he prepares to depart,
he comforts himself by stating, "without enquiring how it
came, or how it went, that in my opinion it was not an
illusion, as long as it lasted, that presence of what did not
exist, that presence without, that presence within, that pres-

ence between, though I'll be buggered if I can understand
how it could have been anything else" (p. 45).

At the end of his stay in the Knott world, Arsene deliberately negates the whole logical system through which he
experienced the Knott illusion, and thus warns Watt of his
fate. Arsene could probably go on with other quests, though
it is doubtful that he ever will, for now he longs to be
transformed "into a stone pillar or a cromlech in the middle
of a field or on the mountain side for succeeding generations
to admire, and for cows and horses and sheep and goats to
come and scratch themselves against and for men and dogs
to make their water against and for learned men to speculate
regarding . . ." (p. 49). One can, however, assume that
Arsene's wish will never come true, and that instead he will
return to the world of man and resign himself to accept
reality as just another illusion.

In contrast with Arsene, Watt "continues to place exclusive focus on the physical aspects of an event," [20] of an object, or of a man, even though Arsene has warned him of
the deceptive quality of things and people in the Knott
world and has told him: "If you want a stone, ask a turnover. If you want a turnover, ask plumppudding" (p. 46).
Watt's perversely logical mind becomes a stumbling block
in the Knott establishment, where the house, the servants,
the master, and all the objects are in a constant state of
transformation, thereby avoiding all classifications—vis-
ual, mental, or verbal. Thus Watt's failure is much more
tragic, and yet much more comic, than Arsene's. Watt's
quest ends in utter confusion, for even after he has left
Mr. Knott's house he continues to fall "into this old error,
this error of the old days" (p. 227) of confusing reality
with illusion.

The sense of harmony that offers a notion of security to
the inhabitants of the material world is destroyed by Watt's
insistence on formulating into speech the Knott meaninglessness. Yet, even though Watt's speech and actions deteri-

[20] Hoefer, *op. cit.*, p. 181.

orate completely, the narration preserves a striking symmetry. Despite its flagrant disorder and suggested incompleteness, the novel presents a formal appearance. The form
transcends the nonsense of its content and comes around full
circle to create an illusion of order. This is accomplished not
only by the obvious circular shape of the narration, which
opens and closes in the material world, but by the unexpected image of Watt, who, in the asylum, performs all his
actions backward, suggesting the possibility of a return to
the beginning of his quest. As he relates his adventures to
Sam, Watt not only reverses the syntactical order of the
language he uses, but wears his clothes back to front, and
walks backward as he staggers away from the narrator. It
seems that by reversing the logical order of speech and of
motion Watt is trying to retrace his mental and physical
steps to the origin of things, to that moment before he
penetrated the Knott illusion. It is as though he wants to
recapture the reality and rationality that were destroyed in
the process of fictional expression. Watt's reversed speech
and motion in the asylum can be interpreted as a need to
return to the primary source of his own self, as a wish to
return to a prenatal condition—to the time and place, prior
to his entrance into the Knott world, prior to his fictional
indoctrination, when he sat in a fetal posture in a ditch
along the roadside, hiding his face from the moonlight,
drinking goat's milk, and listening in his mind to the melo-
dious voices of a mixed choir. [21]

When Watt leaves Mr. Knott's house, retracing his steps
along the road to the railway station where his quest began,
the circle of events almost closes itself as "a strayed ass, or

[21] In an article entitled "Threne and Theme in *Watt*," *Wisconsin Studies in Contemporary Literature*, IV, no. 3 (Autumn, 1963), Sidney Warhaft finds the key to this novel in the threne of the "mixed choir" Watt hears while in the ditch. "In fact," states Mr. Warhaft, "carefully examined, the threne can be found to have a strong synecdochic rele-vance, a meaning central to the whole obscure but uncommonly chal-lenging novel" (p. 261), and he proceeds to show how the "development of Watt toward his fate may be said to parallel the historical develop-ment of man toward his modern condition—and, not so incidentally, to find dark revelation in the threne in the ditch" (p. 275).

goat, lying in the ditch, in the shadow" (p. 223) raises its head as he passes and watches the hero disappear down the road. The roles have been reversed, however, and it is no longer Watt who contemplates dumbfoundedly the journey ahead as he lies in the ditch drinking goat's milk, but the goat (or ass) itself which observes the dumbfounded Watt as he walks away from his failure. This reversal of situations exemplifies the incongruous relationship between the novel's events and characters. In his speech, Arsene describes the change he felt in the Knott world as a "reversed metamorphosis. The Laurel into Daphne. The old thing where it always was, back again" (p. 44). It is through this process of "reversed metamorphosis" that the novel acquires unity. Many events ("if one may speak here of events") reproduce themselves in full circular motion, but each time with enough distortion to create an imperfect and deceptive match.

The final description of Mr. Knott wearing a single shoe ("the black boot, the brown shoe, the black slipper, the brown boot, the black shoe, the brown slipper, on the one foot . . .") reverts to Mr. Nixon's description of Watt, who, when he first met him, had "one of his feet bare" and borrowed five shillings "to buy himself a boot" (p. 23). The association between Watt and Knott both wearing a single shoe may seem irrelevant—as everything else in the novel—but since a Watt-Knott relationship has already been established on an even more absurd level, this allusion reinforces the equation.

As the novel progresses, many incidents occur whose irrelevance would be unexplainable if they did not immediately refer to some previous situation. For instance, upon his arrival at the train station in part one of the novel, Watt bumps into the porter and falls to the ground. This scene is duplicated in part four when Mr. Nolan and Mr. Gorman accidentally knock Watt unconscious as they open the door of the station's waiting room. Thus, twice in the course of his journey, Watt suffers an accidental fall. It was Lady MacCann with a blow of a stone who caused Watt to suffer a moment of weakness, thereby forcing him to rest in the ditch. Lady MacCann reappears in the closing scene when Watt lies unconscious on the floor of the waiting room and she comments on her act: this has been "the scene . . . of terrible . . . terrible . . . events . . . but that now . . . all is well . . . Very good" (p. 243). The effect of the blow is felt some two hundred pages later.

If in the end Watt falls off the ladder of logic, as suggested by Arsene's prediction, as the novel draws to a close one suddenly recalls Mr. Hackett's mention that he, too, fell off a ladder when he was one year old. Therefore, the Watt-Hackett relationship finds another link on a metaphorical level, even though Watt's fall is only a symbolic reflection of Hackett's real fall. Similarly, the reality of Hackett's hunchback is wished on Watt when the porter curses him: "The devil raise a hump on you" (p. 24). In the course of the narration each event, each character, finds a counterpart in some preceding situation or figure as though the plot were literally projecting itself backward, or, as a critic commented: "In the novels of Beckett, the second term of the metaphor is read back into the work by structural and mythico-symbolic devices of plot and characterization." [22] So, in a full elliptical shape, the narration draws a curve between events that may not correspond on a logical plane but that relate on the level of absurdity. Yet this process of duplication never results in a perfect match, since the replica fails to agree with the original, just as reality and the image of reality (fiction) fail to agree in Watt's mind. The Watt-Hackett or Watt-Knott equations remain as incongruous as all the statements Watt makes about the Knott world. He starts his journey from reality, follows the circumference of some imaginary circle (the shape of fiction), and hopes that in the process he will return to reality. Instead he encounters an illusion, and in his effort to render this illusion tangible and rational, to match reality with fiction, he suffers a mental breakdown and is driven to an insane asylum. The circle of his quest remains incomplete, unfulfilled, and meaningless.

Beckett furnishes the critical symbol for the novel's imperfect form and Watt's imperfect quest in the novel itself—it is the subject matter of a picture Watt finds hanging on the wall of Erskine's room, and which causes Watt much anxiety:

A circle, obviously described by a compass, and broken at its lowest point, occupied the middle foreground, of this picture. Was it receding? Watt had that impression. In the eastern background appeared a point, or dot. The circumference was black. The point was blue, but blue! The rest was white. How the effect of perspective was obtained Watt did not know. But it was obtained. By what means the illusion of movement in space, and it almost seemed in time, was given, Watt could not say. But it was given. [pp. 128–129]

Just as the reader wonders how continuity and coherence are achieved in this fragmented novel, Watt struggles to apprehend the illusive composition of the picture. He finds himself speculating as to the trick by which aesthetic order is maintained. He tries to imagine when and how the circle and the dot in the picture will enter together on the same plane, or whether they will ever achieve the inevitable symmetry that a point at the center of a circle has with its circumference, or if eventually the broken circle and the blue dot might not come together and collide. He also wonders about the artist's intention—much as the reader wonders about Beckett's—and whether he meant the point to be in search of the circle, or the circle in search of the point, in "boundless space, in endless time." Watt even tries to see how the picture would look upside down, or on its right side, or on its left side, in each instance seeing the dot shift to a different place within the circle, as though they were mutually exclusive realities. But even "in these positions the picture pleased Watt less than it had when on the wall" (p. 130), and, as usual, unable to satisfy his curiosity, Watt simply drops the whole matter and moves on to some other Knott problems. Though he repeatedly tries to force the issue, the circle of events remains broken at one end, while the inner dot refuses to be situated, apprehended, or pinpointed on a logical plane.

Assuming that the broken circle represents Watt's quest, or the sum of his unfulfilled speculations around some elusive point, and that the dot symbolizes the evasive Mr. Knott and his establishment, then the picture in Erskine's room becomes the metaphor and equation for this novel. However, since the picture is just another "term in a series, like the series of Mr Knott's dogs, or the series of Mr Knott's men, or like the centuries that fall, from the pod of eternity" (p. 131), Watt's futile quest remains forever part of an incomprehensible, universal series of quests which mathematically, geometrically, philosophically, and artistically can reduce, divide, or repeat themselves to infinity and absurdity. The Knott world is for Watt what the universe was for Pascal:". . . an infinite sphere whose center is everywhere, whose circumference is nowhere." [23]

Discussing the mathematical aspect of Beckett's work, Vivian Mercier shows how each novel can be understood according to an equation or a geometrical figure, and of Watt he says: "Watt's career might be represented graphically as the curve of a function which diminishes until it approaches zero and then gradually increases again." [24] Metaphorically, then, Watt advances along the circumference of a broken circle which will never close upon itself, and will therefore never reach its beginning.

During his stay in the Knott establishment, Watt spends most of his time calculating the possibility of arranging or dividing numbers to arrive at the exact measurements of a perfect circle, or at the "root" of reality. But all his calculations fall short, and the mental circle remains imperfect, just as the circular shape of the novel gives the impression of

[23] Pascal, *Pensées* (Paris: Editions Garnier, 1948), p. 87 no. 72: ". . . une sphère infinie dont le centre est partout, la circonférence nulle part."   ..
[24] Vivian Mercier, "Mathematical Limit," *Nation*, CLXXXVIII (Feb. 14, 1959), 144.

being imperfect in spite of its subtly controlled form. Thus language, structure, and content, expertly as all three are manipulated by the author, undergo a disturbing deterioration. On the level of plot, Beckett (through the narrator) pretends to be unable to control the narration; on the aesthetic level, he shows how the novel form is inadequate to gain an understanding of reality; and on the philosophical level, through Watt's absurd quest, he points out the failure of rational thought as a means of acquiring absolute knowledge. Whatever process has been adopted to produce a coherent novel, and whatever method the hero employs to apprehend reality, these are doomed to failure. Eventually Watt is forced to retrace his steps, mentally, physically, and linguistically, just as the events of the novel appear to have been written in the wrong order or in complete disorder.

As the hero of Beckett's last English novel, Watt is perhaps closer by his grotesque personality, his dejected physical appearance, and his irrational mental activities to Beckett's French derelicts than to his immediate ancestors, Belacqua Shuah and Murphy. Yet *Watt* could probably not have been written without the example of *More Pricks Than Kicks* and *Murphy*, which set its form and mood. Therefore, the novel's circular plot extends backward beyond the beginning of Watt's adventures to relate thematically with the works that precede, and projects forward to prepare the shape of the works to come.

FICTIONAL ABSURDITY: EXILE AND ALIENATION

Comment continuer?
Il ne fallait pas commencer,
si il le fallait.

BECKETT, *Nouvelles et Textes pour rien*

*Il n'y a plus
moyen d'avancer.
Reculer est également
hors de question.*

BECKETT, *Mercier et Camier*

V

THE PSEUDOCOUPLE
MERCIER-CAMIER

In 1945 Beckett, who had spent the war years in southern France writing *Watt* and completing the French translation of *Murphy,* returned to Paris and began "the siege in the room." [1] Writing in French, from 1945 to 1950 he produced most of his important works: *Molloy, Malone meurt, En Attendant Godot,* and *L'Innommable.* Three manuscripts, written according to Beckett between 1945 and 1947, remain unpublished: the novel *Mercier et Camier,* the short story *Premier amour,* and the play *Eleutheria.* [2] This jetti-

---

[1] Hugh Kenner, *Samuel Beckett: A Critical Study* (New York: Grove Press, 1961) , p. 24.

[2] *Mercier et Camier* was written in 1945, *Premier amour* in 1945–1946, and *Eleutheria* in 1947. Typescripts of these manuscripts are kept in the library (Special Collections) of the University of California, Santa Barbara. The existence of these unpublished works was first pointed out by Hugh Kenner, who devotes a few pages of his 1961 critical study to a presentation of each manuscript. In turn, Ruby Cohn, in her 1962 book on Beckett (*Samuel Beckett: The Comic Gamut,* [New Brunswick: Rutgers University Press]) , mentions these three manuscripts at various times and offers brief comments on their comic aspect. In neither of these books are the unpublished works analyzed at any length, nor are they viewed thematically and structurally in relation to the rest of Beckett's production. The present chapter is in-

soned material and the three published *Nouvelles,*
"L'Expulsé," "Le Calmant," "La Fin" (also written in
1945–1946), represent Beckett's second creative period: the
transition from the formal intellectualism and social satire
of the English fiction to the more intense existential concern
of the French trilogy and plays.

One may wonder why Beckett refuses to release these
manuscripts for publication. Possibly he finds them inferior
to the rest of his work and considers them lesser products of
his apprenticeship in an adopted language. A more likely
reason, however, is that he meant these simply as first drafts
or experimental sketches for the works to follow. Much of
the dialogue in *Mercier et Camier* is repeated almost word
for word in *Godot,* and many of the situations in which the
two protagonists, Mercier and Camier, find themselves are
reproduced with minor alterations in the trilogy. The journey these two travelers plan to undertake, but constantly
delay with absurd excuses, resembles Molloy's vain quest for
his mother, and Moran's search for Molloy. The couple
concept so evident in Beckett's recent works originated in
this novel. The ambivalent partnership between Mercier
and Camier, suggesting the body and mind dualism, is similar in many respects to the Vladimir-Estragon, Pozzo-Lucky
pairs in *Godot,* or Hamm and Clov in *Fin de partie.* Each
member threatens to leave the other, yet never seems capable of doing so. These are some of the elements found in
this first novel and further explored in later works.

From the play *Eleutheria* Beckett may have derived the
idea of exploiting dramatic situations that lead nowhere and
resolve nothing. Seventeen characters appear in this three-
act play, sixteen of whom are engaged hopelessly in convincing the hero, Victor, to return to his bourgeois family, whom
he deserted to take refuge in a sordid garret. Victor is unable
to formulate his reasons for revolting against society, and

---

tended as an interpretation of the novel *Mercier et Camier* in an effort
to relate this first French narrative to the preceding English fiction,
and to determine to what extent its form and content served as models
for subsequent Beckett works.

therefore fails to give the play a logical direction. To the great exasperation of all those involved in this absurd situation (audience included, since finally one of the "spectators" jumps on stage to argue with the characters in an effort to bring the play to a close), Victor refuses to justify his actions. It becomes evident that the situation cannot be resolved in the usual time allotted a traditional play to unfold its plot. The "spectator" who, in Pirandellian fashion, has taken the liberty of interfering with the actions of the characters criticizes the author of this "flop" who cannot present a play according to the rules. Consulting his program he asks: "Au fait, qui a fait ce navet? (Programme) Beckett (Il dit Béquet), Samuel, Béquet, Béquet, ça doit être un juif groenlandais matiné d'auvergnat." [3] This direct involvement of spectators with characters becomes an essential aspect of Beckett's theater, one that is also exploited in the novels where the reader is repeatedly drawn into the narration. In *Eleutheria* there are many elements of "anti-theater" which Beckett incorporates in his later plays.

In *Premier amour,* Beckett initiates the first-person narrative maintained throughout his later fiction and introduces a true narrator-hero who, in the process of revealing in obscene terms the anguish of his inner self, invents stories of doubtful authenticity. This anonymous "I" is no longer concerned with the reality of the outer world, but with the problem of his own mental existence, his own trivial survival as a fictitious being. In the untiring voice of this egocentric narrator one recognizes the prevailing feature of Beckett's future derelicts. The style and content of *Premier amour* undoubtedly served as a pattern for the three short stories of *Nouvelles et Textes pour rien,* which in turn fixed the tone of the interior monologue developed in the trilogy. It is surprising, then, that Beckett did not publish *Premier amour* together with the other three stories, for they share a common narrator, a common form, a similarity of context, they exploit the same comic effects, and all four achieve the

[3] Beckett, *Eleutheria,* p. 105 of typescript.

same degree of artistic perfection. Perhaps Beckett saw in the structural interplay of the three stories ("L'Expulsé," "Le Calmant," "La Fin") an adequate model for the eventual shape of the trilogy, which does preserve among its novels the same thematic scheme that the stories have with one another.[4]

These unpublished manuscripts furnish valuable clues to Beckett's subsequent works and are therefore essential to the understanding of his creative evolution. For if Beckett draws from outside sources (both literary and philosophical) for the structure of his English fiction, he models his more recent French novels and plays on the bulk of his own preceding achievements. Thus the works that can be gathered in the second period serve as transitional steps between the progressive rejection of social reality on the part of the early protagonists (Belacqua, Murphy, Watt) and the total alienation from society and reality experienced by the later French heroes (Molloy, Malone, The Unnamable). Within the thematic structure of Beckett's universe this material stands as a unifying link relating the pseudorealistic world in which the English fiction evolves to the deteriorated landscape of the French novels of the third period.

The ostentatious intellectualism of Beckett's early literary efforts and the subsequent exaggerated complexity of *Watt's* language and narrative form led to an aesthetic impasse. To renew his creative potentialities Beckett needed a different literary tool, and therefore adopted the French language. When questioned on this linguistic shift he remains extremely evasive, but whatever his reasons they are of little relevance in gaining insight into his achievements. More important is the thematic and structural continuity from the English to the French works. One cannot fail to recognize that the same hand, the same mind, is at work in both languages.

[4] One can read "L'Expulsé" as a draft of *Molloy* (the quest for identity), "Le Calmant" as the equivalent of *Malone meurt* (the creation of fiction as a mental sedative), and "La Fin" as relating to *L'Innommable* (the impasse of fiction).

Beckett's English fiction stands as the substructure for his entire fictional universe. It is upon the aesthetic, thematic, and philosophical groundwork established in *More Pricks Than Kicks, Murphy,* and *Watt* that the unorthodox French experiments are constructed. The characters of the earlier novels serve as prototypes for the later heroes, and their physical ailments and mental idiosyncrasies are reproduced and emphasized in subsequent characters. Moreover, the French fiction not only draws material from the English creations, but also exploits, abuses, mocks, and often parodies these antecedents. In so doing it becomes a biting criticism of traditional realism. This self-generating fiction evolves, however, along consistent lines, despite essential differences in linguistic tone, narrative technique, and setting.

The language in *More Pricks Than Kicks, Murphy,* and *Watt* is primarily academic and scholarly, even though it tends to jest about its own pedantry. It remains Joycean in many ways, and offers flagrant examples of superabundance and self-consciousness. Beckett delights in abusing the vocabulary, distorting the syntax, torturing the diction, until linguistic complexities are made to demonstrate the inadequacy of language as an intellectual and artistic means of communication. By contrast, the language in Beckett's French works is strikingly simple and fluid, in spite of its apparent incoherence. A colloquial tone replaces the eloquent and affected diction of the English prose. The failure of language is now revealed through subtle usage of clichés and verbal banalities. If there are obscurities and ambiguities in the French fiction, these result from the characters' mental confusion, not from the language itself which is deceptively transparent.

The narrative technique in the English novels is basically traditional, with only vague tendencies toward experimentation. *More Pricks Than Kicks* and *Murphy* are presented from a conventional third-person point of view, and if occasionally the author intrudes in the narration, it is to express his dissatisfaction with the form he employs. In *Watt* and also in *Mercier et Camier,* Beckett departs from the omniscient point of view to introduce a narrator whose function is to control and criticize the actions of the characters. This device creates an ambivalent relationship between creator and creation on the one hand, and creation and reader on the other, which reduces aesthetic distance. Here Beckett approaches the technical incongruity which renders his more recent fiction original. In these novels the characters fail to free themselves from social and physical restrictions because they are constantly checked by the narrator's presence. Neither Watt nor Mercier and Camier can alienate themselves completely from social reality.

After his first French novel, Beckett turned to the first-person narrative and gave his heroes the freedom to create the environment in which they were going to exist. Consequently, they became subject to their own creative illusions. No longer limited by realism and credibility, they invented fantastic, absurd, and irrational situations which they were able to negate in a single sentence. Creator and creation were united in an unpredictable subreality. This passing from an objective third-person point of view to a subjective first-person narrative reinforces to a great extent Beckett's deliberate undermining of traditional realism. However, the self-made existence of the French creator-heroes would appear totally meaningless if some remnants of realism were not present to emphasize the absurdity of the fictional condition, for only in relation to a nonabsurd situation can absurdity be exposed. Therefore, even in Beckett's most unrealistic novels one finds a realistic substratum upon which the characters are superimposed.

The shift in setting from the English to the French fiction plays an important part in determining the characters' reactions. The earlier protagonists remain part and parcel of a social world they attempt to escape by withdrawing into the privacy of their minds, or by seeking refuge inside an insane asylum. In contrast, the French heroes exist outside social reality in an irrational environment which can be referred to as fictional absurdity. Exiled from the physical, and unable to reconcile themselves to mental alienation, they fill the gap in which they exist with inventions, lies, and delusions. The extravagant stories they relate are exteriorizations of anguished inner selves. It is as though they were watching their own illusory existence revolve around an elusive center. No longer controlled by an omnipotent creator, no longer presented as human beings given a rational role to perform, they witness and describe their own deceptive progress toward complete disintegration and silence.

In the course of its motion away from reality, Beckett's total universe takes on a geometric form. Belacqua and Murphy advance along a straight line. This line curves in *Watt* to become a broken circle that never closes upon itself. Starting with the first French novel, *Mercier et Camier,* this shape gains a third dimension as it turns inward to form an endless metaphysical spiral whereby "a step forward is, by definition, a step back." [5] While the English protagonists strive to find an asylum within the boundaries of reality, the French heroes are in permanent exile from both society and reality; their predicament is not only more absurd, more pathetic, but also more tragic. For as Beckett himself states in *Murphy*: ". . . asylum (after a point) is better than exile" (p. 73).

The perplexity the English characters show toward the dualism of body and mind, their aspiration to insanity, indolence, doubt, and irresponsibility are attributes that reappear in the French characters, but more deeply pronounced. As the characters evolve from one work to the next, they suffer the full impact of these obsessions, which cause their personality and individuality to undergo complete deterioration. Gradually reduced to mere mental functions, these creatures eventually find themselves vegetating in a landscape whose limits fade into the unreal. In *Mercier et Camier,* however, the characters are still very

[5] Beckett, "Dante . . . Bruno. Vico . . Joyce," *Our Exagmination Round His Factification for Incamination of Work in Progress* (London: Faber and Faber, 1936) , p. 22.

much involved in physical and social activities, and the action of the novel, like that of the preceding English works, remains set in a recognizable and fixed environment (Dublin, it seems, though it is not specified) which gives the narration a semblance of realism. The physical setting in which Mercier and Camier wander preserves many characteristics of the ordinary world, but the situation is made incongruous by the absurd actions of the two protagonists, and particularly by the curious journey they undertake to some unknown destination.

In Beckett's universe, the city as a setting remains the domain of realism and rationality, whereas the countryside represents the region of pure imagination, the landscape of fictional absurdity. To escape social reality and alienate themselves from humanity Beckett's heroes strive to leave the city in order to immerse themselves in the wasteland that lies beyond the city limits, beyond civilization. From the well-defined streets, restaurants, pubs, houses, and public buildings of the English fiction, to the garrets, barns, gutters, benches, and parks of the early French works, to the barren fields, deserted roads, stony beaches, dark forests, and ditches of Beckett's more recent fiction, there is a definite progression into the unreal which corresponds to the characters' exile from society and their gradual metamorphosis from an upright human condition to a reptilian or vegetal status.

More Pricks Than Kicks is set in Dublin, *Murphy* takes place in London, and both of these settings offer identifiable landmarks. *Watt* begins and ends in a city somewhere in Ireland, and Mr. Knott's house, in spite of its seclusiveness, remains within walking distance of the train station. The setting in *Mercier et Camier* is still the city of man, but a city with streets that form a labyrinth of impasses. Mercier and Camier temporarily succeed in wandering into the countryside, but only to return hastily to the city. In *Molloy* and *Malone meurt,* there are some streets, buildings, city walls, and rooms, but one is never quite sure whether these remnants of realism truly belong to the setting or are delusions of the characters' delirious minds. The city becomes a vague memory which haunts these derelicts. In *L'Innommable* the selfless hero appears suspended over a moribund landscape which, in *Comment c'est,* turns into an endless stretch of mud where a wormlike creature crawls in painful agony.

One might say that the first steps into absurdity and irrationality are taken by Watt, and that these steps are carried one stage further in *Mercier et Camier* when the protagonists succeed in departing from the city. On the surface, this first French novel is the story of two men's journey from a city to an unspecified country place, but metaphorically it represents an ascetic quest into the imaginary. Mercier and Camier seem to have decided to put an end to social and physical existence and to alienate themselves from the world of man. Therefore, they depart from reality in an effort to penetrate the realm of illusion. Theirs is a voluntary journey into fictional alienation. Because their quest is marked from the start with the seal of absurdity, and because they are incapable of distinguishing the real from the illusory, all their actions result in confusion and failure. Thus, instead of having his two travelers suffer mental breakdowns as a result of not being able to reconcile themselves to their fate (as with Watt), Beckett places his two heroes beyond rationality, beyond the possibility of ever reaching their goal. Mercier and Camier are plunged into absolute nonsense, and, rather than working their way toward insanity or suicide (like their predecessors), they find themselves caught in an unescapable situation: the impasse of absurdity.

Belacqua and Murphy preserved enough lucidity in the end to be able to commit suicide, and even Watt in his madness was able to recognize the intellectual and artistic failure of his quest. All three progressed toward a definite end. Mercier and Camier, on the contrary, are blind to the futility of their undertaking. They exist in an environment that excludes both rationality and insanity, and prevents any movement either forward or backward. Consequently, they apply the same set of absurd values to every situation they encounter, whether authentic or false, whether in the city or the country.

The hero of a traditional novel is made to believe that he chooses his own fate, and most likely a tragic fate. He never questions his fictional status. The hero of an *absurd* novel, such as *Mercier et Camier,* does not have a fate; he is never permitted to choose one. Only by choice can a meaningless existence be turned into a destiny. Even though such outcasts as Molloy, Malone, or The Unnamable continue to create their own existence in the void of their environment, they are aware of the fraudulence of their roles. Mercier and Camier are denied this lucidity and therefore are more grotesque than Beckett's other French creatures who admit the delusion under which they exist. Mercier and Camier have neither the power to create an illusory life for themselves nor the hope of ever escaping the inferior condition imposed upon them by their creator. Beckett toys with their impotence, and refuses to grant them credibility as human facsimiles or authenticity as fictional inventions. As such they truly deserve the title of "pseudocouple" which they receive from the anonymous narrator-hero of *L'Innommable.*

Torn between the vague suspicion that a meaning exists outside the confinement of fiction, and the complete meaninglessness of their predicament, Mercier and Camier remain locked in a maze of doubt and ignorance. Their situation is rendered absurd by the fact that somewhere outside fiction there is a nonabsurd universe. Already, in his quest for meaning in the deceptive Knott establishment, Watt had encountered this dilemma:

But he had hardly felt the absurdity of those things, on the one hand, and the necessity of those others, on the other (for it is rare that the feeling of absurdity is not followed by the feeling of necessity), when he felt the absurdity of those things of which he had just felt the necessity (for it is rare that the feeling of necessity is not followed by the feeling of absurdity). [6]

[6] Beckett, *Watt* (New York: Grove Press, 1959), p. 133.

The eccentric heroes of Beckett's English novels are either paralyzed by this ambivalence or driven to madness. Since they cannot cope simultaneously with the physical and the mental, the real and the illusory, much less with the rational and the irrational, they cannot give a shape to the broken circle of meaning, nor can they escape the frame forged by the interdependence of two mutually exclusive entities. In utter bewilderment they witness the contingency of the non-absurd to the absurd, of the absurd to the nonabsurd. This partly explains why Beckett's fiction, even in its most realistic and credible situations, remains a paradox.

From the moment the novel *Mercier et Camier* opens, one senses an incongruity in the juxtaposition of the realistic setting and the irrational behavior of the protagonists. This incompatibility of the characters with their environment is made even more evident by the interference of the narrator who insists on widening the gap between the authentic and the counterfeit—between what appears to be reality and what is pure fictional illusion. Through sarcastic comments the narrator draws apart the realism of the novel and its fraudulent aspects, thereby undermining the actions of Mercier and Camier and revealing the absurdity of their quest. Constantly interjecting his presence into the narration, he shows to what extent the two protagonists confuse reality with illusion.

Like Sam in *Watt,* this unidentified narrator enjoys a human relationship with the couple, one which he establishes in the opening lines of the novel: "Le voyage de Mercier et Camier, je peux le raconter, si je veux, car j'étais avec eux, tout le temps." [7] If he wishes, the narrator says, he can relate the journey of Mercier and Camier, since he was with them all the time. However, because he controls the narration as storyteller, he has certain privileges denied his

[7] Beckett, *Mercier et Camier,* p. 1. All quotations and page references from this work are from the original manuscript. I am extremely grateful to Mr. Beckett for granting me permission to quote from the unpublished works. Because he refuses to release these manuscripts for publication, it seems preferable to quote from his own French rather than to attempt a translation, which might abuse his generosity.

fellow characters. He can, if he wishes, rearrange the events in whatever order he chooses. He can distort, exaggerate, or dissimulate the facts, or retain essential information that would perhaps clarify the heroes' adventures. He may even invent incidents totally irrelevant to the couple's journey. His power of selectivity is such that he may deliberately withhold the most important elements of the narration. However, his primary function is to prevent the two travelers from reaching their goal—or rather, to make them believe that they are progressing toward a definite goal, whereas in fact there is none.

Mercier and Camier are under the impression that they can forsake reality simply by leaving the city where their journey originates, and that once they have reached the countryside that lies beyond the city walls they will have penetrated the imaginary world of fiction. Neither of them realizes that the realistic city and its seemingly human inhabitants (themselves included) are already in the realm of make-believe, since fictional realism is but an illusion. Nevertheless, all their actions tend toward rejecting or discarding the material objects and rational concepts which confine man to reality. Thus, whether or not the travelers succeed in leaving the city, they are kept in constant confusion through narrative manipulations which force them to sink deeper and deeper into the illusory. They literally turn in circles, treading the same ground, repeating the same words and gestures. However, for the novel to progress it is essential that time be wasted, and incidents be accumulated, no matter how absurd, irrelevant, or repetitious these may be. Whenever Mercier and Camier seem ready to proceed with their journey, fortuitous excuses (bad weather, night, hunger, sexual need, and so on) offer themselves to delay their departure, and when finally they do manage to catch a train, they immediately invent more unfounded excuses to turn back. It is on this deceptive and utterly absurd basis, clearly established in the opening scene of the novel, that the couple begins its futile journey.

After a night spent away from each other, Mercier and

Camier are to meet according to precise notes in Camier's notebook: "Lundi deux, Saint-Macaire, Mercier, quart de neuf, Square Saint-Ruth" (p. 7) . As to why they are meeting and where they plan to go, they themselves do not know. Nor is the reader given the least information about the journey and its purpose. Only the narrator could reveal this information. Thus, in spite of the specific mention of the meeting place, date, and time, an ambiguous interplay is established between the factual and the absurd. Furthermore, the burlesque manner in which the two travelers finally succeed in keeping their appointment emphasizes the meaninglessness of their purpose.

Camier arrives first at the rendezvous, before Mercier, or at least so he thinks, and after a five-minute wait decides to go for a ten-minute walk around the block. But in fact Mercier has preceded him by ten minutes and, after a five-minute wait, he too has decided to go for a little walk around the block "pour se dérouiller les jambes." In a farcical scene which sets the mood for the whole novel, the two cronies keep missing each other, until finally an hour later they come face to face and embrace at ten to ten, just as the two hands of the clock meet. At this point the narrator presents a diagram (very much like a railroad timetable) in which he lists the time of arrival and departure of Mercier and Camier at their meeting place:

	Arr.	Dép.	Arr.	Dép.	Arr.	Dép.	Arr.
Mercier	9.5	9.10	9.25	9.30	9.40	9.45	9.50
Camier	9.15	9.20	9.35	9.40	9.50		

He concludes by saying: "Que cela pue l'artifice" (p. 3) . The whole novel "stinks artifice," but only because Beckett, more deliberately than ever, wants the reader to recognize that the characters and events of his fiction have less and less in common with real people. Thus, even before the action begins, a period of time has been wasted.

If Mercier and Camier had known that their journey was not meant as a real undertaking, but as an illusory quest into fictional absurdity, they would have accepted the fraudulence of their condition. But it is evident from the specific data of Camier's memorandum that the two protagonists, at least in the early stages of their journey, still function according to normal time-space dimensions, and even within the scope of the Christian calendar, as the reference to the Saint-Macaire indicates, although they are unable to determine the reason for their meeting and the purpose of their journey.

That Beckett should have chosen to have his protagonists meet on the "Saint-Macaire" is quite significant, for it reveals interesting facts about Mercier and Camier. Not only are their names derived from Macaire's, but they share a way of life with the solitary Egyptian monk of the fourth century who withdrew into the desert of Nitria to lead a contemplative life away from the material world. Mercier and Camier also forsake the city and society in order to engage in an ascetic quest—a search for self-knowledge. However, their journey to the mind becomes derisive because they insist on placing emphasis on concrete facts and material objects.

Saint-Macaire of Egypt, whose physical appearance at the age of thirty reflected his inner torment, received the ambivalent nickname of "Le Jeune Vieux." Early in the novel, the two protagonists are reminiscing about the time they spent during the war masturbating "à pleins tubes" while others became war victims. This causes the narrator to remark sarcastically, "Ne déduisez rien de ces paroles en l'air, *Mercier et Camier furent jeunes vieux*" (p. 12 [italics mine]). This direct allusion to Mercier and Camier being "old young" confirms their relation to Macaire. There is undoubtedly irony on the part of the author in suggesting the pious Saint-Macaire as a model for his lewd heroes, but the parallel exemplifies the mocking attitude Beckett assumes toward his creations.[8] The comparison between the

---

[8] In discussing the meeting place of the two travelers in Square Saint-Ruth, Ruby Cohn (*op. cit.*, p. 96) points out another ironic touch on the part of the author, since Square Saint-Ruth was "named, sardonically, for the wife-beating Marshal of France who was killed by cannon-shot in Ireland."

saintly Macaire and the obscene couple becomes even more ironic when one discovers how Mercier and Camier rely exclusively on social and material data to determine the course of their journey. It is primarily their obsession with objects that causes the failure of their ideal quest. Their stubborn preoccupation with their "possessions" (a bicycle, a raincoat, an umbrella, a knapsack, a notebook) is the basic reason for the repeated postponement of their departure and their quick return to the city once they have departed. It seems indeed preposterous for Mercier and Camier to set out on an ascetic quest and at the same time remain obsessed by material objects. Too physical and too sensual to forsake worldly concerns, their intentions are mocked by both author and narrator.

Mercier and Camier are not easily distinguishable from each other, and though they are carefully described, Mercier as "le grand maigre barbu," and Camier as "un petit gros, rougeaud, cheveux rares, multiples mentons, ventre en poire, jambes torses, et des petits yeux de cochon" (pp. 55–56), they appear to be inseparable and yet incompatible parts of the same being: mind and body. A similar confusion of identity exists between two Macaires, both monks of the fourth century, who led identically pious existences, and who have often been taken for each other. One was nick-named "Macaire the tall," the other, "Macaire the young." Ironically, the two Macaires can be said to be prototypes for Mercier and Camier, but Beckett employs the notion of mistaken identity in the couple to demonstrate the dualism of mind and body.

The friendly relationship between Mercier and Camier can be interpreted as an attempt to reconcile the Cartesian cleavage which confronts Beckett's English heroes. This reconciliation, however, is doomed to failure because each member of the couple insists on placing particular stress on the attributes he represents: Mercier the mental, Camier the physical. Therefore, what begins as a congenial and necessary relation between two beings eventually disintegrates into an antagonistic opposition of two exclusive substances.

This is because Mercier and Camier are unable to accept the interdependence of the physical with the mental. Mind and body suffer a final separation in this novel, never again to be reconciled in Beckett's subsequent works. Though Mercier and Camier return to the city at the end of their journey, their dissociation marks the first important stage of fictional disintegration endured to extremes by their successors.

Mercier and Camier's eventual separation results from the confusion of their initial encounter, and the contradictory elements of their quest. Having established contact at the designated place, even though an hour late, it remains for the two travelers to set out immediately on their journey, the ascetic purpose of which is inferred by the reference to Saint-Macaire. However, the specification of their meeting in "Square Saint-Ruth" offers an antithetic aspect. For if idealism is implied in Saint-Macaire, the mention of Saint-Ruth suggests a contrary notion of materialism and sensuality. Thus Mercier and Camier's plight is marked from the beginning by a flagrant contradiction which renders their departure almost impossible. Fortunately, as soon as they meet a sudden downpour of rain forces them to take refuge "dans l'abri en forme de pagode que l'on avait construit à cet endroit, pour servir d'abri contre la pluie et autres intempéries, contre le temps, quoi" (p. 3). Beckett's emphatic use of the word "temps" (meaning both *time* and *weather* in French) gains relevance as one discovers how often the protagonists rely on the excuse of bad weather or lack of time to delay their journey. In order to proceed into the region of the mind, into the desert of fiction, one ought to negate the notions of time, space, integrity, social responsibility, and above all one's obsessions with money and sex. Mercier and Camier fail to do so.

While waiting in the shelter for the rain to stop, they make an inventory of their possessions, watch with some embarrassment but not without pleasure as two dogs fornicate, recapitulate how they decided to meet for this journey, and, finally, since the rain persists, propose to postpone their departure. Suddenly, a guard in green uniform—disabled veteran of the war, symbol of order and responsibility ("Le premier d'une longue série d'êtres malfaisants," comments the narrator) —appears and inquires about a bicycle standing outside the shelter. Mercier and Camier claim to have no knowledge of such a vehicle. An argument ensues, and the guard threatens to call a policeman if the bicycle is not removed in less than five minutes. Forced by the circumstances of the moment, Mercier and Camier admit that the bicycle (perhaps) belongs to them, but convince the guard to allow them to stay in the shelter by bribing him with a shilling. The guard is appeased and disappears, but only to return quickly and suggest that, if they want to spend the night, it will be half a crown.

It is obvious that Mercier and Camier's social dilemma results from their association with members of organized society, with objects, with the physical world in general. Unless they can rid themselves of such encumbrances they will never succeed in departing. They admit that it is because they are disgusted with the society of men, such as the hypocrite guard, that they have decided to desert social and human commitments. However, nature, time, physical needs, material objects, and their own indecision oppose their departure.

While the rain conveniently continues to fall, and the day draws to an end, they plan their course of action: Mercier will go ahead with the raincoat and the bicycle (it is their bicycle after all) to prepare matters at the first stop (wherever that may be), while Camier will follow with the umbrella. The narrator points out "que c'était Mercier, jusqu'à présent, qui avait fait preuve d'allant, et Camier de mollesse. L'inverse était à prévoir d'un moment à l'autre" (p. 16). However, the rain having stopped, they decide to leave together with the bicycle. As they walk away from the shelter, Mercier (the leader) holds on to the handlebar, Camier (the follower) clings to the seat.

Vehicles of all sorts abound in Beckett's universe (trains, streetcars, carts, and so on), but it is the bicycle that serves as the most appropriate means of transportation for the French derelicts. In Beckett's fiction, bicycles (stolen bicycles, missing bicycles, lost bicycles, broken bicycles, forgotten bicycles) play an important part in suggesting the possibility or impossibility of reuniting body and mind. For Beckett a man perched on a bicycle not only represents a reconciliation of Cartesian dualism, but also the ultimate defiance of all natural laws—the perfect image of absurdity. In discussing this means of transportation, Hugh Kenner speaks of a certain "dismemberment" in *Mercier et Camier* of what he calls the "Cartesian Centaur": the perfect union of mind and body, which he describes as "a man riding a bicycle, *mens sana in corpore disposito*." [9] For the Beckettian hero, who is constantly in search of some means to escape the physical world and its restrictions, the bicycle offers itself as the most suitable vehicle for the journey to absurdity.

The picture Mercier and Camier form as they walk away with their bicycle—the more cerebral Mercier leading the way—suggests the temporary reconciliation of mind and body. Yet it is only when man rides the bicycle, when the mind is firmly seated upon the body, that the harmony is achieved. The "pseudocouple" Mercier-Camier would need a tandem to resolve their dilemma, for they are incapable of riding the single bicycle together. It is more of a hindrance to them than a useful means of transporting them forward along their quest. As they walk with their bicycle, each holding his own portion of the vehicle, Mercier complains, "Tu me gênes plus que tu ne m'aides," and Camier replies quite appropriately, "Je ne cherche pas à t'aider, je cherche à m'aider moi" (p. 17). Tired after dragging the bicycle, they decide to stop in a bar (the first in a long series of bars) to discuss the situation. Before entering, they tie the bicycle to a railing, in order to be "plus libre," explains Camier.

Although the history of the bicycle can be traced to Beckett's early English fiction, it is only with the French works that he truly exploits its symbolic and comic aspects and makes of it an element of absurdity. In *More Pricks*

[9] Kenner, *op. cit.*, p. 121.

Than Kicks, Belacqua steals a bicycle to return to the city after a walk in the country with one of his conquests. This gesture already suggests an attempt on his part to reconcile an eccentric mind to an inadequate body. Murphy's obsessive concern with Cartesian dualism is not expressed by an interest in bicycles, but by a passion for an even more curious vehicle: the rocking chair he uses to propel himself into the regions of his mind. Watt does not own a bicycle, nor does he encounter any such machines in the Knott establishment, but he observes bicycles both before and after his stay in the Knott world, and, most significant, when the train arrives which is to take Watt to his final refuge: "It did not take up a single passenger . . . but it discharged a bicycle" (*Watt,* p. 245) . Watt seems to have vanished from the platform, and only a bicycle is left—an inanimate body with no mind to guide it, since Watt has literally lost his mind.

In *Mercier et Camier,* the travelers eventually lose their bicycle, and when Mercier sets out in search of it he finds but a few dismembered parts still tied to the railing. From that point on the protagonists are gradually separated, and in spite of their efforts to reunite, each taking turns leading the other into some sort of concatenation, they end their journey in total ignorance of each other's identity: ". . . from the dismemberment of their bicycle we may date the disintegration of Mercier and Camier's lockstep unity. In the final third of this novel they gradually become nodding acquaintances, like the two wheels which were once sustained by a single frame but are now free to pursue independent careers." [10]

The remarkable thing about Mercier and Camier, or for that matter all of Beckett's French wanderers, is that even though they claim to have somewhere to go, or some quest to fulfill, the direction they choose is of no importance. In Beckett's universe all roads lead to chaos and ignorance, and

[10] *Ibid.,* p. 128.

the characters' motion either forward or backward, outward or inward, reflects the nonsensical progress of the fiction in which they exist—often a non sequitur progress. Yet Beckett's people seem compelled to go on, at least to the end of their story. Condemned to wander in a problematic situation whose ultimate form produces disintegration, they learn to survive by repeating the same actions, and by returning to the same point of departure.

Sitting at the bar, incoherently discussing the plan of their journey, Mercier and Camier come to the conclusion that "il serait inutile, et même téméraire, d'aller plus loin, pour l'instant" (p. 19). They agree to go and spend the night "chez Hélène," a prostitute friend of theirs whose apartment is always conveniently near, no matter where they happen to be, and where Camier can quickly satisfy his sexual desires. Invariably physical needs or material obstacles again offer themselves to prevent their departure. Back in the street, on their way to Hélène's place, they realize that they have lost their way. To determine which direction to take they rely on a trick which consists in throwing their umbrella up in the air, and whichever way it points when it falls they will go: "Le parapluie répondit, à gauche." But whether they go left, right, straight, or back is of little importance; all the streets in the city seem to lead either to a bar or to Hélène's apartment.

At one point in the story, when Mercier and his companion are trying to decide which train to take, they find themselves unable to agree whether to go north, east, west, or south. They finally choose south simply because the railroad station from which trains go south is nearest to where they are. One begins to suspect that Mercier and Camier's journey can never be fulfilled in temporal and spatial terms, as one normally interprets these in reality or even in traditional fiction. Their journey is nondirectional and can lead only to a boundless region which has nothing in common with the ordinary world of man. Those who penetrate that region no longer move in linear time and space but progress in a vacuum of illusions where each step forward results in a backward movement. Thus, every word Mercier and Camier speak, every gesture they make, rather than bringing them closer to a concrete goal or a meaningful experience, draws them further into absurdity and meaninglessness.

Though vaguely sketched in *Mercier et Camier,* the Beckettian quest reveals itself as an exploration of creative consciousness. It is the mind locked in contemplation of the self, but a self that exists in an illusory state. It is the mind observing its own futility as it seeks to apprehend what Beckett calls "the spacious annexe of mental alienation." [11] But even nothingness, or the sublimation of nonexistence, can become a submystical experience: the discovery of the fallen or wounded nature of the self. This act of interrogation of the self by the self becomes for Beckett's creatures a metaphysical and creative undertaking which questions human consciousness in an effort to comprehend human existence. Thus, even though Beckett's heroes succeed in negating the physical world and their own bodies, and succeed in alienating themselves from external reality, in the realm of pure intellect they perform an act of *re-creation*. To go on, to perpetuate themselves fictionally in the midst of disintegration, they fill the existential void with wanton inven-

[11] Beckett, *Proust* (New York: Grove Press, 1957), p. 19. Though describing the Proustian creative process in this essay, Beckett largely predicts his own creative course to come, particularly when he writes (pp. 18–19): "Strictly speaking, we can only remember what has been registered by our extreme inattention and stored in that ultimate and inaccessible dungeon of our being to which Habit does not possess the key, and does not need to, because it contains none of the hideous and useful paraphernalia of war. But here, in that 'gouffre interdit à nos sondes,' is stored the essence of ourselves, the best of our many selves and their concretions that simplists call the world, the best because accumulated slyly and painfully and patiently under the nose of our vulgarity, the fine essence of a smothered divinity whose whispered 'disfazione' is drowned in the healthy bawling of an all-embracing appetite, the pearly that may give the lie to our carapace of paste and pewter. May—when we escape into the spacious annexe of mental alienation, in sleep or the rare dispensation of waking madness." Though Mercier and Camier are trying to "escape into the spacious annexe of mental alienation," they are unable to recognize that "the fine essence of a smothered divinity" is the true fictional experience "accumulated slyly and painfully and patiently under the nose of [their] vulgarity."

tions, absurdities that transcend reality and rationality. Ultimately this creative act represents the affirmation of *being*.

Fiction as the product of an alienated imagination ought not to pose for reality, particularly when it purports to destroy conventional realism. The fallacy of Mercier and Camier in planning their journey into fiction is to rely on terms of the tangible world, and though the criteria of an ascetic or creative quest reject material norms, they impose such norms on every situation that confronts them. In so doing, they create an incongruous interplay between the world of appearances and the mental image of reality. Though Mercier and Camier fail to become genuine creators of fiction, their ambiguous pursuit opens the door on a new fictional dimension, that of the creator-hero contemplating his own futile existence from within the undefinable region of consciousness.

In Beckett's last English novel, Watt's journey to Mr. Knott's house offers conditions similar to that of Mercier and Camier. Watt is also trying to transcend reality in order to apprehend the fictional vista, but his actions follow a precise sequence and remain linear. He takes a train, gets off at a specific stop, walks along a road until he reaches the house of fiction (the Knott establishment), remains there for a designated period of time, leaves, then travels to his final destination: an insane asylum, from which he recollects his adventures. Whether or not this journey can be interpreted symbolically as the evolution of man's intellectual endeavor throughout history, or as man's evolution from birth to senility, the fact remains that Watt progresses in time and space. If he undergoes mental deterioration, it is because he is unable to distinguish what is from what is not, and because he attempts to impose a rational meaning on an irrational situation. In other words, Watt's rationality forbids him to enter the zone of creative consciousness where he would no longer be bound by temporal and spatial dimensions.

Mercier and Camier are involved neither in defining a reality nor in rationalizing their predicament. They are immersed in fictional absurdity. Consequently, it appears useless for them to advance in any direction, and, despite careful specifications of time and place, their journey must be performed beyond the temporal and the spatial. Their quest tends toward an intangible goal which cannot be visualized or apprehended because it cannot be plotted in a logical sequence of events. In this respect, Mercier and Camier find themselves one step further than Watt along the Beckett scale of alienation. No longer functioning as rational beings, but as fraudulent "personnages" who need not conform to any ethical or aesthetic order, they may forsake the logic of human activities, without suffering the consequences of a mental breakdown. Their actions cannot be measured in terms of physical motion; they can be fulfilled only in a static and abstract condition. Thus, if they must take refuge because of rain or night, are forced to delay their departure because their umbrella is broken or forgotten "chez Hélène," or must retrace their steps because they have lost all their possessions, it may disrupt the action of the novel, but it in no way affects or alters the absurdity of their undertaking. Suspended between a pseudorealistic condition and the possibility (or impossibility) of achieving an authentic fictional status, they spend their time procrastinating and arguing over trivial incidents. It seems that Mercier and Camier deliberately refrain from reaching *the age of fictional reason* by remaining uncommitted to fiction. They are literally caught in a state of permanent adolescence on the margin of reality.

Frequently throughout the novel the two protagonists act like irresponsible children lost in a hostile world. But, rather than wishing for a return to the womb, they are inclined to consider death as an alternative (like Belacqua, Murphy, and Watt). On several occasions they propose suicide as a possibility, but, too weak and too lethargic to undertake the act of *felo de se,* they finally prefer to wait for a lucky accident. While wandering through the streets of the city they witness such an accident: an old lady being crushed by an automobile. With great delight they observe the dying woman twist herself weakly on the ground as she gasps for her last breath. This morbid scene revives their courage, and, as they walk away, Camier suggests that one ought not despair of life, and that their turn might also come soon. Camier is not aware that he is here expressing what his successors in Beckett's other French works accept as an irrevocable fact: that fictional existence is a slow death in progress. Therefore, reassured by the hope of a quick death, Mercier and Camier decide once again not to waste any more time and proceed with their journey.

In the following chapter, quite unexpectedly, the two travelers are found on a train, and it seems that they have succeeded in leaving the city. However, they soon realize that they have taken a local train instead of an express, as originally planned, and Mercier accuses his companion of having tricked him so that at each stop they may be tempted to change their minds and return to the city. Mercier and Camier go to all extremes in inventing excuses not to pursue their journey.

On the train they meet a garrulous old man, called Madden, who tells them the depressing and immoral story of his life—a piece of fiction within fiction, very much like the stories Molloy and Malone invent to pass the time in moments of creative delirium. Madden gets off, quite appropriately (his name can be read as an anagram of *damned*) , "au village des damnés." This old man's eccentric behavior, his vulgarity, his verbal incoherence, and particularly his physical appearance ("Il portait des guêtres, un chapeau melon jaune, et une sorte de redingote qui lui descendait jusqu'aux genoux" [12]) announce the personality of Beckett's *fictionally damned heroes* of the trilogy and plays. This encounter with old Madden (madness?) is also reminiscent of Watt's encounter on the train with the talkative Mr. Spiro. In both

[12] Beckett, *Mercier et Camier,* p. 39. Madden's bowler hat and his frock coat which comes down to his knees are permanent attributes of Beckett's French derelicts. These become symbolic elements of the Beckettian fictional costume.

instances these fellow travelers' harangues represent warn-
ings against fictional alienation. However, Mr. Spiro, the
neo-John-Thomist, presents his argument in defense of both
theology and social reality, whereas Madden speaks as
though viewing life from the distorting point of view of
fiction. His story reveals the futility and anguish of fictitious
existence. Insofar as Madden appears in front of Mercier
and Camier as a representative of their eventual condition,
his presence adds to their apprehension. For this reason,
while traveling toward their unknown destination, Mercier
and Camier prefer to sit in the train "le dos tourné au sens
de la marche," [13] as though afraid to face their inevitable
end.

At the next station, the two travelers decide to get off the
train to discuss whether to go on or return to the city. They
can always go back on the excuse that they must recover
their lost possessions: the bicycle, the umbrella, the knapsack. But with night approaching quickly, they are forced to
stop "dans une auberge" whose manager, by a curious coin-
cidence, turns out to be Mr. Gall (the piano tuner in *Watt*),
and where a certain Mr. Graves (Mr. Knott's gardener in
Watt) is also present. It seems then that Mercier and
Camier's journey has led them into the world of Beckett's
former fiction. Watt himself makes an astonishing appearance later in the novel.

When Balzac stumbled onto the idea of having his characters reappear from one novel to the next, he saw in the
device not only a possible means of giving structure to his
fictional universe, but also a way to add immeasurably to the
sense of life, the sense of realism of his creations. His characters could have a past, a history, and acquire larger dimensions when seen from different perspectives. Moreover, this
recurrence of characters suggested the continuum of society

---

[13] While traveling to Mr. Knott's house, Watt is also sitting in the
train "with his back to the engine. . . . Already Watt preferred to have
his back to his destination" *Watt*, p. 26). This emphasizes to what
extent Beckett's people are reluctant to advance toward fictional alienation.

even in the artifice of fiction. Many writers since Balzac have employed this method to give ancestry and a semblance of realism to generations of characters. In Beckett's universe the Balzacian device is not meant to create realism or deepen the characters' personalities. It has an opposite effect: it widens the gap between reality and fiction. By having previous characters appear in subsequent novels, by having their names recur, their actions and idiosyncrasies parodied, by having all his protagonists converge into a single fictional figure, Beckett destroys the notion of credibility and emphasizes the counterfeit aspect of fiction. Every time a former hero reappears he undergoes a further touch of disintegration, a further stroke of dehumanization. The narrator-heroes of Beckett's trilogy recall earlier characters to their sides in order to bring them to the same degree of alienation as themselves. They change the earlier characters' names, reduce their personalities, question their past experiences, as though in complete control of the creative process. In fact, sitting at the desk of their imagination, Beckett's French creator-heroes even contrive new playmates to share the loneliness of their existence.

In *Mercier et Camier* Beckett finds not only the key to fictional absurdity, but the entrance into his former fiction. From that point on he parodies his own creative efforts, and, rather than exploit reality directly, he builds each successive novel on the content and structure of his preceding achievements. Gradually the French heroes incorporate into themselves all the attributes of their predecessors, and eventually reach a stage where they can no longer determine in which novel they belong, or whether they are "the teller" or "the told." Such a predicament, however, affords an insight into fictional ambiguity which permits the later creations to ridicule the characters of earlier works who believed themselves human and socially compromised. By a subtle identification with the author, Beckett's French creator-heroes force their predecessors to depend on the whims of their imagination. The Unnamable sees Murphy, Watt, "the pseudocouple Mercier-Camier," [14] Molloy, Malone, and all the others revolve around him as though they were planets caught in the gravitational force of his mind. Thus, by transplanting figures from his earlier works into *Mercier et Camier*, Beckett establishes the basis of what may be termed *total fictional integration and disintegration*.

The numerous characters with whom Mercier and Camier come in contact during the course of their journey perform a specific function in determining the outcome of the couple's quest. As in *Watt*, these characters may be grouped into three categories. First there are those who portray humanity, then a number who seem borrowed from traditional fiction, and finally those whom Beckett resurrects from his previous novels. The first category consists of the usual puppets who exist in civil order ("les êtres malfaisants") : the guard, policemen, barmen, prostitutes, children, and the solid citizens whom Mercier and Camier encounter in the streets of the city. These inferior beings conform to the rules of social reality and are unmarked by fictional alienation. They insist on dealing with Mercier and Camier as though they were still members of the *human clique*. The second category is composed of stereotyped figures referred to as "personnages," who act as though they have had prior fictional experience, not necessarily in Beckett's own novels. Their function is to offer their personalities and existences as models for Mercier and Camier. They try to convince the two travelers that fictional authenticity lies in traditional realism. The third category is represented by the legitimate ancestors of the couple. Mercier calls one of them "un vieux copain de cauchemar" (p. 46) . These displaced persons are introduced in the novel to lead Mercier and his companion to their proper Beckettian destination: the region of fictional absurdity.

[14] Beckett, *The Unnamable* (New York: Grove Press, 1958) , p. 11. The Unnamable sees Mercier and Camier as "Two shapes then, oblong like man, entered into collision before me. They fell and I saw them no more. I naturally thought of the pseudocouple Mercier-Camier" (*idem*) .

The travelers are thus faced with three possible ways of life: they can remain in the city and go on believing that the people with whom they associate and the setting that surrounds them represent reality; they can join with traditional characters and be assigned trivial roles in some bourgeois novel; or they can follow their forebears and, under their guidance, ultimately lose both identity and credibility to become characters within characters. [15] In other words, fictitious existence reveals itself to Mercier and Camier under the guise of familiar figures out of Beckett's own fiction, or in the presence of stereotyped characters who could belong in any nineteenth-century novel and who pretend to be exemplary creations.

Old Madden and Monsieur Conaire, fellow travelers whom Mercier and Camier encounter during their journey (Madden on the train, Conaire in the inn), appear in the role of traditional models and confront the inadequate couple with the image of their accomplished existence. These are travelers who have supposedly reached their destination and discovered their true identity. Though Madden resembles the ageless wanderers of Beckett's trilogy, and like them enjoys telling extravagant stories, by his personality he remains worthy of a Dickens novel. As for Monsieur Conaire, though announcing the bourgeois Pozzo of *Waiting for Godot,* he is rather reminiscent of a Flaubert character. The comparison is not too farfetched, for indeed Mercier and Camier themselves often act as idiotically as Bouvard and Pécuchet, who could pass for their prototypes. Monsieur

[15] The concept of characters being integrated into other characters has been discussed by Edith Kern in her excellent article entitled "Moran-Molloy: The Hero as Author," *Perspective,* XI, no. 3 (Autumn, 1959), 183–193. Miss Kern follows Moran's gradual identification with Molloy and explains that Molloy appears to Moran "as a chimera that haunts and possesses him" (p. 186). She concludes by saying that "Moran's escape from time, habit, and intelligence and his surrender to the Molloyan, the Dionysian element within him are to a certain degree paralleled in Beckett's own artistic development" (p. 192). Mercier and Camier are also progressing toward fictional integration; however, when they encounter their "Dionysian" counterpart (it is Watt who presents himself in this role) they refuse to be "possessed" by him.

Conaire makes an unusual entrance into the novel and into the inn where the two protagonists have stopped. That he represents traditional fiction is evident from his physical appearance:

Une homme entra dans la salle. Il portait une casquette, un imperméable ceinturé bardé de pattes et de poches, une culotte de cheval et des chaussures d'alpiniste. Ses épaules encore vaillantes pliaient sous le poids d'un sac éclatant et bosselé et il tenait à la main un immense bâton. Il traversa la salle d'un pas incertain, en traînant bruyamment ses semelles cloutées.   [pp. 50–51]

The narrator adds a sarcastic note to this description by stating: Il est des personnages dont il convient de parler dès le début, car ils peuvent disparaître d'un moment à l'autre, et ne jamais revenir" (p. 51). Indeed, this outmoded character, who walks into the novel with an uncertain step, definitely seems out of place, but he lasts only a few pages before disappearing completely.

Monsieur Conaire claims that he has an appointment with Camier in this particular hotel (symbolic meeting place of fictitious beings). Such a statement on the part of this unexpected character is puzzling since Mercier and Camier never seem to know where exactly they are going, and have stopped at Mr. Gall's establishment purely by chance. To the great disappointment of Monsieur Conaire, Mercier and Camier, who have taken a room to rest, refuse to see anyone. This refusal to keep their appointment (if such an appointment was ever made) prevents Monsieur Conaire from performing the role he was intended for: that of offering his person as a typical example of fictional success. [16]

[16] Ruby Cohn (*op. cit.*, p. 98) interprets Monsieur Conaire's name as a pun on Descartes' "conarium" (the meeting place of matter and mind), and suggests that when Camier refuses to keep his appointment with Monsieur Conaire he is performing a "symbolic 'conarectomy,' removing any possible meeting ground for mind and body." One could argue that if Monsieur Conaire is introduced in this novel to reconcile the two parts of Cartesian dualism as personified by Mercier (the mind) and Camier (the body), then Beckett is poking fun at the Cartesian theory in having the sensual bourgeois Monsieur Conaire perform this task. Ruby Cohn is perhaps closer to the truth when she

The following day, when Camier finally comes face to face with Monsieur Conaire, whom apparently he does not know, Camier tells him to mind his own business and not interfere with his and Mercier's actions. In rejecting Monsieur Conaire, Camier is brushing aside fictional realism. But this stubborn gentleman insists on describing how he arrived in the hotel exhausted, was told that Camier refused to see him, and waited all night for him to appear. Unexpectedly, Camier admits, with his usual effrontery, that for awhile he did think of Monsieur Conaire: "Puis je n'ai plus pensé à vous, mais pas du tout, pas un instant. C'était comme si vous n'aviez jamais existé, Monsieur Conaire. Non, je me trompe, c'était comme si vous aviez cessé d'exister. Non, ce n'est pas ça, c'était comme si vous existiez à mon insu" (p. 68). It seems then that Camier does know Monsieur Conaire, and that at one time he had promised to take him along on his journey with Mercier. Yet if this journey was originally planned as an attempt to reach traditional fiction so that the two travelers might acquire fictitious status, they changed their minds and no longer need the company and guidance of Monsieur Conaire. No doubt Camier's promise was made when he still had a specific function in society and knew nothing of fictional existence. Camier's former profession is revealed when Monsieur Conaire presents the visiting card he received from Camier when they arranged this meeting. The card reads:

> Francis Xavier Camier
> Enquêtes et Filatures
> Discrétion Assurée

That Camier should have been at one time a private investigator—a person thoroughly trained for the most intricate quests—renders his present condition doubly ironic and suspect since he is now incapable of expressing the least

---

states that Conaire, being "phonetically close to a French obscenity and vulgarity, underlines the philosophic frustration" (*idem*). One could add that, in failing to recognize Monsieur Conaire's function, Mercier and Camier emphasize the aesthetic frustration of their quest.

certainty about his own identity, his actions, and the course of his journey with Mercier. This exemplifies the degree of alienation already suffered by the couple. It is interesting to note that in the second part of *Molloy* Moran also sets out in search of Molloy (his alter ego) in the role of a private detective. Although Moran fails to fulfill his quest, in the process he undergoes complete mental and physical deterioration, and eventually succeeds in identifying himself with Molloy, who in the first part of the novel appears as an accomplished fictional derelict.

Because Mercier and Camier refuse to acknowledge the artifice of fiction and fail to accept alienation as a primary condition of fictional existence, they remain ambiguously trapped in the vacuum that exists between the world of the Conaires and that of the Molloys. Undoubtedly it would be easier for them to follow Monsieur Conaire into pseudorealism than to pursue their journey into absurdity—but they are not forsaking the world of man to become conventional characters in a bourgeois novel. Therefore, they cannot allow themselves to associate with such antiquated "personnages" as Conaire, and quickly turn away from him to proceed with their own "idiotic" quest, whatever it may be. Meanwhile, Monsieur Conaire suffers a moment of despair as he remembers the pleasant setting, the dog and the marquise, he has left behind in order to come and perform in this absurd story. As he disappears from the scene, the narrator intrudes again to remark: "En voilà déjà un de liquidé, sauf malheur" (p. 69) . Because Conaire appears in the role of a bourgeois character, he is doomed to quickly become obsolete, and must be liquidated.

The next morning Mercier and Camier are found wandering in a desolate landscape where "rien n'y poussait, rien d'utile aux hommes, c'est à dire" (p. 57) . Having disposed of their intruder and broken relations with both man and traditional fiction, they are nearing the moribund countryside of the trilogy where human attributes lose their functional qualities. While walking, Camier reads the pages of his notebook which he then tears one by one and scatters on the ground. He also empties the contents of his pockets and casts everything away: locks of hair, buttons, an embroidered handkerchief, shoelaces, a toothbrush, a rubber band, a garter, pieces of cloth—all the remnants of the past. Free of material souvenirs, he exclaims: "Voilà, je me sens plus léger" (p. 58). This disposal of all personal property suggests that the travelers have at last recognized the idealistic purpose of their quest and are now getting rid of all ties with their former human existence. Shortly thereafter, they decide to dispose of their raincoat, the last of their worldly possessions. In this final discarding of the raincoat, Mercier and Camier are symbolically rejecting all the paraphernalia of the bourgeois world and bourgeois novel:

Si on jetait l'imperméable? dit Camier.
A quoi sert-il?
Il retarde l'action de la pluie, dit Mercier.
C'est un linceul, dit Camier.
N'exagérons rien, dit Mercier.
Veux-tu que je te dise toute ma pensée? dit Camier.
Celui qui le porte est gêné, au physique comme au moral, au même titre que celui qui ne le porte pas.
Il y a du vrai dans ce que tu dis, dit Mercier.
Il regardèrent l'imperméable. Il s'étalait au pied du talus.

[p. 69]

In comparing the raincoat to a shroud, Camier is not only suggesting the burial of the past, but also the death of material life. To discard this last vestige would enable them to transcend the human condition, particularly since the raincoat delays the action . . . of the rain. Mercier might as well have said the action of fiction. As they progress toward fictional independence, the two heroes must eliminate all physical and moral ties with reality. Thus Camier's reference to the raincoat as an inconvenience to the one who wears it both "au physique comme au moral" suggests a degree of lucidity in regard to their situation. Looking at the raincoat spread on the ground, they wonder if they should insult this remnant of materialism:

Si je l'apostrophais? dit Mercier.
On a le temps, dit Camier.

Mercier réfléchit.
Adieu vieille gabardine, dit-il.
Le silence se prolongeant, Camier dit:
C'est ça, ton apostrophe?
Oui, dit Mercier.
Allons-nous en, dit Camier.
Alors on ne le jette pas? dit Mercier.
On le laisse là, dit Camier. Pas la peine de se fatiguer.
J'aurais voulu le lancer, dit Mercier.
Laissons-le là, dit Camier. Peu à peu les traces de nos corps
s'effaceront. Sous l'effet du soleil il se repliera, comme une feuille
morte.
Et si on l'enterrait? dit Mercier.
Ce serait de la sensiblerie, dit Camier.

[p. 70]

They are intent on comparing the raincoat to a dying aspect
of some anterior life. They would indeed enjoy burying it in
the ground, and with it the traces of their bodies. But, as
Camier points out, it would be mere sentimentality, a feeling that may still be valid in traditional fiction, but not in
the absurd world of Mercier and Camier. Yet, as they walk
away from the spot where they have left the raincoat, they
succumb to a feeling of irritation and apprehension: irritation because of the failure of their past, apprehension because of the unknown fate that lies ahead. Looking back at
the raincoat, Mercier asks:

On n'a rien laissé dans les poches, au moins?
Des billets poinçonnés de toutes sortes, dit Camier, des allumettes
usées, sur des bouts de marge de journal des traces oblitérées de
rendez-vous irrévocables, le classique dernier dixième d'un crayon
épointé, quelques feuilles crasseuses de papier à cul, quelques ca-
potes d'étanchéité douteuse, et de la poussière. Toute une vie,
quoi.
Rien dont nous ayons besoin? dit Mercier.
Puisque je te dis toute une vie, dit Camier.   [p. 71]

One can date Mercier and Camier's exile from social
reality from the moment they dispose of their raincoat. It is
a whole way of life—"toute une vie"—that they are leaving
behind, but, as Mercier emphasizes, nothing they need at the
present. It is their pseudoidentity as human beings that

remains in the pockets of the raincoat—the shroud of the past. The scene sums up the travelers' journey. It expresses their nostalgia for the world they are forsaking, and reveals their apprehension as they now face the illusory condition for which they were destined. This stirring scene of the raincoat's disposal stands as the turning point of their journey.

The tragicomic nature of the dialogue projects forward into the absurd verbal exchange of Didi and Gogo in *Waiting for Godot,* and with the same poignancy reveals the anguish that permeates all Beckett fiction. However, Mercier and Camier have not yet discovered their true destination, are not yet ready to accept fictional indifference, and therefore cannot resign themselves to the useless waiting of Vladimir and Estragon, or the meaningless wandering of the other Beckettian derelicts. Having renounced their last tie with the material world, they should be free to advance fully into fictional absurdity, but instead they decide to return to the city and try to recover their lost possessions: the knapsack, the bicycle, the umbrella. Invigorated by this thought, they immediately set out on foot.

How long it takes them to return to their starting point is not specified, for as they reach the suburbs of the city the narrator notes that "ils avaient perdu la notion du temps" (p. 75). Night approaching quickly, they decide to take refuge "chez Hélène." She allows them to stay for a day or two, and produces the umbrella which she has fixed. Rejoiced by this good fortune, they spend the next few days making love to her and enjoying the bottles she has ordered: "Des hommes moins tenaces qu'eux auraient pu céder à la tentation d'en rester là, mais avec eux rien à faire" (p. 76). The next afternoon finds them back in the street, ready to go on. However, since it is quite late in the day, and they cannot decide where to go and how to proceed, they rush to a bar to discuss the situation, "car c'est dans les bars que les Mercier et Camier de ce corps céleste parlent avec le plus de liberté, et avec le plus de profit" (p. 77). They make a list of thirteen important items for their journey, all of them totally irrelevant, and finally reach the conclusion that they must return "chez Hélène" and postpone all action until the next day and perhaps even the day after that.

When finally, two days later, at noon, they reappear in the street, they notice that they have again forgotten the umbrella. Camier rushes upstairs, and after a long and suspicious absence returns with the umbrella. Once more before setting out they debate, reason, argue as to whether or not they should open the umbrella (it rains again), or simply throw it away. When finally they agree, the umbrella refuses to open. They curse "cet abri portatif . . . ce parasol . . . qui a dû faire ses débuts vers 1900 . . . quand le siècle avait deux mois" (p. 79), and Camier rushes back to Hélène to get it repaired. On his return—after an even longer period of time: "C'est toujours un peu plus long la deuxième fois" (p. 82)—he announces that it will take about half an hour for the umbrella to be fixed, and even until the next morning since he told Hélène not to rush.

Thus, after some eighty pages of futile gestures and incoherent words, they are once more standing under the same porch, in the same place as before, back where they started. Nothing has happened, nothing has changed, nothing has been resolved, and the two companions face the same futile situation. As the novel proceeds into its second half, one realizes that nothing will ever happen, and that Mercier and Camier are trapped in the Beckettian impasse of indecision. One is here on the brink of Beckett's "theater of the absurd" where nothing is ever resolved. As in the second act of *Waiting for Godot,* where Vladimir and Estragon return on stage to repeat the same empty words, to perform the same meaningless gestures as in the first act, in a state of hopeless expectancy, Mercier and Camier must now attempt to resume their endless quest, and allow the circular plot to unfold chaotically to the last part of the novel.

The second part of the novel, like the second act of *Godot,* in spite of its apparent repetitious meaninglessness, gains intensity and pathos as the protagonists' relationship begins to deteriorate. Their conversation becomes less and less coherent, or rather, since it was already quite nonsensical, it reaches a stage of complete illogical rambling, very much like the verbal exchanges of the two bums in *Godot,* who never seem to be talking about the same thing at the same time. As Mercier and Camier sink deeper into fictional confusion they develop a mutual animosity and blame each other for the failure of their quest. In the last pages of the novel their anxiety is underlined by the frantic manner in which they hurry through the streets of the city in a last effort to recover their possessions. But these endless corridors of absurdity bring the travelers back to deserted squares. Yet they must do something! Go somewhere! They cannot stand in the same spot, "comme deux cons." They decide to proceed "obliquement devant nous" (p. 100), and Mercier again takes the initiative and tells Camier to wait for the umbrella while he goes ahead in search of the knapsack and the bicycle. They agree to meet later in a bar.

Camier arrives first at the rendezvous and, while waiting for his partner, listens to a theological discussion between some strangers who argue the moral issue of injecting sperm from a nonmarital provenance. The question is totally irrelevant to Camier's problem, but it fascinates him enough so that he tries to interject a few words in the conversation, only to be immediately told to "shut up." When finally Mercier arrives they celebrate their reunion over a drink, and furtively hold hands under the table since it would appear suspicious for them to embrace in public. There is an ambivalent sensuality in Mercier and Camier's relationship which can be explained only in the light of their symbolic association as body and mind. The unity of the Beckettian couple is maintained in function of a common interest in worldly possessions. Once these possessions are removed the couple begins to disintegrate.

Mercier has bad news for his friend. He was unable to find the knapsack, and the bicycle: "Il en subsiste, solidement enchaîné à la grille, ce qui peut raisonnablement subsister, après plus de huit jours de pluie incessante, d'une bicyclette à laquelle on a soustrait les deux roues, la selle, le timbre et le porte-bagage. Et le réflecteur, ajouta-t-il, j'allais l'oublier.

Quelle tête j'ai" (p. 100). Mercier (the mental) seems to be
losing his mind as soon as he can no longer rely on material
objects. In turn, Camier tells his companion that he has
thrown away the umbrella. For the first time the travelers
are completely free of all their possessions, and could now
escape the world of man. But instead they succumb to
physical and mental embarrassment:

Nous avançons péniblement—.
Péniblement! s'écria Mercier.
Malaisément . . . malaisément par des rues sombres et relative-
ment abandonnées, à cause de l'heure sans doute, et du temps
incertain, sans savoir qui mène, ni qui suit.   [p. 101]

Even though materially dispossessed, and unable to determine who leads and who follows, they continue hopelessly to
plan, discuss, argue the course of their journey in concrete
terms. But their relationship suffers a crucial blow, and
gradually their actions and thoughts become less and less
coördinated as they degenerate into a series of disjointed
gestures and incoherent words. They do manage, however,
to leave the city once more, but not before getting involved
in a violent argument with a policeman who refuses to direct
them to a brothel—"une maison de tolérance," as Mercier
calls such places. Infuriated, they kill the policeman and
rush away from the scene of the crime. This melodramatic
but symbolic murder of the law enforcer compels the two
outlaws to leave the city and with it the reality of a world
with which they can no longer cope, and from which they
are now morally and humanly banished.

After wandering for days and nights through a desolate
countryside, in a state of hallucination, supporting each
other as they stumble, fall, crawl, from roads to ditches, like
the blind leading the blind, Mercier finally asks his companion:

Enfin, qui es-tu, Camier?
Moi? dit Camier. Je suis Camier, Francis Xavier.
C'est maigre, dit Mercier.
A qui le dis-tu, dit Camier.
Je pourrais me poser le même question, dit Mercier.
Je pensais que tu me connaissais, dit Camier.
                                              [p. 120]

Mercier and Camier do not realize that by leaving the city they have lost their identity as human beings as well as human facsimiles. Having penetrated the no-man's-land of Beckett's absurd fiction, they are slowly moving toward integration into the Beckettian state of anonymity, where names undergo frequent changes, and where personalities and individualities are no longer distinguishable. Mercier and Camier, however, insist on calling themselves by their "given" names, and thus fail to respond to their newly acquired selflessness. At this stage, they are on the verge of becoming united into a single being, into a single abstraction: the reduction of the physical into the mental. Alienated from reality, deprived of all their worldly possessions, they need only to reconcile themselves to their loss of identity to become as unnamable as the hero of Beckett's last volume of the trilogy. Instead, they continue to rely on names and personal attributes to identify themselves, and therefore are forced to separate. Like two strangers, avoiding each other, they return to the city presumably to resume that state of physical being, that state of human nothingness which was theirs prior to the novel. Emptied of their former existence, dispossessed of their former selves, they are unable to accept the faceless and nameless condition offered them by the Beckettian predicament.

Their story does not end here. The Beckett quest is endless in its ambiguity and self-perpetuation. A last effort is made to reconcile the couple and to grant Mercier and Camier fictional authenticity. Appropriately enough, it is Watt—himself an accomplished hero of the Beckett universe—who appears in the last scene of this novel to attempt the reconciliation. Watt accosts Camier in the street and asks if he knows Mercier, who is then standing in front of "une vitrine de chapelier," possibly considering whether or not to buy himself a hat—no doubt a bowler of the kind worn by all Beckett heroes who are engaged in fictional absurdity and creativity. In Beckett's universe the bowler hat may be interpreted as a symbol of imagination, but Mercier hardly deserves such a hat.

Watt claims that he has known the couple since the cradle, but Camier does not seem to remember him. Watt admits smilingly that he has not yet gained notoriety, though he might someday be recognized as an important literary figure, at least, he adds, by a select audience. Mercier does remember a certain Murphy, "qui vous ressemblait un peu, en beaucoup plus jeune," he tells Watt, "mais il est mort, il y a dix ans, dans des circonstances mystérieuses. On n'a jamais retrouvé son corps, figurez-vous" (p. 137). This unexpected allusion to Murphy's death and the appearance of Watt in this novel mark the first acknowledgment of a family tie among Beckett's creations. From that point on it is as fictional relatives, and no longer as members of the community of men, that Beckett's people evolve and reappear from one work to the next. Beckett finds here a means of creating an illusory continuity in his fiction, and

in these intramural pleasantries, which contain the germ of *The Unnamable* . . . we discern Beckett's sudden realization of the way to lay the present book at rest. If he simply stops writing it he will not violate its decorum, since it has all the time existed, in an essentially lyric mode as an amusement of its creator, an amusement fiercely pursued.[17]

Already in *Watt* the ambiguity of the novel's conclusion and its apparent incompleteness suggested a narrative form that remained deliberately open for eventual re-creation. Thus Watt's resurrection in *Mercier et Camier* is totally justified, even though Watt appears inconsistent with his former personality.

In the role he plays in this novel, Watt takes on a much more superior and self-assured attitude than the rather submissive one he knew in his own fiction. After all, he now ranks (in 1945) as Beckett's most accomplished hero, Belacqua and Murphy being dead and long forgotten, and the others not yet born. It is then in the function of a fictional guide that Watt commands the situation, orders Mercier and Camier about, suggests that they should "tutoyer" each other, and even invites them to a bar (Watt, the milk-drinking hero!) to discuss their problem. As the curious trio walks down the street arm in arm, like the Three Musketeers, Watt wonders how Dumas (Alexandre Dumas?) would react to such unusual characters. Indeed, the three ludicrous figures appear very much out of place in the realistic setting of the city. A policeman stops them and angrily remarks: "Ceci est un trottoir, pas une piste de cirque." Watt appeases the outraged policeman by telling him that his two companions are mentally deranged and that "le grand se croit Saint Jean-Baptiste . . . tandis que le petit hésite entre Jules César and Monsieur Erskine Childers." Watt's fraudulent statement emphasizes the irony of the situation since it was he who suffered mental disorder in his own novel. However, Watt goes on to explain, as for himself, "je me résigne à rester dans le rôle que la naissance m'a collé" (p. 138).

In the bar, Watt suffers a moment of violent rage and slams his cane on the table as he shouts: "La vie au poteau!" No doubt he means real life, or the pseudoexistence Mercier and Camier refuse to forsake. The barman threatens to "kick them out," and Watt calms down. While he dozes off, Mercier and Camier wonder where they have seen "this guy" before; they do not realize that it was in the "cradle" of Beckett's mind. Watt reminds them somewhat of old Madden, who also tried to tell them something. Suddenly Watt springs up again, and again slams his cane on the table, breaking the glass top, and this time shouts: "La vie aux chiottes!" Instinctively Mercier and Camier make a dash for the door and, just before running out, in a last glance, observe Watt disappear like a ghost as he screams madly: "Vive Quin!" Mercier wonders who this Quin could be, and concludes: "Ça doit être quelqu'un qui n'existe pas" (p. 145). In any event, they are glad that this stranger "qui pue la décomposition" has vanished, perhaps to return to oblivion in his own obscure fictional world. [18] So, in spite of

---

[18] It is of interest to note that when Beckett was writing *Mercier et Camier*, the novel *Watt* had not yet been released for publication.

Watt's efforts, Mercier and Camier fail to take their legitimate place among Beckett's family of alienated heroes. By refusing to recognize Watt as their ancestor and archetype they acquire for themselves the condescending title of "the pseudocouple."

Back in the street Mercier and Camier walk together for awhile toward the canal where Mercier now resides in what he describes as a hospital for those who suffer from skin diseases. Sitting on a bench by the water, they reminisce about their unfulfilled journey, talk about Hélène's parrot, their lost possessions and lost identities, and finally bid each other adieu as the novel ends on a melancholic note. Like Flaubert's Bouvard and Pécuchet, the protagonists separate to return to their own private loneliness and contemplate the failure of their quest.

As one closes this book, it becomes evident that "we are on the brink of the trilogy; that Mercier and Camier, the narrator, and Beckett who holds the pen, constitute a converging series whose terms are difficult to distinguish; and that this fiction is less close to any other reality than the mental world of a man sitting in a room before a sheaf of paper." [19]

After *Mercier et Camier*, Beckett abandons the third-person narration; but even though he allows his characters to participate in the creative act, they remain his own private fancies. Having been dragged from the closed system of social reality to the unescapable region of the mind, their only hope for survival is to be exteriorized into fiction. From the moment they begin their journey into consciousness, Beckett's heroes know they will never reach their goal, and that they are forever exiled from reality. Yet, while stumbling and crawling toward an impossible and unexplainable experience, they continue to act and think humanly, too humanly, or, as Molloy explains subsequently, as though describing not only his own destiny but also that of his predecessors:

[19] Kenner, *op. cit.*, p. 76.

But I am human, I fancy, and my progress suffered, from this state of affairs, and from the slow and painful progress it had always been, whatever may have been said to the contrary, was changed, saving your presence, to a veritable calvary, with no limit to its stations and no hope of crucifixion. . . . Yes, my progress reduced me to stopping more and more often, it was the only way to progress, to stop.   [*Molloy*, p. 105]

Though Mercier and Camier never reach their goal, their repeated hesitations, their futile efforts, their absurd actions, and above all their ambiguous association with former Beckett characters serve to prepare their successors' way to "calvary, with no limit to its stations and no hope of crucifixion. . . ."

Where now?
Who now?
When now?
Unquestioning.
I, say I.

BECKETT, *The Unnamable*

VI

THE EXPULSION

Starting with the unpublished short story *Premier amour* and the three *Nouvelles,* "L'Expulsé," "Le Calmant," "La Fin," [1] Beckett adopts the first-person narrative. The author, narrator, and protagonist, who in preceding works formed a triangular relationship which determined the structure of the novels, now merge into a single anonymous being. In the predominant role he acquires as creator-hero, this omnipotent creature not only controls the tale, invents stories within stories and characters within characters, ridicules or negates his own inventions, but also gains the unusual power to attack the author, the reader, and the beings portrayed in traditional fiction. While the hero seemingly fabricates his own existence and the setting in which he performs, the fiction falls into an apparent state of irresponsibility and chaos. In his newly achieved status, this Beckettian derelict governs a twofold perspective: he reflects upon the fraudulence of fictional existence, and mocks the medi-

[1] The three short stories "L'Expulsé," "Le Calmant," "La Fin" were published in 1955 with a total of thirteen texts in *Nouvelles et Textes pour rien* (Paris: Editions de Minuit). An editor's note states: "Les *Nouvelles* sont de 1945, les *Textes pour rien* de 1950."

ocrity of the human condition. As such the incoherent monologue of this solitary figure fixes the anguished and ambivalent tone of Beckett's subsequent fiction.

Of these four stories, *Premier amour* is the only one to preserve a pretense of plot. After the death of his father, which the anonymous hero associates, "à tort ou à raison . . . dans le temps," [2] with his own marriage, he is forced to leave the paternal home. Exiled from his fellowmen, perturbed by an uncomprehensible past, he wanders through the streets of an unidentified city in search of a refuge. While walking aimlessly, or stretching on a bench, or hiding in a stable, he mutters to himself, reminisces incoherently, tells himself stories which he points out are totally false, digresses from these tales into more absurd fictions, reflects upon "la drôle de nouvelle" in which he finds himself, curses the fictional predicament, and all this in obscene and scatological terms.

One day he encounters a prostitute called Lulu, whose name he immediately changes to Anne, and with whom he believes he has fallen in love. He attempts to define his feelings for the prostitute, but falls into gross contradictions. Yet he is convinced that his love is sincere, since he catches himself writing the girl's name with his finger "sur de vieilles merdes de vache." Eventually the prostitute offers to share her apartment with him. He nonchalantly appropriates one of the two rooms, and after having emptied the room of all its furniture, except for a sofa in which he settles as though lying in a coffin, refuses all human relations with the girl—particularly sexual intercourse. One night, while he is asleep, the girl manages to get into bed with him. Some time later she announces that she is pregnant. The hero refuses to be held responsible for the initial act, and suggests various methods for disposing of the unborn child. When Lulu rejects his suggestions, he abandons her. While sneaking out of the apartment he explains that after all he was not

[2] Beckett, *Premier amour*, p. 1 of a typescript of the original unpublished manuscript. Page references and quotations from this story are taken from the typescript.

married to the girl, though earlier in the story he clearly stated the contrary.

The three other stories ("L'Expulsé," "Le Calmant," "La Fin") have even less of a credible plot, and, though published as a group, show little continuity from one to the other. They can be read as the same story rewritten on three different occasions. The anonymous heroes of these stories (or perhaps it is the same character) have also been expelled from a house or an institution and appear condemned to wander through the streets of a city seeking refuge, a bed, a container, and above all seeking an identity. In the process, like the narrator-hero of *Premier amour,* they invent incongruous stories they doubt and finally negate.

Having suffered a brutal expulsion from the house of his deceased father, the hero of "L'Expulsé" remains sprawled in the gutter for awhile as he contemplates his lot. Then, proceeding through the city, which he claims not to know very well, on two occasions he is stopped by policemen who point out that the sidewalk is for pedestrians and the street for vehicles. The hero wonders in which of these categories he belongs, and when the second policeman insists "que le trottoir était à tout le monde, comme s'il était évident que je ne pouvais être assimilé à cette catégorie" (p. 24), he begins to question his human appearance, and whether he belongs in the world of man. As a last resort, he hires a passing "fiacre" and asks the coachman to take him to the zoo. But he quickly changes his mind about his destination and with the help of the coachman tries to find a room to rent. However, since his repulsive physical appearance causes most doors to close in his face, the hero accepts the coachman's invitation to spend the night in the stable with his horse. During the night, disgusted with the coachman and the horse, which, he claims, have gotten into the story in spite of him, he sneaks out through the window, and asks himself why he bothered to tell this absurd story. Next time, perhaps, he will invent a different one or tell the same one, since all stories are alike.

In an astonishing opening statement, the hero of "Le

Calmant" claims that he no longer remembers when he died. Therefore, to remain calm and pass the time, he decides to tell himself a story, like the one his father used to tell him when he was a child, about a certain Joe Breem, or Breen. As he begins his tale, the hero sees himself being expelled from an institution, and wandering through the streets of a city where he encounters all sorts of people and animals that stare at him as though he were a strange creature from some other world. A stranger, whom he meets on a bench, and who tells him the sad story of his love affair with a certain Pauline, gives the hero a little vial, which supposedly contains "le calmant." The hero puts the vial in his pocket and goes on with his story, soon realizing that it is a complete waste of time. As he struggles with his narration, he comments on its progress, or its lack of progress: "Tiens, des arbres. . . . Me voilà acculé à des futurs. . . . Quelle est cette horreur chosesque où je me suis fourré?" [3] But since Joe Breem, or Breen, is not waiting for him, he need not worry whether or not he reaches the end of his story. Finally, the hero is so confused that he can no longer distinguish in which tale he really belongs—Beckett's story, the stranger's story, his father's story, or his own. In any event, he explains: "Je m'en voudrais d'insister sur ces antinomies, car nous sommes bien entendu dans une tête" (p. 61). Meanwhile he has forgotten about "le calmant."

It is the hero of "La Fin" who eventually swallows the contents of the vial. He too has been expelled from an institution, and while wandering through the city reflects upon the coat, hat, shoes, and the little money he was given before his expulsion. However, he is quickly swindled out of his money and must resign himself to begging at street corners. Since his physical appearance and particularly the putrid smell he emits force the passersby away from him, he contrives ingenious means for having the charitable people drop their pennies or buttons in his cup without having to

[3] Beckett, "Le Calmant," *passim.* Unless otherwise indicated, page references given in the text with quotations from the *Nouvelles* are from the 1955 edition of *Nouvelles et Textes pour rien* (see n. 1).

approach him. Eventually he manages to leave the city, and for awhile lives in a cave by the sea with a man whom he claims to have known in some "époque antérieure." But because the noise of the sea prevents him from sleeping, he moves inland and takes refuge inside a deserted barn. There he finds an abandoned rowboat for which he builds a cover, and it is while lying inside this coffinlike box that he finally swallows "le calmant" as he waits for the water to rise through the little hole he has pierced in the side of the boat, and thinks without regret of the "récit que j'avais failli faire, récit à l'image de ma vie, je veux dire sans le courage de finir ni la force de continuer" (p. 123).

It is obvious from the extravagant and repetitive plot of these four stories that Beckett is not interested in creating realistic and credible situations. On the contrary, he seems rather intent on avoiding all aesthetic and ethical norms. The social and moral indifference exhibited by the heroes of the stories reveals Beckett's condescending attitude toward the human condition. Moreover, through the creative eccentricities of his narrator-heroes, Beckett mocks the efforts of the artist engaged in the presumptuous task of trying to apprehend reality, of trying to represent man in a condition true to life. By deliberately treading the same narrative ground, the author exposes the futility of human actions and particularly the absurdity of the creative act. In having grotesque and irresponsible heroes wander in a city that preserves many characteristics of the real world, Beckett creates an ambiguity of situation which illustrates to what extent the fictional predicament is a product of social and mental alienation.

By having the narrator-heroes of the stories shape their own existences outside the standards of human life, by having them control their behavior outside social morality, Beckett succeeds in alienating them from the setting. Even though they appear as caricatures of man superimposed on a quasi-realistic background, they overcome the creative frustration of their predecessors who could not escape common reality. As a result of this ambivalent juxtaposition, these narrator-heroes gain insight into the creative process, at the same time disclosing the fraudulence of fiction. In this respect the four stories mark a crucial step in Beckett's creative evolution.

The controlled artificiality of the English novels and of *Mercier et Camier* is based on the author's unemotional relationship with his creations. By adopting an equivocal attitude toward his characters, Beckett pretends not to be responsible for their eccentricity, their antisocial behavior, and above all their failure to communicate their experiences in logical terms. Yet as omnipotent author he drives these characters into failure, and renders their actions meaningless. Within these novels, Beckett often introduces a narrator who participates in the actions of the characters, interferes with their existence, criticizes their performance, their lack of credibility, and even their failure to cope with the social world. But in spite of his seemingly privileged role, this narrator does not escape the author's sarcasm. He is used as a decoy which can be blamed for the narration's incongruity, while from behind the scene the author subtly manipulates the fiction's form and content. By becoming himself a fictional target—as demonstrated particularly by Sam in *Watt*—the narrator acquires the same dubious status as the characters. Placed in an ungrateful position, he can claim neither authenticity as an inventor of fiction nor credibility as a fictitious hero. His condition is no better than that of the characters who also fail to determine whether they are genuine replicas of man or mere puppets.

In Beckett's universe one can then establish a scale of values on which to gauge not only the degree of reality of the characters, but also the ambiguity of their relationship to the author or narrator. It is in function of this ambiguity that they impose their personality on the narration, or become self-sufficient creator-heroes. In the English fiction and in *Mercier et Camier,* the characters are like Eurydice condemned to follow Orpheus, knowing that at any moment their creator can look back and force them to disappear. Though they struggle to acquire an identity, their efforts are rendered useless and derisive because they are perversely led into error, ignorance, and failure. As soon as Beckett frees his creations and allows them to relate their own experiences in the first person, even though these experiences may be totally false, the characters escape the overpowering control of the omnipotent creator. They become themselves creators of fiction as they invent stories within stories and fictitious companions which in turn they transform, reduce, or cause to disappear from one page to the next. As first sketched in the four French stories, the Beckettian creator-hero is no longer playing the inferior role of Eurydice; he now appears as an Orphean figure given the power to create and destroy not only his own inventions, but also his own illusory self. Eurydice and Orpheus are united in him, and as he advances on his infernal quest, as he observes his existence in progress, often "sans le courage de finir ni la force de continuer," this double-headed creature forces his twin self to vanish behind him. He has become both "the teller" and "the told," as one of these anonymous beings explains. Expelled from reality into an intangible world, exiled into fictional illusion, the French creator-hero descends time after time into the depth of Hades (his own consciousness) to bring back an identity which repeatedly eludes him. It is as though he penetrates "un monde contra-dictoire, où l'esprit devient matière, puisque les valeurs apparaissent comme des faits, où la matière est rongée par l'esprit, puisque tout et fin et moyen à la fois, où, sans cesser d'être dedans, [il se voit] du dehors." [4]

Having launched his creations on this deceptive fictional path, Beckett continues to supply them with fictitious raw material: an illusory existence and an appropriate setting in which to pursue their endless quest. He does so by hiding behind the tortured mask of his creator-heroes and by forc-

[4] Jean-Paul Sartre, "Aminadab," in *Situations I* (Paris: Gallimard, 1947) , p. 138. Sartre's discussion of the fantastic in Maurice Blanchot's fiction is applicable to Samuel Beckett's own distortions of reality.

ing them to believe that they are perpetuating themselves as well as the fiction in which they perform. Often these selfless beings, "caricatures de ce qui fut autrefois des hommes," [5] turn in anger and frustration toward their concealed creator and protest: "Encore s'il me décernait la troisième personne, comme à ses autres chimères, mais non, il ne veut que moi, pour son moi." [6]

Thus the French stories unfold as free associations of the confused thoughts of the narrator-heroes, with little actual concern for order or logical continuity, and at times with such absurd situations and such incoherent language that one marvels how aesthetic unity is achieved. Though Beckett controls all the strings of fictional illusion, the heroes' inventions and lies defy all rational and realistic norms. These creatures show so little respect for organized society, or for man as a deserving individual, that they reveal themselves as morally and artistically aberrant. Yet, in spite of their mental and physical depravities, in spite of their anomalism, these alienated beings acquire such universality that they are able to reflect quite profoundly on the mystery of the self, on the dilemma of existence.

The anonymous heroes of the four stories share one essential experience which they keep remembering as it becomes an obsessive leitmotif throughout the narration: their brutal expulsion from the security of a bourgeois home. This expulsion represents the passage from the world of reality into fictional absurdity. It is often described as a painful birth—the ejection from the womb, or rather the symbolic extraction from the mind of the creator. Having been kicked down the stairs of his paternal home, the hero of "L'Expulsé" preserves the fetal position, even in the gutter where he has rolled: "Je m'accoudai, curieux souvenir, au

---

[5] Geneviève Bonnefoi, "Textes pour rien?" *Les Lettres Nouvelles,* no. 36 (March, 1956), 425. *Nouvelles et Textes pour rien* has been greatly ignored by critics; this is one of the few articles devoted to this important Beckett work.

[6] Beckett, *Nouvelles et Textes pour rien,* "Texte 4," p. 155.

trottoir, j'assis mon oreille dans le creux de ma main et me mis à réfléchir à ma situation, pourtant familière" (pp. 13–14) . That he should find his situation "familière" points out his affinity with all the other Beckett creations who have also been expelled from the author's mind, and who repeatedly assume the fetal posture to evade cruel reality. Though most Beckett heroes appear as senile men, their initial appearance is usually described as a birth. Therefore, as they wander through the fictional world as full-grown figures, born aged, they are denied all memories of a past, and, if at times they seem to remember such a past, it is because they invent memories to fill the void of their fragile existence.

The narrator-heroes of the four stories wander through the streets of the city like lost children in search of a father, a mother, or a past. In the process, these outcasts mutter to themselves and curse those who are responsible for their expulsion, those who have given them life (even though fictitious) and forced them into their present condition. Later, in his own fiction, Molloy calls this hidden procreator "the hypothetical imperative." It is the driving force that compels the Beckettian derelicts to go on and on toward an unknown and unattainable goal; it is the omnipotent master who puts words into their twisted mouths.

In the course of their endless quest in fiction, Beckett's heroes long for a place to hide, a place to rest, a place to stop: a room, a bed, a box, a pot, a container of some sort, or, as one of them explains, "un berceau ou un tombeau." These containers also become symbolic vehicles for the journey to nothingness, to death and disintegration. But if eventually the heroes succeed in appropriating or even inventing such vehicles, they fail to progress toward their desired goal. Their deceptive wanderings may suggest a quick and meaningless passage through life, but they afford little change in the heroes' fate.

Such a fraudulent existence, which negates as it shapes the substance of which it is made, builds itself on an accumulation of words and events repeated endlessly. In all their misguided creativity the French heroes are confronted with the futility of their undertakings and realize that the stories and identities they invent are basically false. The hero of "L'Expulsé" concludes the tale of his adventures by stating: "Je ne sais pas pourquoi j'ai raconté cette histoire. J'aurais pu tout aussi bien en raconter une autre. Peut-être qu'une autre fois je pourrai en raconter une autre. Ames vives, vous verrez que cela se ressemble" (p. 40). If all stories are false, if all fiction can be made to say whatever the hero chooses, then all stories are alike, or can be made alike. But, being committed to his fictional role, the creator-hero is compelled to go on, if only to attain a semblance of identity and authenticity.

The heroes of the stories may pretend to be in search of a refuge, of a condition, and even of a meaning for their vacant existence, but they know that their search will never succeed. Nevertheless, they go on seeking an improbable and impossible rest, a means of evading the futility of their creative function. While repeating the same words, the same movements, from one story to the next, they provide themselves with the chance of stumbling into silence, into immobility, or into "le bon agrégat," as one of these storytellers hopes:

Bien choisir son moment et se taire, serait-ce le seul moyen d'avoir être et habitat? Mais je suis ici, cela au moins est certain, j'ai beau le dire et le redire, cela reste vrai. Je ne me rends pas compte. Moins vrai, moins certain, que lorsque je me dis sur terre, venu au monde et assuré de le quitter, c'est pourquoi je le dis, patiemment, en variant, en essayant de varier, car on ne sait jamais, il s'agit peut-être seulement de tomber sur le bon agrégat. Pour ne plus être ici enfin, n'avoir jamais été ici. . . . Le bon agrégat, mais il y en a quatre millions de possibles, voire de probables, selon Aristote, qui savait tout.[7]

Undoubtedly, these derelicts are seeking the aggregate of form and matter of which every being is composed (according to Aristotle). But since there are four million such aggregates, their only hope of finding the right one is to remain present and pursue their vain quest, relying on the chance of meeting the proper conditions. It is quite unlikely

[7] *Ibid.*, "Texte 8," p. 186.

that they will ever encounter these conditions, since they are exiled not only from the material world, but also from their own selves. Cut off from the original source of life, and suspended in a state of complete alienation, they cannot advance toward a definite end. They cannot disappear.

Death never comes to these "Dying Gladiators," [8] as Horace Gregory calls them, nor do they have the courage or strength to commit suicide. Lethargically stretched on a public bench, like the hero of *Premier amour,* or inside an empty carriage which reminds the hero of "L'Expulsé" of a hearse, or inside the jettisoned rowboat for which the hero of "La Fin" has built a cover that he pulls over himself as though sliding into a coffin, these Beckettian Oblomovs refuse to assume the least responsibility for their survival, and allow themselves to drift heedlessly toward oblivion. Yet in the process these undying creatures achieve an immortality that transcends the temporal limits of human existence. Caught in a static state of stupefaction, they reflect upon the ambiguity of their condition, and see themselves simultaneously as *outsiders* in Beckett's fiction and *insiders* in their own creations. Eventually they no longer distinguish whether they are the creator of the story or its protagonist. This equivocal situation may appear comical, but it is above all tragically absurd. However, this absurdity does not imply total nihilism, for in being made conscious of their twofold condition Beckett's characters gain the power to transform the negative aspect of their existence into an affirmation of life. Even as fictitious beings they transcend the fraudulence of their status to regain contact with reality, and, whether lying in a ditch, crawling in the mud, or planted in a pot, their state of consciousness reveals itself as a human experience.

Beckett's people are not necessarily vegetating in lethargy and depravity because they oppose a decadent social system,

[8] *The Dying Gladiators* (New York: Grove Press, 1961). An early version of Horace Gregory's "Beckett's Dying Gladiators" appeared in *Commonweal,* LXV (Oct. 26, 1956), 88–92.

as often occurs in traditional fiction, but rather because they are in rebellion against the limitations of the human condition. Thus, while removing themselves from the social and physical reality of the world of man they become stubbornly preoccupied with their own illusory selves, and develop a natural indifference to all the governing aspects of human life. However, within the region of the inner self, they encounter a more distressing situation as they face the dilemma of fictional existence. Beckett's creator-heroes may exist free of all memories and social commitments, outside conventions, traditions, and even history, but they cannot avoid the artistic question Beckett puts before them, of how to survive fictionally. The anguish they suffer does not relate to what might have been or what ought to be, but to a fictional void which is the essence of the Beckettian experience. Because the French creator-heroes are locked in aesthetic contemplation, the irrationality of their actions and reflections becomes a revaluation of literature.

When the characters of a traditional bourgeois novel become part and parcel of their environment, of the paraphernalia of their daily life, and submit to circumstances and objects, they cease to exist and begin to vegetate. Beckett's derelicts also vegetate and appear obsessed by their surroundings and personal possessions, at times suffering utter panic at the loss of their belongings; but these objects and surroundings are functionally irrelevant. Their obsession with objects, like all other aspects of their existence, is a pretense. Even though they stubbornly indulge in such activities as searching for a lost bicycle or a lost pencil stub, repairing a broken umbrella, exchanging a dirty hat for another dirty hat or a torn shoe for another torn shoe, the creator-heroes are in a position to negate these trifles with a few well-chosen words.

Objects and physical setting are obsolete in Beckett's French fiction, and if the characters seem unable to free themselves of their obsessive presence it is not because they are part of a social system, but because these objects serve as creative inspiration—means of perpetuating fictional absurdity. The heroes' interest in objects is purely gratuitous, and whether they discuss a hat, a shoe, a stone, or a carrot, they place the same value, or rather the same absence of value, on all objects. If bicycles, hats, shoes, bags, pencils, pebbles, and so on insist on reappearing, they do so devoid of all functional meaning, and therefore acquire the same fraudulence as the characters themselves. The presence of these objects serves to contrast tangible forms with the intangibility of fiction, just as Beckett introduces a quantity of pseudorealistic characters next to his inventive protagonists in order to create an incongruous interplay between social reality and fictional alienation.

As the narrator-heroes of the stories wander aimlessly among the dismal remnants of a realistic world, they scatter, along with the vague memories they attach to their doubtful pasts, all the objects they were given before their expulsion. But no sooner have they forsaken material ties than they contrive ingenious techniques for begging, as though wishing to recapture their lost possessions, at the same time mocking the needs of humanity. Standing at street corners, these improvised beggars observe with indifference the *real* people of a world from which they have been banished. In turn, these people observe the Beckettian derelicts with curiosity and contempt, for indeed they offer a most puzzling and repulsive physique. They all wear the same kind of discolored greatcoat, the same filthy bowler hat tied to the buttonhole with a shoelace, the same worn-out shoes. They all share a putrid smell from both the feet and the mouth, and exhibit numerous physical ailments: stiff legs, cysts, pustules on the top of the skull, sores in the anus, decaying teeth, failing sight. Moreover, their attitude toward their fellow characters (one can hardly say fellowmen) is cruel, obscene, and inhuman.

Among the many people they meet in the city there are children with whom they associate, prostitutes who try to seduce them, policemen who threaten to lock them up, and stable citizens who look upon them as though they were unbelievable creatures from some other planet. They also encounter animals (goats, horses, donkeys, rats) which stare at them with puzzled animal looks, for if these derelicts seem barely human, neither can they claim to belong to the animal kingdom. Grotesque chimeras transplanted from the eccentric imagination of their creator into a realistic setting, their physical appearance betrays the incompatibility of their origin.

Some of the people they encounter in the streets keep reappearing with obsessive insistence, while others quickly vanish out of sight. Two of these figures offer by their actions revealing facts about the narrator-heroes' condition. One is a political speaker, the other a cyclist. While begging at a busy street corner, minding his own business, the hero of "La Fin" is brought into evidence by a man perched on top of an automobile who, in the midst of a vehement public address about "Union . . . frères . . . Marx . . . capital . . . bifteck . . . amour," turns contemptuously toward the unconcerned hero of the story and shouts: ". . . regardez-moi cette loque, ce déchet. S'il ne se met pas à quatre pattes, c'est qu'il a peur de la fourrière. Vieux, pouilleux, pourri, à la poubelle. . . . Regardez-moi ce supplicié, cet écorché" (p. 112). In his role as fictitious outcast, Beckett's hero does appear incongruous, objectionable, and out of place in a social setting. It is the uselessness, the parasitic condition of such beings that the realist citizen attacks. But from the indifferent point of view of the displaced fictional hero, this sort of sociopolitical harangue is totally meaningless. The hero of the story is pleased to be considered as human detritus, and as he staggers away from the gesticulating orator he wonders what kind of madman or religious fanatic this might be.

For the Beckettian derelict, it is the man inside, the socially preoccupied individual who appears pathological, insane, and psychotic. Within his own free world of artistic illusions, the fictional hero of an absurd novel need not be engaged in social or human activities, nor is he required to justify his useless existence. As narrator-narrated his responsibility is to himself, just as the creator's responsibility is to his creation. Therefore, one cannot condemn the heroes of the stories for their lack of social consciousness or their lack of ethical values. They cannot be judged morally, socially, or politically as the public speaker of "La Fin" pretends to do.

A much more pleasing encounter is with the strange cyclist whom the hero of "Le Calmant" sees during his wandering through the city. For the deformed heroes of Beckett's fiction, the image of a man precariously balanced on a two-wheeled vehicle represents the one possible means of achieving unity between the physical and the mental. Because most Beckett creatures fail miserably in their attempts to achieve such harmony, the vision of a stable bicycle rider remains for them a tempting but unattainable aspiration. What is particularly fascinating about the cyclist of "Le Calmant" is that he rides his bicycle while reading a newspaper that he holds with both hands before his eyes, from time to time ringing the bicycle bell without even looking up. Such dexterity, such elegant equilibrium, such incredible balance between mind and body—each functioning independently of one another—create an unforgettable feeling of admiration and frustration in the clumsy hero of the story who, like most of his fellow creatures, can hardly drag himself on his own stiff legs. This expert cyclist performs his feat in total defiance of the laws of nature and common sense. As such he represents the ultimate in irrationality.

Among the crippled and senile Beckett heroes, this utterly detached cyclist who rides his machine while reading a newspaper, unconcerned with what his feet are doing while his mind is occupied elsewhere, stands as a perfect model of fictional absurdity. He performs a deed conceivable only beyond the norms of reality and rationality. All Beckett's derelicts strive to achieve such physical and mental independence; all would forsake past, present, and future for a single moment of such perfection, as "across the entire

Beckett landscape there passes no more self-sufficient image of felicity." [9] Furthermore, the absurdity of this man's actions is reinforced by his complete indifference to his destination. He simply passes swiftly across the hero's field of vision and disappears like a dot on the horizon. The hero's only consolation is to remark that they both travel in the same direction, but the cyclist quickly outstrips him. In all its graceful mobility, this figure remains the symbol of accomplished absurdity, the kind of absurdity that shapes aesthetic illusion. It is somewhere between the extremes of the socially preoccupied political speaker and the totally indifferent cyclist that the Beckettian hero seeks his identity.

Like the cyclist of "Le Calmant," the heroes of the stories have no definite goal, nor are they concerned with the purpose of their quest. Nevertheless, they are obsessed by the problem of motion. Each step they take, whether mental or physical, is marked by suffering, and yet their creative progress is nondirectional, nonsensical because it cannot be plotted within the frame of an actual world. Forced to calculate their advance in abstract terms, they rely on free associations of images and words gathered on the basis of unpredictability. Though they struggle to have their stories and existence move in a specific direction, they are repeatedly faced with illusions: the deceptive content of their inventions and lies. Yet to affirm their identities and give themselves the sensation of progress, they persist in accumulating words and in reshaping their doubtful memories. Often they must repeat the same words and relate the same stories to maintain a semblance of progress. Expelled from the mind of a creator who refuses to acknowledge his responsibility, the narrator-heroes become useless parasites who can justify their presence only by inventing situations in which to survive fictionally. These inventions serve as sedatives to cure the pain of existing in a fraudulent condition: "Je vais donc me raconter une histoire, je vais donc essayer

[9] Hugh Kenner, *Samuel Beckett: A Critical Study* (New York: Grove Press, 1961) , p. 122.

de me raconter encore une histoire, pour essayer de me calmer . . ." (pp. 41–42).

Because fiction never changes anything, these stories within the story, in which the heroes depict themselves as central figures, never achieve their purpose, never lead anywhere, and become as meaningless as their inventor. The hero of "La Fin" concludes about himself and his fiction: "Je songeai faiblement et sans regret au récit que j'avais failli faire, récit à l'image de ma vie, je veux dire sans le courage de finir ni la force de continuer" (pp. 122–123). He ends his tale with the sensation of having performed an empty verbal exercise, but in the process he has exposed the false coherence and significance of fictional alienation, and openly admits that the content of his story is a poor substitute for the real life he has never known. Cornered in "l'horreur chosesque" into which he has driven himself, he realizes that the form of his fiction "masks the formlessness" of his existence, and since the language he uses to tell his stories "is not reality itself, but only an inadequate and distorting substitute for reality," [10] he comes to doubt the very words he speaks, the very words of which he is made. No longer able to match reality with its symbolic counterpart (language), he sinks into silence and nonexistence.

Built on a language whose destiny is "to communicate silence by words," [11] and to negate its rational meaning, the absurd fiction invented by the heroes rises on a structure that uses its own deceptive foundation to reach higher levels of absurdity. Beckett creates a story about a character who in turn invents a story about himself. From the depth of this double illusion, the creator-hero believes that his fiction is reality, but it is only the by-product of an imaginary source.

[10] Judith Radke, "Doubt and Disintegration of Form in the French Novels and Drama of Samuel Beckett" (unpublished doctoral dissertation, University of Colorado, 1961), p. 49. In an interesting chapter entitled "Fiction and the Lie" (pp. 50–118), Miss Radke shows how Beckett's French heroes in the process of inventing their fiction "question the validity of the novel as a literary genre."

[11] As quoted from Maurice Blanchot by Neal Oxenhandler in his "Paradox and Negation in the Criticism of Maurice Blanchot," *Symposium*, no. 1 (Spring, 1962), 37.

This is how the hero of "La Fin" explains, in rather obscene terms, this fictitious superimposition: "Se tailler un royaume, au milieu de la merde universelle, puis chier dessus, ça c'était bien de moi" (p. 119). Thus, while author and hero are indistinguishable, while Orpheus and Eurydice are united in an impasse of make-believe, the reader cannot determine who of the two is the bigger liar, and which of their fiction is the bigger lie. Reality, subreality, and illusion are interwoven into an intricate scheme rendered even more ambiguous by the hero's claims to authorship.

As portrayed by Beckett's characters, man appears alienated from the source of his existence, cut off from reality and surrounded by the illusions he substitutes for the resulting void. The anonymous speaker of "La Fin" expresses his dubious condition by wondering: "C'est à se demander parfois si on est sur la bonne planète. Même les mots vous lâchent, c'est tout dire. C'est le moment peut-être où les vases cessent de communiquer, vous savez les vases." [12] Communication between reality and fiction is perhaps possible on the level of the story created by the author as background for the plot, but on the level of the hero's own fiction there is no longer any possibility of communication with reality, only an ambivalent interplay between two fraudulent settings: that of Beckett's story and that of the hero's inventions.

Yet throughout the narratives there are recurring images which seem to emerge directly from a reality that the heroes of the stories either try to recapture or forsake completely. It is as though a thin thread of realism (an umbilical cord) ran from the characters to their obscure origin, as though their present condition were related to a former existence as rational beings. For the heroes of the stories it is the memory

[12] Beckett, "La Fin," pp. 118–119. The allusion may be to André Breton's *Les Vases communicants*, though undoubtedly meant ironically. For if Breton and the surrealist writers visualized a possible communication of the real and the surreal through verbal expression, thus linking the vision of the subconscious with conscious perception, for Beckett's physically, mentally, and verbally alienated heroes such communication is no longer possible.

of a dead father and the presence of the curious hat they all wear which serve as connections with the past and furnish the hope of a possible future. Somehow father and hat are associated on a creative level. Father and hat stand as the initial causes for the heroes' expulsion into absurdity. It is from the moment his father bought him his first hat that the hero of "L'Expulsé" dates the beginning of his fictional misery:

Comment décrire ce chapeau? Et pourquoi? Lorsque ma tête eut atteint ses dimensions je ne dirai pas définitives, mais maxima, mon père me dit, Viens, mon fils, nous allons acheter ton chapeau, comme s'il préexistait depuis l'éternité, dans un endroit déterminé. Il alla droit au chapeau. Moi je n'avais pas voix au chapitre, le chapelier non plus. Je me suis souvent demandé si mon père n'avait pas pour dessein de m'humilier, s'il n'était pas jaloux de moi qui étais jeune et beau, enfin, frais, alors que lui était déjà vieux et tout gonflé et violacé. Il ne m'était plus permis, à partir de ce jour-là, de sortir tête nue, mes jolis cheveux marron au vent. Quelquefois, dans une rue écartée, je l'ôtais et le tenais à la main, mais en tremblant. Je devais le brosser matin et soir. Les jeunes gens de mon âge, avec qui j'étais malgré tout obligé de frayer de temps en temps, se moquaient de moi. Mais je me disais, Le chapeau n'y est pas pour grand'chose, ils ne font qu'y accrocher leurs saillies, comme au ridicule le plus saillant, car ils ne sont pas fins. J'ai toujours été étonné du peu de finesse de mes contemporains, moi dont l'âme se tordait du matin au soir, rien qu'à se chercher. Mais c'était peut-être de la gentillesse, genre celle qui raille le bossu sur son grand nez. A la mort de mon père j'aurais pu me délivrer de ce chapeau, rien ne s'y opposait plus, mais je n'en fis rien. Mais comment le décrire? Une autre fois, une autre fois.   [pp. 14–15]

This hat will have many occasions to be described, discussed, and cursed in the course of Beckett's subsequent fiction as it becomes a permanent attribute of the future heroes' personalities. Symbol of propagation of the Beckettian race, this hat is the link between generations of fictitious derelicts. It is passed on from one to the other, thereby preventing the characters from completely obliterating the past, reality, and above all their affinity with the procreator who originally furnished the hat "comme s'il préexistait depuis l'étermité, dans un endroit déterminé." In the minds

of the heroes, the father who inflicts the hat upon his progenies is equated with the creator who inflicts fictional life
upon his characters. Beckett's outcasts accept the hat as a
symbol of predetermined condition based on a set of illusory
values—symbol of a counterfeit ancestry. But the hat also
contributes to their creative power, for not only is it a means
of self-perpetuation, but also a source of inventiveness, an
element of creativity.

The narrator-heroes of all four stories make numerous
allusions to their hats whenever they find nothing else to
talk about and want to occupy fictional time. Hats give them
aesthetic pleasure, though more often they are a cause of
suffering. The hero of "La Fin" explains: "J'ôtai mon chapeau qui me faisait mal" (p. 86)—a statement repeated
almost textually by Vladimir in *Godot* as he exchanges his
own hat for the one Lucky has forgotten on stage: "Le mien
me faisait mal. Comment dire? Il me grattait" (p. 123). Like
all other objects the heroes find, drag, or lose in their fiction,
hats are sources of artistic inspiration. They serve as pretexts
for performing an absurd vaudeville act in order to force the
action of a static play into a semblance of progress. They are
excuses for instigating an irrelevant argument or presenting
a detailed description to fill up space in a novel. The possession of a hat marks for the Beckett hero the beginning of
alienation, the first step toward creative consciousness. It
shows fictional maturity as the head reaches perhaps not "ses
dimensions . . . définitives, mais maxima." As such, devoid
of its functional value, the hat helps the characters to
achieve independence.

In *More Pricks Than Kicks*, the socially inclined Belacqua never boasts of having a hat, and perhaps the reason
Murphy fails to acquire fictional authenticity and perishes
of a human death is that "Murphy never wore a hat, the
memories it awoke of the caul were too poignant, especially
when he had to take it off" (*Murphy*, p. 73). Though Watt
never becomes a true inventor of fiction since he relies on
Sam for the narration of his adventures, he deserves a hat

because his mental breakdown places him on the brink of fictional alienation. Watt's hat is meticulously described:

Watt wore, on his head, a block hat, of a pepper colour. This excellent hat had belonged to his grand-father, who had picked it up, on a racecourse, from off the ground, where it lay, and carried it home. Then mustard, now it was pepper, in colour.

[*Watt,* p. 218]

It is the first time in Beckett's fiction that a hat relates a character to his ancestors—in this instance, Watt to his grandfather. It may also be relevant to note that the stone Lady MacCann throws at Watt, while he is on his way to Mr. Knott's house, does not strike Watt's head or body, but his hat. Symbolically, one can date Watt's mental deterioration from the moment his hat is struck by the stone.

In Beckett's first French novel, Mercier and Camier do not wear hats, although at the end of their unsuccessful journey Mercier is seen standing in front of "la vitrine d'un chapelier" considering no doubt whether or not to buy a hat. Had he and his partner fulfilled their quest, this hat would become a status symbol for fictional alienation. Only in the stories, where the anonymous narrator-heroes are exiled from social reality, does the hat become a means of perpetuating the fictitious predicament.

The relationship between the hat (symbol of creativity) and the father (procurer of the head cover) corresponds on a metaphorical level to the ambiguous relationship between the concealed creator and his imaginative heroes. From the day their fathers die, the protagonists of the stories are expelled from the material world. Similarly, from the moment Beckett grants his characters freedom to relate their own experiences in the first person, they find themselves fictionally alienated. Father and author are metaphorically related, just as hat and skull—from which all fiction comes forth—are intricately united. Though they may deny this fact, Beckett's creator-heroes are the product of a mind, and since the hat symbolizes imagination, it is in relation to their hats that they fulfill their creative ability. One might say that it is while "talking through their hats" that Beckett's heroes discover their affinity with the author. Without their hats they feel insecure and unimaginative, for not only do the hats cover the sores on their skull, but they literally become part of that skull. The hero of "La Fin" declares: "Je ne pouvais me promener tête nue, vu l'état de mon crâne. Ce chapeau était d'abord trop petit, puis il s'habitua" (p. 78). The narrator-heroes can think and perform their artistic feats only with their hats on.

Metaphorically, Beckett is the father who furnished "ce salaud de chapeau" to his characters in order to subject them to self-creativity. He remains the original inflicter of torments, the force that launched these creatures on their absurd and endless fictional paths. It is to their fathers, and to all other creators (Beckett included), that the heroes of the stories refer when they curse "ces assassins . . . ces pourris," who imposed life and hat upon them, torturing them into fiction. Throughout Beckett's French works the heroes allude to some unidentified "they" (Molloy calls these "hypothetical imperatives") who, like the father and creator, remain safely outside the boundaries of fiction, "dans le monde des vivants," and refuse to acknowledge their creative responsibility. Beckett's derelicts hold a personal grudge against these people, a grudge they reiterate as they wander from "the spermarium to the crematorium." For if the father is responsible for his offsprings' birth and expulsion from the womb, he is also responsible for having committed them to fictional alienation, for subjecting them to the slow death in progress which fiction represents.

The hero of *Premier amour* exemplifies the connection between creativity and death when, at the beginning of his fraudulent story about his love affair with the prostitute Lulu, he states: "J'associe, à tort ou à raison, mon mariage avec la mort de mon père, dans le temps. Qu'il existe d'autres liens, sur d'autres plans, entre ces deux affaires, c'est possible. Il m'est déjà difficile de dire ce que je crois savoir" (p. 1). Like all his fellow creatures, this hero claims a defective memory. Therefore, to fix in time the beginning of his fiction, he must return to his father's grave to check on the tombstone the date of his father's death, which supposedly corresponds to the beginning of his legal (or illegal) union with Lulu—or rather the beginning of his fictional lie, since at the end of the tale he denies having been married to Lulu. Like all other Beckett fiction, this story is stamped with the seal of death and fraud. The Orphean hero descends into the region of the dead (his father's grave) to recapture the meaning of his present condition; but, as with Orpheus, when he looks back upon that meaning it disappears.

The further one advances into the Beckettian universe the more helical it becomes as it moves away from reality and rationality. Whether riding a real or an imaginary bicycle, walking along a deserted road, crawling in a ditch, or sitting in a room telling themselves stories of dubious authenticity, Beckett's heroes progress along a deceptive path made in the image of their own identities—a path that vanishes behind them and never leads anywhere. Though these wanderers believe themselves in motion, they are actually standing still, gradually fading into nonexistence, darkness, silence, nothingness. Such meaningless, nonethical, nonsocial, nonsensical endeavors may appear questionable, but it is the artist's privilege to create whatever world he chooses and to respect only those rules he invents to govern his art, for "art has always been this—pure interrogation, rhetorical question less the rhetoric—whatever else it may have been obliged by the 'social reality' to appear, but never more so than now, when social reality . . . has severed the connexion." [13]

While the Beckettian creature gradually forsakes "social reality" to draw inward into his own consciousness, he en-

[13] Beckett, "Denis Devlin," *Transition* 27 (April-May, 1938), p. 289. In this review of Denis Devlin's book of poetry entitled *Intercessions,* Beckett makes some striking statements about art and the artist in relation to society: "The time is not perhaps altogether too green for the vile suggestion that art has nothing to do with clarity, does not dabble in the clear and does not make clear . . ." (p. 293).

counters the illusion of fictional life. The identity he ascribes to himself being based on artistic lies, the more he probes the inner self the greater the meaninglessness of his discovery. Yet this act of reflection, this search of the self by the self in the privacy of a mind, eventually reaches beyond the creative madness of the hero and opens up into a quasi-mystical experience. But this experience never becomes a transcendental revelation. The Beckettian quest exploits its own absurdity to affirm in existential terms the anguish of human fate; it does not purport to offer spiritual salvation. The selfless Beckett hero is driven on and on into an infinite inner world to be confronted in the end with his own void.

As a fictitious being shaping his own existence, he becomes conscious of the fragility of his fraudulent condition, of his absurd immortality. But he must continue to seek his own self even if it means destroying it in the process. This predicament resembles the one described by Eddington in which a man finds a strange footprint on some unknown shore. To explain its origin, he builds theories upon theories. Having finally reconstructed the being who left this mark, he discovers that it is himself.[14] It is this necessary quest, this process of discovering one's own identity, which forces Beckett's creatures into an endless cycle of painful birth and hopeless death.

Throughout Beckett's fiction, from the 1934 *More Pricks Than Kicks* to the 1961 *Comment c'est,* images of physical birth are equated with the act of creating fiction—the act of a writer sitting in front of a white sheet of paper deliberately inventing people, a world, a reality that destroys *reality.* While this fiction progresses, it becomes a process of disintegration into death. However, because Beckett's heroes are permitted to observe themselves being created, they acquire a profound and unusual insight into life and death. Their self-made condition is in fact death in progress, or as one of

[14] As described by Sartre, *op. cit.,* p. 126.

the French creatures says of himself, as though speaking of a work of literature nearing its completion (a work in progress) : "Je suis en progrès, il était temps, je finirai par pouvoir fermer ma sale gueule, sauf prévu." [15] This desire for silence, for annihilation of one's being, is a form of creative impotence. Beckett's French creator-heroes recognize that whether or not they go on with their stories they accomplish nothing, and, in the end, are no better, no worse, than if they had remained silent. Their futile artistic gesticulations, rather than offering an ending for their fiction, force them back to an absurd beginning. They achieve, gain, learn nothing, and perhaps suffer a slight regression toward the obscure source from which they sprang—a source as deceptive as the goal they seek.

Suspended in a universe open at both ends and including within its paradoxical frame the formula for its own creation and its own destruction, Beckett's French heroes view their fictional existence as a form of life born out of a delirious state of mind. Therefore, they act and think more like lunatics than rational beings. Fallen angels of fiction, they take it upon themselves "to make a mess" out of their fictitious condition. Like their creator, whom a French critic describes as "un bâtisseur de ruines qui sape son édifice à mesure qu'il l'élève," [16] these creator-heroes are builders of ruins, inventors of fraudulent situations they can abolish in a single sentence. Witness Moran's statement at the end of his vain search for Molloy: "Then I went back into the house and wrote, It is midnight. The rain is beating on the windows. It was not midnight. It was not raining" (Molloy, p. 241). Temporarily sustained by the lie of fiction, the illusion of progress, "the entire laborious order [of their stories] collapses back into chaos, with a meaningful order conjured by its absence." [17]

[15] Beckett, Nouvelles et Textes pour rien, "Texte 4," p. 157.
[16] Maurice Nadeau, Littérature présente (Paris: Corrêa, 1952), p. 279.
[17] Josephine Jacobsen and William R. Mueller, The Testament of Samuel Beckett (New York: Hill and Wang, 1964), p. 42.

At the end of their fictional escapades the heroes of
Beckett's English fiction had the choice of returning to social
reality to succumb in the hands of some incompetent doctors
(Belacqua Shuah), of committing suicide or encountering
an accidental death (Murphy), or of accepting insanity as a
last refuge and remaining locked within the walls of a
mental institution (Watt). The undying French heroes are
denied such a choice, and no longer hope for a "classic"
ending to their fiction. Like incurable poker players they are
committed to their *mise en jeu,* and, win or lose, they cannot
withdraw from the game until all cards are played, all the
while knowing that the deck of fictional cards can be dealt
and redealt endlessly. As they persist in their creative speculations, they encounter the gambler's doubt and suffer "from
the hallucination that what has been left behind is still
before [them]." [18] While dreaming of salvation, or hoping
for a quick death, or attempting to disappear into silence,
they inflict upon themselves the punishment of having to go
on gambling with their false existence. The rules of the
creative game forbid them to withdraw their stakes in the
middle of a hand. Whether they stop, advance, wait, hesitate, or turn back, they are caught in the impasse of creativity.

Condemned to an existence they must perpetuate until
they run out of words—since literature is made of words—or
until they run out of space—since fictional life is contained
in the pages of a book—these creatures cannot desert the
roles they have chosen for themselves. Though they have
little hope of ever seeing an end to their existence, and since
language and fiction can be made endless by the process of
repetition, they must continue to speak, to exist verbally in
the vacuum of fictional illusion. It is the almost moribund
Malone who sums up the futility of the Beckettian predicament: "And when all is said and done there is nothing more
like a step that climbs than a step that descends or even that
paces to and fro forever on the same level" (*Malone Dies,* p.
45).

[18] Beckett, *Proust* (New York: Grove Press, 1957), p. 44.

To fail artistically and accept one's failure as a raison d'être is the essential attitude of Beckett's French heroes. The further removed they are from reality and rationality the greater is their hope of rendering failure into a "howling success." Though Beckett has never formulated a precise aesthetic position for himself, this notion of failure as an artistic goal is implicit throughout his work, and is specifically expressed in his critical essays where he makes revealing statements about art and the condition of the artist in society.

In a series of *Three Dialogues* with Georges Duthuit, though dealing with painters rather than writers, Beckett discusses the dilemma of the modern artist ". . . who is helpless, cannot act, in the event cannot paint, since he is obliged to paint. The act is of him, who helpless, unable to act, acts, in the event paints, since he is obliged to paint." [19] Debating this Zeno-like paradox, Beckett—"disguised as an Irish pawn who quails before a Frenchman's dialectic" [20]— plays the straight man's role to Georges Duthuit, who simulates the position of a critical censor. Defending the abstract art of his friend, the Dutch painter Bram van Velde, whom he has championed since the early thirties and whose work may have influenced his more than that of any writer, Beckett pursues an ambiguous line of thought. Duthuit warns him appropriately to "try and bear in mind that the subject under discussion *is not yourself,* nor the Sufist Al-Haqq, but a particular Dutchman by name van Velde, hitherto erroneously referred to as an *artiste peintre.*" [21]

The irony of the argument emerges out of a clownish dialectical interplay between the two critics. However, B. manages to assert his position against that of his opponent D.:

My case, since I am in the dock, is that van Velde is the first to desist from . . . estheticised automatism, the first to submit

[19] Samuel Beckett with Georges Duthuit, "Three Dialogues," *Transition*, no. 5 (1949), 101.
[20] Kenner, *op. cit.*, p. 28.
[21] Beckett and Duthuit, *op. cit.*, p. 102.

wholly to the incoercible absence of relation, in the absence of terms or, if you like, in the presence of unavailable terms, *the first to admit that to be an artist is to fail, as no other dare fail,* that failure is his world and the shrink from it desertion, art and craft, good housekeeping, living. No, no, allow me to expire. I know that all that is required now, in order to bring even this horrible matter to an acceptable conclusion, is to make of this submission, this admission, this fidelity to failure, a new occasion, a new term of relation, and of the act which, unable to act, obliged to act, he makes, an expressive act, even if only of itself, of its responsibility, of its obligation.[22]

It is evident from the above passage, and in the light of Beckett's own creations, that his conviction about failure being the only possible "expressive act" of the modern artist goes beyond his admiration for the work of his painter friend, Bram van Velde. Beckett is undoubtedly thinking of his own creative endeavor—that of an artist who (in 1949 when the *Three Dialogues* were published) has alienated himself from society and deliberately chosen failure as an artistic goal. For more than twenty years, Beckett ("the man in the room," as Hugh Kenner calls him) lived and worked exiled from his native land and tongue, exiled from social reality as he created his own personal reality. Only in recent years has society taken its revenge, recognizing his talent and placing him in the ranks of major literary figures. Meanwhile, exile, alienation, and failure have become the property of his creations.

Beckett's French characters are not presented as individuals performing semirational actions in a realistic environment. Their condition transcends the boundaries of a single life, of a particular society, of a specific moment in history, to become the expression of man's universal fears, hopes, anxieties, desires, and doubts. Each French hero is a symbol of the human race, a cross-bearer for man's original sin of existence, and when, in the midst of his despair, Vladimir cries out: "But at this place, at this moment of time, all mankind is us, whether we like it or not" (*Waiting for Godot,* p. 51), he is speaking for all of Beckett's derelicts.

[22] *Ibid.,* p. 103 (italics mine).

Placed on the periphery of human life, reduced to nonde-script identities, these subhuman creatures represent the evolution of mankind from the ape to the mystery of its future condition. In his French works Beckett no longer satirizes, as he did in his English fiction, the mediocrity of certain types of people, or certain social institutions; in-stead, he confronts the reader with the crude image of *being*—the image of a creature stripped of all human attrib-utes, who, while crawling naked like a worm in the mud, reveals the secret of the creative process as well as the agony of the process of life, whether real or fictitious.

APPENDIX

APPENDIX

Three of Samuel Beckett's works discussed in the present study are unpublished: the novel *Mercier et Camier,* the short story *Premier amour,* and the three-act play *Eleutheria.* Summaries of these works are incorporated in chapters v and vi. Recently, Mr. John Fletcher of the University of Toulouse pointed out the existence of another unpublished Beckett manuscript: an unfinished novel written in 1932 and entitled *Dream of Fair to Middling Women.* I am indebted to Mr. Fletcher for the information reported here concerning this manuscript. The collection of short stories *More Pricks Than Kicks,* published in 1934, is extremely difficult to obtain. For convenience's sake a summary of its content is also included in this appendix.

DREAM OF FAIR TO MIDDLING WOMEN

According to Beckett, this unfinished novel (214 pp.) was written in 1932, in a Paris hotel. It appears to be a first draft of *More Pricks Than Kicks,* and its protagonist is also named Belacqua. In Beckett's own typing, faded and somewhat untidy, with several handwritten corrections, this typescript consists of two long chapters numbered 2 and 3. A first chapter was projected, covering Belacqua's boyhood, but was never written. Only a few lines exist on a single page to signify chapter one. Evidently Beckett found the draft of his hero's biography so long that he dropped it in favor of a series of sketches about his life in the form of short stories. Extracts from this manuscript became, after some revision, "Sedendo et Quiescendo," in *Transition,* no. 21 (March, 1932) ; "Text," in *The New Review* (April, 1932) ; "A Wet Night," and "The Smeraldina's Billet Doux," in *More*

Pricks Than Kicks (1934) . Other short passages, and groups of words, were also incorporated in *More Pricks Than Kicks* and the collection of poems *Echo's Bones and Other Precipitates* (1935) . Thus, of the ten short stories of *More Pricks Than Kicks*, only two really came from this first draft. The title of this work may be a parody of Chaucer, of Tennyson, or perhaps of Henry Williamson's *Dream of Fair Women: A Tale of Youth after the Great War*, a pompous novel published in 1924, the third part of a tetralogy entitled *The Flax of Dream*. The title of Beckett's novel also ironically reflects its subject matter, for the narrative deals with at least three women, though others were due to figure in subsequent unwritten chapters.

SUMMARY

Belacqua is waving goodbye from (Dublin's?) Carlyle Pier to the Smeraldina-Rima, a rather plump German-speaking female with whom he has just fallen deeply in love. She is leaving for Vienna to study music. Soon after, Belacqua drops his local girl friend and sets out after the Austrian lady. The music academy where she studies is located in or near Vienna, and Belacqua takes lodging nearby. Every morning she visits him and fixes his tea. One day, over tea, she betrays his trust and rapes him. From this point on their relationship declines; but before it ends, Belacqua receives an invitation from a male friend to visit him in Paris. Belacqua spends a few months in the French capital before returning to Vienna, and fits in a platonic affair with the Syra-Cusa, a tempestuous woman. Meanwhile, the Smeraldina is sending Belacqua fervent love letters ("The Smeraldina's Billet Doux") . After a final disastrous visit to Vienna (the waning lust affair of "Sedendo et Quiescendo") , around New Year's Eve Belacqua returns to Dublin, where he is introduced to the aloof pseudointellectual Alba, who has just shaken off her admirer Jem Higgins (the love letter written by Higgins to Alba is mentioned in "A Wet Night") . They carry on an intense but totally platonic love affair. They go to a party together ("A Wet Night"), after which Belacqua takes Alba home. He reappears in a rainy Dublin street in the early hours of morning. However, the author insists that no sexual intercourse took place. The typescript abruptly ends here.

MORE PRICKS THAN KICKS

This collection of ten short stories was published in London by Chatto and Windus in 1934. Prior to the book's publication only one of the short stories appeared in a somewhat different version, "Dante and the Lobster," in *This Quarter* (December, 1932). The book is now very rare, and I am grateful to Professor Hugh Kenner for the use of his photographed copy of the original edition. Two of the stories from *More Pricks Than Kicks* have been reprinted since their first publication: "Yellow," in *New World Writing*, no. 10 (1956), and "Dante and the Lobster," in the *Evergreen Review*, no. 1 (1957). The ten stories are entitled: "Dante and the Lobster," "Fingal," "Ding-Dong," "A Wet Night," "Love and Lethe," "Walking Out," "What a Misfortune," "The Smeraldina's Billet Doux," "Yellow," and "Draff." They all share the same protagonist, Belacqua Shuah, and show particularly his love life.

SUMMARY

In the opening story, "Dante and the Lobster," the protagonist Belacqua Shuah is preoccupied with his three obligations: lunch, which he prepares meticulously while pondering an impenetrable passage from Dante's *Paradiso*, at the same time casually reflecting on the execution of the murderer, MacCabe; his Italian lesson, to which he goes and where again he debates Dante with his female instructor; and a lobster, which he must deliver to his aunt, and later on watches being boiled alive—to his great consternation. Contrasting divine mercy (Dante's allusion to the man in the moon: Cain with the crown of thorns) and earthly justice (the execution of MacCabe—son of Cain and Abel?) to the martyrdom of the lobster, Beckett sets a highly intellectual but sardonic tone to his book.

The second story, "Fingal," introduces the first of Belacqua's lady loves, the "pretty, hot and witty" Winifred Coates. While taking a stroll in the Dublin countryside, from the top of a hill Belacqua points to the nearby Portrane Lunatic Asylum and tells Winnie: "My heart's right there" (p. 27), thus showing a flagrant aspiration to lunacy. Suddenly he abandons the girl and returns to the city on a stolen bicycle to enjoy a good drink in a "pub" and a "memorable fit" of laughter. This story reveals a corner of Belacqua's tormented mind and his unmotivated eccentricity.

In "Ding-Dong," a narrator-friend of Belacqua appears, who gratuitously relates the hero's anxiety and states how having reached "the last phase of his solipsism, before he toed the line and began to relish the world, with the belief that the best thing he had to do was to move constantly from place to place" (p. 43), Belacqua comes to realize the uselessness of his existence. In this Turgenev-like situation one gains insight into Belacqua's indolent and extravagant temperament. Avoiding all social involvements by moving from one furnished room to another, Belacqua finally ends up in a pub where he buys "four seats in heaven" from a woman peddler.

"A Wet Night," a story of some fifty pages, brings Belacqua, after an evening spent wandering aimlessly in the streets in the rain, to a Christmas Eve party where Alba Perdue begs him to see her home. He gives in easily, and "when Belacqua that uneasy creature came out of Casa Alba in the small hours of the morning" (p. 113), he suffers such a "belly-ache" that he finds himself forced to sit down on the sidewalk until a policeman enjoins him to move on. Here the hero's antisocial attitude bitingly satirizes the pseudointellectual milieu in which he and his friends evolve.

With Ruby Tough in the next story, "Love and Lethe," Belacqua has arranged a suicide pact. Having worked out all the details with precision, he picks up the girl at her house in a huge, fancy, rented car he can hardly drive. They proceed to a secluded spot on a mountainside, but instead of committing the act of *felo de se* as planned, they share a bottle of whisky, forget their intent, and come "together in inevitable nuptial," which amounts to the same thing, since, as the author quotes ironically, "in the words of one competent to sing of the matter, *L'Amour et la Mort*—caesura—*n'est qu'une mesme chose*" (p. 139).

Resigned to go on living, Belacqua appears in the next story, "Walking Out," engaged to be married to Lucy. She is so taken by Belacqua that she follows him, on her jennet, as he takes daily walks in the woods with his bitch to enjoy his favorite pastime: spying on lovers who indulge in *their* favorite intimate pastime. While riding toward her fiancé, who has taken a shortcut, Lucy is struck by a "superb limousine" driven by a drunken lord, and becomes crippled for life, "her beauty dreadfully marred" (p. 154). Nevertheless, they do marry, and spend their domestic life sitting at home playing the gramophone.

In "What a Misfortune," Lucy now being dead, Belacqua directs his attention and passion to Miss Thelma née bboggs. With the help of his faithful friend, Hairy Quin, he prepares for and eventually suffers the wedding ceremony, which, described in comic detail for some fifty pages, represents a social satire of the Irish Protestant bourgeoisie.

However, "Thelma née bboggs perished of sunset and honeymoon that time in connemara. Then shortly after that they suddenly seemed to be all dead, Lucy of course long since, Ruby duly, Winnie to decency, Alba Perdue in the natural course of being seen home" (pp. 255–256). Belacqua then turns to the only available female in sight, a plump German-speaking girl, the Smeraldina, with whom he had previously established a sentimental relationship in *Dream of Fair to Middling Women*. "The Smeraldina's Billet Doux" is presented under the form of a love letter from the German girl. Writing in a most distorted language, misspelling outrageously, mixing German expressions and constructions with her broken English, the Smeraldina reveals her extreme sentimentality and her overflowing passion for Belacqua.

"Yellow" is set in a hospital where Belacqua is to undergo a double surgical operation—of neck and toe. The patient's stream of incoherent thoughts reveals his fear and disgust as he watches the nurses, doctors, medical assistants, and cleaning personnel prepare for his ordeal. He reaches such a state of anxiety that he finds himself pondering a little question: "Was it to be laughter or tears?" (p. 236). Should he laugh at the whole situation like Democritus, or weep like Heraclitus? Eventually Belacqua dies of heart failure on the operating table; the doctor, who was in great form—he had just returned from a wedding ceremony—"had clean forgotten to auscultate him!" (p. 252).

In the final story, "Draff," Mrs. Shuah, none other than the German Smeraldina, is reading Belacqua's obituary in the newspaper when Hairy Quin, Belacqua's best friend, comes in to help with the last details of the funeral. Having dutifully attended to Belacqua's burial, they turn to each other for consolation: "Why not come with me," says Hairy, "now that all this has happened and be my love?" The Smeraldina fails to understand at first, and only after repeated and involved explanations, to the point where poor Hairy "conked out," does she grasp Hairy's intention and murmur: "Perhaps after all, this is what darling Bel would wish" (pp. 276–277). The cemetery groundkeeper watching the scene cannot decide whether it should be termed romantic or classical; "perhaps classico-romantic would be the fairest estimate," he concludes. Satisfied, he sings a little song, enjoys a bottle of stout, wipes away a tear, and makes himself comfortable. An ironical statement, no doubt spoken by the omniscient author, closes the book: "So it goes in the world" (p. 278).

BIBLIOGRAPHY

BIBLIOGRAPHY

NOTE: This bibliography consists of two sections—a chronology (immediately following) and a selected bibliography of Beckett criticism.

A Chronology of Beckett's Works

1929

Dante . . . Bruno. Vico . . Joyce. (Essay on Joyce.)
First published in *Our Exagmination Round His Factification for Incamination of Work in Progress*. Paris: Shakespeare and Co., 1929. Pp. 3–22. Reprinted in *Transition*, no. 16–17 (June, 1929), 242–253. Reissued in London: Faber and Faber, 1936; New York: New Directions, 1939, 1962.
Assumption. (Short story.)
Transition, no. 16–17 (June, 1929), 268–271. Reprinted in *Transition Workshop* (New York, 1949). Pp. 41–43.

1930

For Future Reference. (Poem.)
Transition, no. 19–20 (June, 1930), 342–343.
Whoroscope. (Poem.)
Paris: Hours Press. 6 pp. (98 lines, 17 footnotes). Reprinted in *Poems in English*. London: Calder, 1961; New York: Grove Press, 1963.

1931

Anna Livia Plurabelle. (Translation from James Joyce with Alfred Péron.)
Nouvelle Revue Française, no. 212 (May, 1931), 633–646.
Proust. (Essay on Marcel Proust's *A la recherche du temps perdu*.)
London: Chatto and Windus. 72 pp. Reprinted by Grove Press New York, 1957; Calder, London, 1958.
Return to the Vestry. (Poem.)
The New Review, I, no. 3 (Aug.–Oct., 1931), 98–99.
Alba. (Poem.)
Dublin Magazine, VI, no. 4 (Oct.–Dec., 1931), 4. Included in *Echo's Bones*.
Text. (Poem.)
The New Review, I, no. 4 (Winter, 1931–1932), 338–339.

1932

Dream of Fair to Middling Women. (Unfinished novel.)
Unpublished manuscript written in 1932. 214 pp.
Sedendo et Quiesciendo [*sic*]. (Short story.)
Transition, no. 21 (March, 1932), 13–20. (From *Dream of Fair to Middling Women*.)
Text. (Prose fragment.)
The New Review, II, no. 5 (April, 1932), 57. (Excerpt from *Dream of Fair to Middling Women*.)
Dante and the Lobster. (Short story.)
This Quarter (Dec., 1932), pp. 222–236. Revised version included in *More Pricks Than Kicks*, 1934.

1934

Home Olga. (Poem acrostic on James Joyce's name.)
Contempo, III (Feb., 1934), 3. Reprinted in Richard Ellman's *James Joyce*. New York: Oxford University Press, 1959. P. 714.
More Pricks Than Kicks. (Collection of ten short stories.)
London: Chatto and Windus. 278 pp. Titles of stories are: "Dante and the Lobster" (reprinted in *Evergreen Review*, I, no. 1, 1957, 24–36), "Fingal," "Ding-Dong," "A Wet Night," "Love and Lethe," "Walking out," "What a Misfortune," "The Smeraldina's Billet Doux," "Yellow" (reprinted in *New World Writing*, no. 10 [New York: Mentor, 1956], pp. 108–119), "Draff."
Gnome. (Poem.)
Dublin Magazine, IX, no. 3 (July–Sept., 1934), 8 (4 lines).
Case in a Thousand. (Short story.)
The Bookman, no. 515 (Aug., 1934), 241–242.

1935

Echo's Bones and Other Precipitates. (Collected poems.)
Paris: Europa Press. 26 pp. Reprinted with German translations by Eva Hesse in *Samuel Beckett: Gedichte*, Limes Verlag. ed., Wiesbaden, 1959; and in *Poems in English*, London: Calder, 1961; and New York: Grove Press, 1963.

1936

Malacoda. (Poem from *Echo's Bones*.)
Transition, no. 24 (June, 1936), 8. Reprinted in *Transition Workshop* (New York, 1949). P. 204.
Enueg II and Dortmunder. (Poems from *Echo's Bones*.)
Transition, no. 24 (June, 1936), 8–10.
Cascando. (Poem in three parts.)

Dublin Magazine, XI, no. 4 (Oct.–Dec., 1936) , 3–4. Reprinted in *Gedichte* and *Poems in English.*
Seven Poems by Paul Eluard. (Translated from the French.)
  Thorns of Thunder, ed. G. Reavey. London: Europa Press and Stanley Nott, 1936. First published in *This Quarter* (Sept., 1932) , 86–98.

1938

Murphy. (Novel.)
  London: Routledge. 282 pp. Reprinted in New York: Grove Press, 1957; London: Calder, 1963.
Denis Devlin. (Review of Denis Devlin's *Intercessions.*)
  Transition, no. 27 (April–May, 1938) , 289–294.
Ooftish. (Poem.)
  Transition, no. 27 (April–May, 1938) , 33.

1945

Mercier et Camier. (Unpublished novel in French.)
  Written, according to Beckett, in 1945. 150 pp. Two excerpts entitled "Madden" and "The Umbrella" were translated into English with the author's permission by Hugh Kenner and Raymond Federman, published in *Spectrum,* IV, no. 1 (Winter, 1960) , 3–11.
Premier Amour. (Unpublished short story in French.)
  Written, according to Beckett, in 1945. 32 pp.
La Peinture des van Velde, ou le Monde et le pantalon. (Article.)
  Cahiers d'Art, Paris (1945–1946) , pp. 349–356.

1946

Suite. (Short story.)
  Les Temps Modernes, no. 10 (July, 1946) , 107–119. Revised version entitled "La Fin" in *Nouvelles et Textes pour rien,* 1955.
Poèmes 38–39. (Twelve poems numbered I to XIII; number XI is missing.)
  Les Temps Modernes, no. 14 (Nov., 1946) , 288–293. Reprinted in *Gedichte,* 1959, pp. 54–76 (translations by Elmar Tophoven) .
L'Expulsé. (Short story.)
  Fontaine, X, no. 57 (Dec., 1946-Jan., 1947) , 685–708. Revised version published under the same title in *Nouvelles et Textes pour rien,* 1955.

1947

Eleutheria. (Unpublished three-act play.)
  Written, according to Beckett, in 1947–1948. 133 pp.
Murphy. (Novel translated into French by the author.)
  Paris: Bordas. 201 pp. Reprinted in Paris: Les Editions de Minuit, 1953.

1948

Peintres de L'Empêchement. (Article on Bram and Geer van Velde.)
Derrière le Miroir, no. 11–12 (June, 1948), 4–5, 7.
Three Poems. (With French versions.)
Transitions 48, no. 2 (June, 1948), 96–97. Reprinted (English texts only) in *Poetry Ireland*, no. 5 (April, 1949), 8; and in *Gedichte* (French texts with German translations by Elmar Tophoven), pp. 80–90.

1949

Three Dialogues. (Discussion between Samuel Beckett and Georges Duthuit on the painters Tal Coat, Masson, and Bram van Velde.)
Transition 49, no. 5 (Dec., 1949), 97–103. Extracts translated into French by Samuel Beckett were reprinted in *Nouvelle N. R. F.*, no. 54 (June, 1957), 1125–1126, and in the book *Bram van Velde*. Paris: Georges Fall, 1958.

1951

Molloy. (Novel in French.)
Paris: Editions de Minuit. 272 pp. Reprinted with the story "L'Expulsé" in the collection *Le Monde en 10–18*. Paris: U. G. E., 1963.
Malone meurt. (Novel in French.)
Paris: Editions de Minuit. 217 pp. Excerpts previously published in *Les Temps Modernes* (Sept., 1951), 385–416.

1952

En Attendant Godot. (Two-act play in French.)
Paris: Editions de Minuit. 163 pp. Scholarly edition annotated by Germaine Brée and Eric Schoenfeld. New York: Macmillan, 1963. 120 pp.

1953

L'Innommable. (Novel in French.)
Paris: Editions de Minuit. 262 pp. Excerpt entitled "Mahood" published in *Nouvelle Nouvelle Revue Française* (Feb., 1953), pp. 214–234.
Watt. (Novel in English.)
Paris: Olympia Press. 279 pp. Reprinted by Olympia Press, 1958; New York: Grove Press, 1959; London: Calder, 1963. Excerpts published in *Envoy*, I, no. 2 (Jan., 1950), 11–19; *Irish Writing*, no. 17 (Dec., 1951), 11–16, and no. 22 (March, 1953), 16–24; *Merlin*, I, no. 3 (Winter, 1952–1953), 118–126.

1954

Hommage à Jack B. Yeats. (Article.)
  Les Lettres Nouvelles, no. 14 (April, 1954), 619–620.
The End. (Short story translated from the French.)
  Merlin, II, no. 3 (Summer–Autumn, 1954), 144–159. Translated
  by Richard Seaver in collaboration with the author. Reprinted
  in *Evergreen Review,* IV, no. 15 (Nov.–Dec., 1960), 22–41;
  Writers in Revolt (New York: Frederick Fell, 1963), pp. 348–
  366.
Waiting for Godot. (Two-act play translated from the French.)
  New York: Grove Press, 1954; London: Faber and Faber, 1956.
  Translated by the author.

1955

Nouvelles et Textes pour rien. (Collection of short stories and
  texts.)
  Paris: Editions de Minuit. 220 pp. Contains three stories,
  "L'Expulsé," "Le Calmant," "La Fin," and thirteen texts num-
  bered from I to XIII. A note from the editor states that the
  Nouvelles were written in 1945, the *Textes* in 1950.
Trois Poèmes. (Poems.)
  Cahiers des Saisons, no. 2 (Oct., 1955), 115–116. Reprinted in
  Gedichte, 1959 (German translations by Elmar Tophoven).
Molloy. (Novel translated from the French.)
  Paris: Olympia Press; New York: Grove Press. 241 pp. Trans-
  lated by Patrick Bowles in collaboration with the author.
  Excerpts previously published in *Merlin,* II, no. 2 (Autumn,
  1953), 89–103; *Paris Review,* no. 5 (Spring, 1954), 124–135;
  New World Writing, no. 5 (April, 1954), 316–323.

1956

Malone Dies. (Novel translated from the French.)
  New York: Grove Press, 1956; London: Calder, 1958; Har-
  mondsworth: Penguin Books, 1962. 120 pp. Translated by the
  author. Excerpts in *Transition 50,* no. 6 (Oct., 1950), 103–106;
  Irish Writing, no. 34 (Spring, 1956).
Yellow. (Short story.)
  New World Writing, no. 10 (New York: Mentor, 1956), 108–
  119. Reprinted from *More Pricks Than Kicks,* 1934.

1957

Fin de partie. (One-act play.) Acte Sans paroles. (Mime.)
  Paris: Editions de Minuit. 124 pp. (*Fin de partie,* 108 pp., *Acte
  sans paroles,* 12 pp.) *Fin de partie* was reprinted in *Vingt pièces
  en un acte,* ed. O. Aslan. Paris: Seghers, 1959.

All That Fall. (Radio play in one act.)
>London: Faber and Faber. 37 pp. New York: Grove Press. 59 pp.
Reprinted in *Krapp's Last Tape and Other Dramatic Pieces.*
New York: Grove Press, 1960.

Tous ceux qui tombent. (Radio play translated from the English.)
>Paris: Editions de Minuit. 77 pp. Translated by Robert Pinget
and the author. Previously published in *Les Lettres Nouvelles,*
no. 47 (March, 1957), 321–351.

Ten Poems. (From *Echo's Bones.*)
>*Evergreen Review,* I, no. 1 (1957), 179–192. Includes: "The
Vulture," "Enueg I," "Enueg II," "Sanies I," "Sanies II," "Se-
rena I," "Serena II," "Serena III," "Da Tagte es," "Echo's
Bones."

From an Abandoned Work. (Prose fragment.)
>*Evergreen Review,* I, no. 3 (1957), 83–91. Reprinted in Lon-
don: Faber and Faber, 1958. Earlier version published in *Trinity News,* III, no. 17 (1956), 4.

1958

The Unnamable. (Novel translated from the French.)
>New York: Grove Press. 179 pp. Translated by the author. Pub-
lished in one volume with *Molloy* and *Malone Dies* in 1959 in
New York: Grove Press; London: Calder; Paris: Olympia Press.
418 pp. Excerpts published in *Texas Quarterly,* no. 2, (Spring,
1958); *Chicago Review,* XII, no. 2 (Summer, 1958); *Spectrum,*
II, no. 1 (Winter, 1958).

Fourteen Letters. (From Samuel Beckett to Alan Schneider.)
>*The Village Voice.* New York, March 19, 1958. Published with
Beckett's permission, these letters (the first dated 27 December
1955, the last 4 March 1958) retrace the genesis of *Fin de
partie.*

Endgame and Act without Words. (One-act play and mime translated from the French.)
>New York: Grove Press. 91 pp. London: Faber and Faber. 60 pp.

Anthology of Mexican Poetry. (Translations from the Spanish.)
>Bloomington: Indiana University Press, 1958 (UNESCO Publi-
cation). 213 pp. Compiled by Octavio Paz; translated by Samuel Beckett. Reprinted in London: Thames and Hudson, 1959.

Krapp's Last Tape. (One-act play.)
>*Evergreen Review,* II, no. 5 (Summer, 1958), 13–24. Reprinted
in *Krapp's Last Tape and Other Dramatic Pieces,* 1960.

1959

Gedichte. (Bilingual collection of poems.)
>Wiesbaden: Limes Verlag, 1959. Contains *Echo's Bones,* twelve
French poems written 1937–1939, and six written 1947–1949.

La Dernière Bande and Cendres. (One-act play and radio play.)
Paris: Editions de Minuit. 72 pp. *La Dernière bande* was trans-
lated by Pierre Leyris and the author, *Cendres* by Robert Pinget
and the author. First published in *Les Lettres Nouvelles,*
no. 1 (March 4, 1959), 5–13, and no. 36 (Dec. 30, 1959), 3–14.
Text for Nothing I. (Translated from the French.)
Evergreen Review, III, no. 9 (Summer, 1959), 21–24. Trans-
lated by the author.
Act without Words II. (Mime translated from the French.)
New Departures, no. 1 (Summer, 1959), 89–91. Reprinted in
Krapp's Last Tape and Other Dramatic Pieces, 1960.
L'Image. (Prose fragment from *Comment c'est.*)
X (London), I, no. 1 (Nov., 1959), 35–37.
Embers. (Radio play.)
Evergreen Review, III, no. 10 (Nov.–Dec., 1959), 24–41. Re-
printed in *Krapp's Last Tape and Other Dramatic Pieces,* 1960.

1960

Krapp's Last Tape and Other Dramatic Pieces. (Collected plays.)
New York: Grove Press. 141 pp. Contains *Krapp's Last Tape,
All That Fall, Embers, Act without Words I, Act without
Words II.*
From an Unabandoned Work. (Prose fragment.)
Evergreen Review, IV, no. 14 (Sept.–Oct., 1960), 58–65. Ex-
cerpts from *Comment c'est* translated by the author.
Madden and The Umbrella. (Translations from an unpublished
novel.)
Spectrum, IV, no. 1 (Winter, 1960), 3–11. Excerpts from
Mercier et Camier translated by Hugh Kenner and Raymond
Federman, with the author's permission.
The Old Tune. (Translation from the French.)
Paris: Editions de Minuit. Bilingual edition containing the
original text of a radio play by Robert Pinget, *La Manivelle,*
with the English translation by Beckett, *The Old Tune.* 62 pp.
Beckett's English translation reprinted in *Evergreen Review,*
V, no. 17 (March–April, 1961), 47–60.
Bram van Velde. (A study of the painter's work.)
New York: Grove Press. 64 pp. In collaboration with Georges
Duthuit and Jacques Putnam. Translated from the French by
Samuel Beckett and Olive Classe.

1961

Comment c'est. (Novel in French.)
Paris: Editions de Minuit. 177 pp. Excerpt differing slightly
published in *L VII* (Brussels), no. 1 (Summer, 1960), 9–13.

Happy Days. (Two-act play.)
New York: Grove Press. 64 pp. Reprinted in London: Faber
and Faber, 1962; and in *Plays and Players*, London (Nov.,
1962) .

1962

The Expelled. (Short story translated from the French.)
Evergreen Review, VI, no. 22 (Jan.–Feb., 1962) , 8–20. Trans-
lated by Richard Seaver in collaboration with the author.
From How It Is. (Prose fragment.)
Paris Review, no. 28 (Summer–Fall, 1962) , 113–116. Excerpt
from the English version of *Comment c'est*. Translated by the
author.
Words and Music. (Radio play.)
Evergreen Review, VI, no. 27 (Nov.–Dec., 1962) , 34–43.

1963

Poems in English. (Collected poems.)
New York: Grove Press. 64 pp. Previously published in London:
Calder, 1961. 53 pp.
Cascando. (Radio play.)
Evergreen Review, VII, no. 30 (May–June, 1963) , 47–57. Trans-
lated from the French by the author.
Oh les beaux jours. (Two-act play translated from the English.)
Paris: Editions de Minuit. 89 pp. Translated by the author.

1964

Play. (One-act play.)
London: Faber and Faber. 48 pp. Includes "Words and Music"
and "Cascando."
Second Testament. (Poem translated from the French.)
"Le deuxième testament" by Alain Bosquet in *Alain Bosquet:
Selected Poems* (Bilingual Edition) . New York: New Direc-
tions, 1963. Pp. 60–63. Translated by Samuel Beckett.
How It Is. (Novel translated from the French.)
New York: Grove Press. 147 pp. London: Faber and Faber.
160 pp. Translated by the author. Excerpt in *Transatlantic Re-
view*, no. 13 (1963) , 5–15.

A Selected Bibliography of Beckett Criticism

Abel, Lionel. "Joyce the Father, Beckett the Son," *New Leader*,
XLII, no. 46 (Dec. 14, 1959) , 26–27.
Allsop, Kenneth. *The Angry Decade*. London: Peter Owen, 1958.
Pp. 37–42.
Alter, André. *"En Attendant Godot* n'était pas une impasse.

Beckett le prouve dans sa seconde piéce," *Le Figaro Littéraire,* Jan. 12, 1957, Pp. 1, 4.

Anders, Günther. "Sein Ohnt Zeit zu Beckett's Stück *En Attendant Godot,*" *Die Antiquiertheit des Menschen Über die Seele im Zeitalter der Zweiten industriellen Revolution.* Munich: C. H. Beck, 1956. Pp. 213–231.

Anon. "Puzzling about Godot," *Times Literary Supplement,* April 12, 1956, p. 221.

———. "The Train Stops," *Times Literary Supplement,* Sept. 6, 1957, p. 604.

———. "The Play's the Thing," *San Quentin News,* Nov. 28, 1957, p. 1.

———. "Paradise of Indignity," *Times Literary Supplement,* March 28, 1958, p. 168.

———. "Life in the Mud," *Times Literary Supplement,* April 7, 1961, p. 213.

———. "The Core of the Onion," *Times Literary Supplement,* Dec. 21, 1962, p. 988.

Anouilh, Jean. "Du Chapitre des chaises," *Le Figaro,* April 23, 1956, p. 1.

Atkinson, Brooks. "*Endgame,*" *New York Times,* Jan. 29, 1958, p. 32.

———. "Abstract Drama," *New York Times,* Feb. 16, 1958, sec. 2, p. 1.

———. "Village Vagrants," *New York Times,* Jan. 31, 1960, sec. 10, p. 1.

Bajini, Sandro. "Beckett o l'emblema totale," *Verri,* III, no. 2 (April, 1959), 70–88.

Barbour, Thomas. "Beckett and Ionesco," *Hudson Review,* II (Summer, 1958), 271–277.

Barrett, William. "Real Love Abides," *New York Times Book Review,* Sept. 16, 1956, p. 5.

———. "The Works of Samuel Beckett Hold Clues for an Intriguing Riddle," *Saturday Review of Literature,* XL (June 8, 1957), 15–16.

———. "I've Been Reading," *Columbia University Forum,* II, no. 2 (Winter, 1959), 44–48.

Bataille, Georges. "Le Silence de Molloy," *Critique,* XLVIII (May 15, 1951), 387–396.

Beigbeder, Marc. "Le Théâtre à l'âge métaphysique," *L'Age Nouveau,* IX, no. 85 (Jan., 1954), 30–41.

———. *Le Théâtre en France depuis la Libération.* Paris: Bordas, 1959. Pp. 142–144.

Belmont, Georges. "Un Classicisme retrouvé," *La Table Ronde,* no. 62 (Feb., 1953), 171–174.

Bentley, Eric. "The Talent of Samuel Beckett," *New Republic*, CXXXIV, no. 20 (May 14, 1956), 20–21.

Bernard, Marc. "Review of Fin de partie," *Les Nouvelles Littéraires*, May 9, 1957, p. 10.

Blanchot, Maurice. "Où maintenant? Qui maintenant?" *Nouvelle Nouvelle Revue Française*, II, no. 10 (Oct., 1953), 678–686.

———. *Le Livre à venir*. Paris: Gallimard, 1959. Pp. 256–260.

Bloch-Michel, Jean. *Le Présent de l'indicatif*. Paris: Gallimard, 1963. *Passim.*

Boisdeffre, Pierre de. *Une Histoire vivante de la littérature d'aujourd'hui*. Paris: Le Livre Contemporain, 1959. Pp. 303–304, 682–684.

———. *Une Histoire vivante de la littérature d'aujourd'hui*. Paris: Perrin, 1962.

Bonnefoi, Geneviéve. "Textes pour rien?" *Les Lettres Nouvelles*, no. 36 (March, 1956), 424–430.

Bowles, Patrick. "How Beckett Sees the Universe: *Molloy*," *Listener*, LIX, no. 1525 (June 19, 1958), 1011–1012.

Boyle, Kevin. "Molloy: Icon of the Negative," *Westwind*, V, no. 1 (Fall, 1961).

Brick, Allan. "The Madman in his Cell: Joyce, Beckett, Nabokov and the Stereotypes," *Massachusetts Review*, I, no. 1 (Oct., 1959), 40–55.

Briggs, Ray. "Samuel Beckett's World in Waiting," *Saturday Review of Literature*, XL (June 8, 1957), 14.

Brooke-Rose, Christine. "Samuel Beckett and the Anti-novel," *London Magazine*, V, no. 12 (Dec., 1958), 38–46.

Capron, Marcelle. "Fin de partie," *Combat*, May 2, 1957, p. 2.

Chadwick, C. "*Waiting for Godot:* A Logical Approach," *Symposium*, XIV, no. 4 (Winter, 1960), 252–257.

Champigny, Robert. "Interprétation de *En Attendant Godot*," *PMLA*, LXXV, no. 3 (June, 1960), 329–331.

Chapsal, Madeleine. "Un Célèbre inconnu," *L'Express*, Feb. 8, 1957, pp. 26–27.

Clurman, Harold. "Theater," *Nation* (May 5, 1956), pp. 387–390.

———. *Lies Like Truth*. New York: Macmillan, 1958. Pp. 220–222, 224–225.

Cmarada, Geraldine. "*Malone Dies:* A Round of Consciousness," *Symposium*, XIV, no. 3 (Fall, 1960), 199–212.

Cohn, Ruby. "The Comedy of Samuel Beckett: 'Something old, something new—,'" *Yale French Studies*, no. 23 (Summer, 1959), 11–17.

———. "Still Novel," *Yale French Studies*, no. 24 (Fall, 1959), 48–53.

————. "Preliminary Observations," *Perspective,* XI, no. 3 (Autumn, 1959), 119–131.

————. "A Note on Beckett, Dante and Geulincx," *Comparative Literature,* XII, no. 1 (Winter, 1960), 93–94.

————. "*Watt* in the Light of *The Castle,*" *Comparative Literature,* XIII, no. 2 (Spring, 1961), 154–166.

————. *Samuel Beckett: The Comic Gamut.* New Brunswick: Rutgers University Press, 1962. 340 pp.

————. "Comment c'est: de quoi rire," *French Review,* XXXV, no. 6 (May, 1962), 563–569.

————. "Plays and Players in the Plays of Samuel Beckett," *Yale French Studies,* no. 29 (Spring–Summer, 1962), 43–48.

————. "Philosophical Fragments in the Works of Samuel Beckett," *Criticism,* VI, no. 1 (Winter, 1964), 33–43.

Corrigan, Robert W. "The Theatre in Search of a Fix," *Tulane Drama Review,* V, no. 4 (June, 1961), 21–35.

Curtis, Anthony. "Mood of the Month—IV," *London Magazine,* V, no. 5 (May, 1958), 60–65.

Davie, Donald. "Kinds of Comedy: All That Fall," *Spectrum,* II, no. 1 (Winter, 1958), 25–31.

Davin, Dan. "Mr. Beckett's Everymen," *Irish Writing 34* (Spring, 1956), pp. 36–39.

Delye, Huguette. *Samuel Beckett, ou la philosophie de l'absurde.* Aix-en-Provence: Faculté des Lettres, 1960.

Dhomme, Sylvain. "Des Auteurs à l'avant-garde du théâtre," *Cahiers de la Compagnie Madeleine Renaud-Jean-Louis Barrault,* III, no. 13 (1955), 112–118.

Dobrée, Bonamy. "The London Theatre," *Sewanee Review,* LXVI, no. 1 (Winter, 1958), 146–160.

Dort, Bernard. "Godot," *Les Temps Modernes,* VIII, no. 90 (May, 1953), 1842–1845.

Drews, Wolfgang. "Die Grossen Unsichtbaren: VII: Godot," *Theater und Zeit,* VI, no. 6 (Feb., 1959), 107–109.

Dreyfus, Dina. "Vraies et fausses énigmes," *Mercure de France,* no. 1130 (Oct., 1957), 268–285.

Driver, Tom F. "Beckett by the Madeleine," *Columbia University Forum,* IV, no. 3 (Summer, 1961), 21–25.

Eastman, Richard M. "The Strategy of Samuel Beckett's Endgame," *Modern Drama,* II, no. 1 (May, 1959), 36–44.

Ellman, Richard. *James Joyce.* New York: Oxford University Press, 1959. *Passim.*

Esslin, Martin. "The Theater of the Absurd," *Tulane Drama Review,* IV, no. 4 (May, 1960), 3–15.

————. "Samuel Beckett," in *The Novelist as Philosopher.* Ed. John Cruickshank. London: Oxford University Press, 1962. Pp. 128–146.

Federman, Raymond. "Comment c'est," *French Review*, XXXIV, no. 6 (May, 1961), 594–595.

———. "The Fiction of Mud," in *On Contemporary Literature*. Ed. Richard Kostelanetz. New York: Avon Books, 1964. Pp. 255–261.

Fiedler, Leslie. "Search for Peace in a World Lost," *New York Times*, April 14, 1957, sec. 7, p. 27.

Fletcher, John. "Comment c'est," *Lettres Nouvelles*, no. 13 (April, 1961), 167–171.

———. "Samuel Beckett et Jonathan Swift: vers une étude comparée," *Annales publiées par la Faculté des Lettres de Toulouse, Littératures X*, Année XI, fasc. 1 (1962), 81–117.

———. "Beckett's verse: Influences and Parallels," *French Review*, XXXVII, no. 3 (Jan., 1964), 320–331.

———. "Beckett et Proust," *Annales publiées par la Faculté des Lettres de Toulouse, Caliban I* (Jan., 1964), Pp. 89–100.

———. *The Novels of Samuel Beckett*. London: Chatto and Windus, 1964. 256 pp.

Fowlie, Wallace. "The New French Theatre," *Sewanee Review*, LXVII, no. 4 (Autumn, 1959), 643–657.

———. *Dionysus in Paris*. New York: Meridian, 1960. Pp. 210–217.

Frank, Nino. "Scherzi di Beckett," *Il Mondo*, VII, no. 40 (Oct. 4, 1955), 10.

Fraser, G. S. "Waiting for Godot," *Times Literary Supplement*, Feb. 10, 1956 (published anon). Reprinted in *English Critical Essays: Twentieth Century*. London, 1958. Pp. 324–332.

Friedman, Melvin J. "The Achievement of Samuel Beckett," *Books Abroad*, XXXIII, no. 3 (Summer, 1959), 278–280.

———. "Samuel Beckett and the Nouveau Roman," *Wisconsin Studies in Contemporary Literature*, I, no. 2 (Spring–Summer, 1960), 22–36.

———. "The Novels of Samuel Beckett: An Amalgam of Joyce and Proust," *Comparative Literature*, XII, no. 1 (Winter, 1960), 47–58.

———. "Book Reviews," *Wisconsin Studies in Contemporary Literature*, III, no. 3 (Fall, 1962), 100–106.

Frye, Northrop. "The Nightmare Life in Death," *Hudson Review*, XIII, no. 3 (Autumn, 1960), 442–449.

Gerard, Martin. "Molloy Becomes Unnamable," *X*, I, no. 4 (Oct., 1960), 314–319.

Gessner, Niklaus. *Die Unzulänglichkeit der Sprache*. Zurich: Juris-Verlag, 1957. 127 pp.

Gibbs, Wolcott. "Enough Is Enough Is Enough," *New Yorker*, XXII (May 5, 1956), 83–84.

Giraud, Raymond. "Unrevolt among the Unwriters in France Today," *Yale French Studies*, no. 24 (Summer, 1959), 11–17.

Gold, Herbert. "Beckett: Style and Desire," *Nation*, CLXXXIII (Nov. 10, 1956), 397–399.

Goth, Maja. *Franz Kafka et les lettres francaises*. Paris: José Corti, 1956. Pp. 120–122, 255.

Gransden, K. W. "The Dustman Cometh," *Encounter*, XI (July, 1958), 84–86.

Gray, Ronald. *"Waiting for Godot*: A Christian Interpretation," *Listener*, LVII (Jan. 24, 1957), 160–161.

Gregory, Horace. "Beckett's Dying Gladiators," *Commonweal*, LXV (Oct. 26, 1956), 88–92. Reprinted in *The Dying Gladiators and Other Essays*. New York: Grove Press, 1961. Pp. 165–176.

———. "Prose and Poetry in Samuel Beckett," *Commonweal*, LXXI (Oct. 30, 1959), 162–163.

Grenier, Jean. *"En Attendant Godot,"* *Le Disque Vert*, I, no. 3 (July–Aug., 1953), 81–86.

Gresset, Michel. "Le 'parce Que' Chez Faulkner et le 'donc' chez Beckett," *Lettres Nouvelles*, no. 19 (Nov., 1961), 124–138.

Grossvogel, David I. *The Self-conscious Stage in Modern French Drama*. New York: Columbia University Press, 1958. Pp. 324–334.

———. *Four Playwrights and a Postscript: Brecht, Ionesco, Beckett, Genet*. Ithaca, New York: Cornell University Press, 1962. Pp. 86–131.

Guggenheim, Peggy. *Out of This Century*. New York: Dial Press, 1946. *Passim*.

———. *Confessions of an Art Addict*. New York: Macmillan, 1960.

Guicharnaud, Jacques. *Modern French Theater from Giraudoux to Beckett*. New Haven: Yale University Press, 1961. Pp. 193–220.

Hamilton, Carol. "Portrait in Old Age: The Image of Man in Beckett's Trilogy," *Western Humanities Review*, XVI, no. 2 (Spring, 1962), 157–165.

Hamilton, Kenneth. "Boon or Thorn? Cary and Beckett on Human Life," *Dalhousie Review*, XXXVIII, no. 4 (Winter, 1959), 433–442.

Hartley, Anthony. "Samuel Beckett," *Spectator*, CLXXXI (Oct. 23, 1953), 458–459.

Harvey, Lawrence E. "Art and the Existential in *En Attendant Godot*," *PMLA*, LXXV, no. 1 (March, 1960), 137–146.

Hayes, Richard. "Nothing," *Commonweal*, LXIV, no. 8 (May 25, 1956), 203.

Hesla, David H. "The Shape of Chaos: A Reading of Beckett's *Watt*," *Critique*, VI, no. 1 (Spring, 1963), 85–105.

Hicks, Granville. "Beckett's World," *Saturday Review of Literature*, XLI (Oct. 4, 1958), 14.

Hobson, Harold. "Samuel Beckett, Dramatist of the Year," *International Theatre Annual*, no. 1 (London, 1956).

Hoefer, Jacqueline. "Watt," *Perspective,* XI, no. 3 (Autumn, 1959), 166–182.

Hoffman, Frederick, J. *Samuel Beckett: The Language of Self.* Carbondale: Southern Illinois University Press, 1962. 177 pp.

Hooker, Ward. "Irony and Absurdity in the Avant-Garde Theater," *Kenyon Review,* XXII, no. 3 (Summer, 1960), 436–454.

Hubert, Renée R. "The Couple and the Performance in Samuel Beckett's Plays," *L'Esprit Créateur,* II, no. 4 (Winter, 1962), 175–180.

Jacobsen, Josephine, and William R. Mueller. *The Testament of Samuel Beckett.* New York: Hill and Wang, 1964. 178 pp.

Johnston, Denis. "Waiting with Beckett," *Irish Writing,* no. 34 (Spring, 1956), 23–27.

Karl, Frederick R. "Waiting for Beckett," *Sewanee Review,* LXIX, no. 4 (Autumn, 1961), 661–676.

Kennebeck, Edwin. "The Moment of Cosmic Ennui," *Commonweal,* LXI, no. 13 (Dec. 31, 1954), 365–366.

Kenner, Hugh. "Samuel Beckett vs. Fiction," *National Review* (Oct. 11, 1958). Pp. 248–249.

———. "The Beckett Landscape," *Spectrum,* II, no. 1 (Winter, 1958), 8–24.

———. "The Cartesian Centaur," *Perspective,* XI, no. 3 (Autumn, 1959), 132–141.

———. "The Absurdity of Fiction," *Griffin,* VIII, no. 10 (Nov., 1959), 13–16.

———. "Samuel Beckett: The Rational Domain," *Forum,* III, no. 4 (Summer, 1960), 39–47.

———. "Voices in the Night," *Spectrum,* V, no. 1 (Spring, 1961), 3–20.

———. *Samuel Beckett: A Critical Study.* New York: Grove Press, 1961. 208 pp.

———. *Flaubert, Joyce and Beckett: The Stoic Comedians.* Boston: Beacon Press, 1963. 107 pp.

Kermode, Frank. "Beckett, Snow and Pure Poverty," *Encounter,* XV, no. 1 (July, 1960), 73–77.

Kern, Edith. "Drama Stripped for Inaction: Beckett's Godot," *Yale French Studies,* no. 14 (1954–1955), 41–47.

———. "Moran-Molloy: The Hero as Author," *Perspective,* XI, no. 3 (Autumn, 1959), 183–193.

———. "Beckett's Knight of Infinite Resignation," *Yale French Studies,* no. 29 (Spring–Summer, 1962), 49–56.

Kott, Jan. "Le Roi Lear autrement dit Fin de partie," *Les Temps Modernes,* no. 194 (July, 1962), 48–77.

L. J. "En attendant Godot de Samuel Beckett, au Théâtre Hébertot," *Le Figaro Littéraire,* June 30, 1956, p. 12.

Lalou, René. "*Malone meurt,*" *Les Nouvelles Littéraires,* Nov. 8, 1951, p. 6.

Lamont, Rosette C. "The Metaphysical Farce: Beckett and Ionesco," *French Review,* XXXII, no. 4 (Feb., 1959), 319–328.

Lebesque, Morvan. "Le Théâtre aux enfers: Artaud, Beckett et quelques autres," *Cahiers de la Compagnie Madeleine Renaud-Jean-Louis Barrault,* VI, nos. 22–23 (1958), 191–196.

Lee, Warren. "The Bitter Pill of Samuel Beckett," *Chicago Review,* X, no. 4 (Winter, 1957), 77–87.

Lemarchand, Jacques. "Fin de partie," *Le Figaro Littéraire,* May 11, 1957, p. 14.

———. "Fin de partie," *Nouvelle Nouvelle Revue Française,* IX, no. 54 (June, 1957), 1085–1089.

Leventhal, A. J. "Mr. Beckett's *En Attendant Godot,*" *Dublin Magazine,* XXX, no. 2 (April–June, 1954), 11–16.

———. "Close of Play: Reflections on Samuel Beckett's New Work for the French Theatre," *Dublin Magazine,* XXXII, no. 2. (April–June, 1957), 18–22.

———. "Samuel Beckett, Poet and Pessimist," *Listener,* LVII (May 9, 1957), 746–747.

Littlejohn, David. "The Anti-realists," *Daedalus,* XCII, no. 2 (Spring, 1963), 250–264.

Loy, J. Robert. " 'Things' in Recent French Literature," *PMLA,* LXXI (1956), 27–41.

Lukacs, Georges. *La Signification présente du réalisme critique.* Paris: Gallimard, 1960 (Essais XCV). *Passim.*

McCoy, Charles. "Waiting for Godot: A Biblical Approach," *Florida Review,* no. 2 (Spring, 1958), 63–72.

Maciel, Luis Carlos. *Samuel Beckett et a Solidão.* Porto Alegre (Brasil) : Cadernos do Rio Grande, 1959. 111 pp.

Magny, Olivier de. "Samuel Beckett ou Job abandonné," *Monde Nouveau-Paru,* XI, no. 97 (Feb., 1956), 92–99.

———. "Panorama d'une nouvelle littérature romanesque," *Esprit,* XXVI, nos. 7–8 (July–Aug., 1958), 3–18.

———. "Ecriture de l'impossible," *Les Lettres Nouvelles,* no. 13 (Feb., 1963), 125–138.

Mailer, Norman. *Advertisements for Myself.* New York: New American Library, 1959. Pp. 289–294.

Mannes, Marya. "A Seat in the Stalls," *Reporter,* Oct. 20, 1955, p. 43.

Marcel, Gabriel. "Atomisation du théâtre," *Les Nouvelles Littéraires,* June 20, 1957, p. 10.

Marissel, André. *Beckett.* Paris: Editions Universitaires, 1963. 123 pp.

———. "L'Univers de Samuel Beckett: un noeud de complexe," *Esprit,* no. 320 (Sept., 1963), 240–255.

Mauriac, Claude. "Samuel Beckett," *Preuves,* no. 61 (March, 1956) , 71–76.

———. "Samuel Beckett," *Le Figaro Littéraire,* Aug. 11, 1956, p. 2.

———. "Samuel Beckett," in *The New Literature.* Trans. Samuel I. Stone. New York: George Braziller, 1959. Pp. 75–90. Original French title, *L'Alittérature contemporaine.* Paris: Albin Michel, 1959.

Mauroc, Daniel. "*Watt,*" *Table Ronde,* no. 70 (Oct., 1953) , 155–156.

Mayoux, Jean-Jacques. "Le Théâtre de Samuel Beckett," *Études Anglaises,* X, no. 4 (Oct.–Nov., 1957) , 350–366.

———. "Samuel Beckett et l'univers parodique," in *Vivants Piliers.* Paris, 1960. Pp. 271–291.

Mercier, Vivian. "Beckett and the Search for Self," *New Republic,* CXXXIII (Sept. 19, 1955) , 20–21.

———. "Savage Humor," *Commonweal,* LXVI (May 17, 1957) , 188.

———. "Mathematical Limit," *Nation,* CLXXXVIII (Feb. 14, 1959) , 144–145.

———. "How to Read Endgame," *Griffin,* VIII, no. 5 (June, 1959) , 10–14.

———. "Samuel Beckett and the Sheela-Na-Gig," *Kenyon Review,* XXIII, no. 2 (Spring, 1961) , 299–328.

Micha, René. "Une nouvelle littérature allégorique," *Nouvelle Nouvelle Revue Française,* III, no. 16 (April, 1954) , 696–706.

Miller, Karl. "Beckett's Voices," *Encounter,* XIII, no. 3 (Sept., 1959) , 59–61.

Mintz, Samuel I. "Beckett's *Murphy:* A 'Cartesian' Novel," *Perspective,* XI, no. 3 (Autumn, 1959) , 156–165.

Montgomery, Niall. "No Symbols Where None Intended," in *New World Writing,* no. 5. New York: New American Library of World Literature, 1954. Pp. 324–337.

Monticelli, R. "L'Ultima avanguardia," *Il Sipario,* no. 164 (1959) , 38–44.

Moore, John R. "Farewell to Something," *Tulane Drama Review,* V, no. 1 (Sept., 1960) , 49–60.

Morse, Mitchell. "Beckett and the Contemplative Life," *Hudson Review,* XV, no. 4 (Winter, 1962–1963) , 512–524.

Muller, André. "Techniques de l'avant-garde," *Théâtre Populaire,* no. 18 (May, 1956) , 21–29.

Murray, David. "A Review of *Murphy* and *Malone Dies,*" *Dalhousie Review,* XXXVII, no. 1 (Spring, 1957) , 104, 106.

Nadeau, Maurice. "Samuel Beckett, l'humour et le néant," *Mercure de France,* CCCXII, no. 1056 (Aug., 1951) , 693–697.

———. "Samuel Beckett ou le droit au silence," *Les Temps Modernes*, VII, no. 75 (Jan., 1952), 1273–1282.

———. *Littérature présente*. Paris: Corrêa, 1952. Pp. 274–279.

———. "Beckett: la tragédie transposée en farce," *L'Avant-scène*, no. 156 (1957), 4–6.

———. "Comment c'est," *L'Express*, Jan. 28, 1961, pp. 25–26.

———. *Le Roman Français depuis la guerre*. Paris: Gallimard, 1963 (Collection Idées). Pp. 155–159.

Nicoletti, G. "Théâtre d'aujourd'hui. Ionesco et Beckett," *Biennale di Venezia*, VIII, no. 30 (1958), 33–37.

Noon, W. T. "Modern Literature and the Sense of Time," *Thought*, XXXIII, no. 131 (Winter, 1958–1959), 571–604.

Norès, Dominique. "La Condition humaine selon Beckett," *Théâtre d'Aujourd'hui*, no. 3 (1957), 9–12.

Olles, Helmut. "Samuel Beckett," *Welt und Wort*, XV, no. 6 (June, 1960), 173–174.

Paris, Jean. "The Clock Struck 29," *Reporter*, XV, no. 39 (Oct. 4, 1956), p. 39.

Paulding, Gouverneur. "Samuel Beckett's New Tale," *New York Herald Tribune Book Review*, Sept. 16, 1956, p. 5.

Piatier, Jacqueline. "Comment c'est," *Le Monde*, Feb. 11, 1961, p. 9.

Pingaud, Bernard. "Molloy," *Esprit*, XIX, no. 9 (Sept., 1951), 423–425.

———, ed. *Ecrivains d'aujourd'hui*. Paris: Grasset, 1960. Pp. 93–100.

———. "Molloy, douze ans après," *Les Temps Modernes*, no. 200 (Jan., 1963), 1283–1300.

Politzer, Heinz. "The Egghead Waits for Godot," *Christian Scholar*, XLII (March, 1959), 46–50.

Pouillon, Jean. "Molloy," *Les Temps Modernes*, VII, no. 69 (July, 1951), 184–186.

Poulet, Robert. *La Lanterne magique*. Paris: Debresse, 1956. Pp. 236–242.

Pritchett, V. S. "Irish Oblomov," *New Statesman*, LIX (April 2, 1960), 489.

Pronko, Leonard C. "Beckett, Ionesco, Schéhadé: The Avant-Garde Theatre," *Modern Language Forum*, XLII (Dec., 1958), 118–123.

———. *Avant-Garde: The Experimental Theater in France*. Berkeley and Los Angeles: University of California Press, 1962. Pp. 22–58.

Radke, Judith. "Doubt and the Disintegration of Form in the French Novels and Drama of Samuel Beckett." Unpublished doctoral dissertation, University of Colorado, 1961. 276 pp.

Radke, Judith. "The Theatre of Samuel Beckett: 'Une durée à animer,' " *Yale French Studies*, no 29 (Spring–Summer, 1962), 57–64.

Rainoird, Manuel. "*En attendant Godot*," *Monde nouveau*, XI, no. 103 (Aug.–Sept., 1956), 115–117.

Rexroth, Kenneth. "Point Is Irrelevance," *Nation*, CLXXXII (April 14, 1956), 325–328.

Rhodes, S. A. "From Godeau to Godot," *French Review*, XXXVI, no. 3 (Jan., 1963), 260–265.

Rickels, Milton. "Existentialist Themes in Beckett's *Unnamable*," *Criticism*, IV, no. 2 (Spring, 1962), 134–147.

Robbe-Grillet, Alain. "Samuel Beckett, auteur dramatique," *Critique*, IX, no. 69 (Feb., 1953), 108–114.

———. *Pour un nouveau roman*. Paris: Gallimard, 1964 (Collection Idées). Pp. 121–136.

Rousseaux, André. "L'Homme désintégré de Samuel Beckett," in *Littérature du Vingtième Siècle*. Cinquième série. Paris: Albin Michel, 1955. Pp. 105–113.

S. A. "Balzac a-t-il inspiré *En attendant Godot*?" *Le Figaro Littéraire*, Sept. 17, 1955, p. 12.

Schneider, Alan. "Waiting for Beckett," *Chelsea Review*, no. 2 (Autumn, 1958), 3–20.

Schumach, Murray. "Why They Wait for Godot," *New York Times Magazine*, Sept. 21, 1958, pp. 36, 38, 41.

Seaver, Richard. "Samuel Beckett: An Introduction," *Merlin*, I, no. 2 (Autumn, 1952), 73–79.

Selz, Jean. "L'Homme finissant de Samuel Beckett," *Les Lettres Nouvelles*, V, no. 51 (July–Aug., 1957), 120–123.

Shenker, Israel. "Moody Man of Letters," *New York Times*, May 6, 1956, sec. 2, pp. 1, 3.

Simon, Alfred. "Samuel Beckett et les rendez-vous manqués," *Esprit*, XXI, no. 4 (April, 1953), 595–598.

———. "Le Degré zéro du tragique," *Esprit*, no. 323 (Dec., 1963), 905–909.

Spender, Stephen. "Lifelong Suffocation," *New York Times Book Review*, Oct. 12, 1958, p. 5.

———. "What Is a Man's Life, a Joke or Something Sacred?" *New York Times Book Review*, Feb. 25, 1962, pp. 7, 32.

Stottlar, James. "Samuel Beckett: An Introduction and an Interpretation." Unpublished master's thesis, Columbia University, 1957.

Strauss, Walter A. "Dante's Belacqua and Beckett's Tramps," *Comparative Literature*, XI, no. 3 (Summer, 1959), 250–261.

Tindall, William York. "Beckett's Bums," *Critique: Studies in Modern Fiction*, II, no. 1 (Spring–Summer, 1958), 3–15.

Unterdecker, John. "Samuel Beckett's No-Man's Land," *New Leader*, XLIII, no. 12 (May 18,1959), 24–25.

Vahanian, Gabriel. "The Empty Cradle," *Theology Today*, XIII (Jan., 1957), 521–526.

Verdot, Guy. "Beckett continue d'attendre Godot," *Le Figaro Littéraire*, March 3, 1960, p. 3.

Vigée, Claude. "Les Artistes de la faim," *Comparative Literature*, IX, no. 2 (Spring, 1957), 97–117.

Walker, Roy. "Love, Chess and Death: Samuel Beckett's Double Bill," *Twentieth Century*, CLXIV (Dec., 1958), 533–544.

Warhaft, Sidney. "Threne and Theme in *Watt*," *Wisconsin Studies in Contemporary Literature*, IV, no. 3 (Autumn, 1963), 261–278.

Wellwarth, G. E. "Life in the Void," *University of Kansas City Review*, XXVIII, no. 1 (Oct., 1961), 25–33.

Worsley, T. C. "Cactus Land," *New Statesman and Nation*, L (Aug. 13, 1955), 184–185.

INDEX

INDEX

NOTE: Numbers in italics refer to subjects discussed at length; fictitious characters are listed with the title of the work in which they appear.

65217

823.91
B396F

Federman, Raymond
Journey to chaos

LIBRARY
OHIO DOMINICAN COLLEGE
COLUMBUS, OHIO 43219